Historical Problems:
Studies and Documents

Edited by

PROFESSOR G. R. ELTON
University of Cambridge

13

POLITICS AND THE BENCH
The Judges and the Origins of the English Civil War

In the same series

1. ANTI-CATHOLICISM IN VICTORIAN ENGLAND
   by E. R. Norman

2. GERMANY IN THE AGE OF BISMARCK
   by W. M. Simon

3. PROBLEMS OF EMPIRE, 1757–1813
   by P. J. Marshall

4. RURAL SOCIETY, 1200–1350
   by J. Z. Titow

5. THE WOMAN MOVEMENT
   in The United States and England
   by William L. O'Neill

6. AGRARIAN PROBLEMS IN THE SIXTEENTH CENTURY AND AFTER
   by Eric Kerridge

7. GOVERNMENT AND SOCIETY IN FRANCE, 1461–1661
   by J. H. Shennan

8. THE ROYAL SUPREMACY IN THE ELIZABETHAN CHURCH
   by Claire Cross

9. THE CITY IN AMERICAN HISTORY
   by Blake McKelvey

10. THE CROWN LANDS 1461–1536
    by B. P. Wolffe

11. THE RISORGIMENTO AND THE UNIFICATION OF ITALY
    by Derek Beales

12. THE AGE OF LLOYD GEORGE
    by K. O. Morgan

14. THE DISSOLUTION OF THE MONASTERIES
    by Joyce Youings

15. MEDIEVAL MONARCHY IN ACTION
    by Boyd H. Hill

POLITICS AND THE BENCH

The Judges and the Origins of
the English Civil War

W. J. Jones
Professor of History, University of Alberta

LONDON: GEORGE ALLEN & UNWIN LTD
NEW YORK: BARNES AND NOBLE INC

BRITISH ISBN 0 04 942094 1 *cased*
             0 04 942095 x *paper*

    U.S. ISBN 389 04512 8

Printed in Great Britain
in 10 point Plantin type
by Cox & Wyman Ltd,
London, Fakenham and Reading

TO RIYAD

The Long Parliament's hostility towards Councillors and bishops is well known. Appreciation of this phobia can become distorted unless it is realized that the Justices of the great central courts of common law were also assailed. They were the most significant group to be impeached in the early months, and the nature of their predicament would be even more apparent had not death removed some assumed culprits. This book attempts to sketch some of the background.

It is not a history of the law, of the legal profession, or of institutions. Students especially interested in the great cases or in particular policies and men should turn to other works. Indeed the familiarity of much of the material provided the author with his greatest literary problem; the historian's worst conundrum, reminiscent of filling old bottles with new wine, is often provided not by his central theme but by the necessity of placing it in context. Early Stuart England represents a well-tramped field, but despite the value of recent studies our overall narrative impression is still partially dominated by the marriage of Clarendon and Rushworth achieved by S. R. Gardiner. There is so much that remains to be done on institutions, politics and procedures. The challenge and the prospects are exciting. Indeed it has always been rewarding to work amid a group of historians who are so ready to exchange information. Institutions are not separate entities, and so those who work with institutions recognize that others continually amend and supplement their own studies. In this little book, it should be evident that my greatest debt is to all the authors mentioned in the footnotes.

The crisis of the story comes with the meeting of the Long Parliament. This assembly, concerned with most grievances, found little time in the months before civil war to do much beyond eradicating or tackling immediate issues. Yet some of the most incisive stresses on the administrative structure of Early Stuart England were not particularly occasioned by the policies of Charles I. Their force is too often confused with the drama of his collapse. If asked to explain the point of this book, I would reply that it illustrates that point when legal justification becomes politically unacceptable. There are, however, other themes. Early Stuart England is often described in terms of demarcation which would have been confusing to contemporaries. Historians, in consequence, have unconsciously employed terminologies which do not fit the situation.

The spelling of quotations has been modernized. In giving dates, I have used the Julian Calendar and I have begun the year from I

January. Transcriptions of Crown copyright records in the Public Record Office appear by kind permission of the Controller of Her Majesty's Stationery Office. Document 3 appears by permission of Lady Elizabeth de Villiers and the Council of the Royal Historical Society. I am grateful to the General Editor of this series for his advice and criticism. In respect of fellowships and assistance, I must acknowledge the interest of the Guggenheim Foundation and the Canada Council.

W.J.J.

University of Alberta
September 1970

CONTENTS

AUTHOR'S NOTE vii

INTRODUCTION xiii
1 Introduction 13
2 Judges and Lawyers 32
3 The 1620s 53
4 Projects and Extraordinary Courses 84
5 Condemnation 123

DOCUMENTS
1 The judges and the House of Lords, 1614 151
2 *Ignoramus*, 1615 154
3 James I instructs the House of Lords about its judicial responsibilities, March 10, 1621 155
4 The judges discuss the nature of a Parliament, 1623 157
5 Sir Edward Coke comments on the nature of a Parliament 159
6 Part of the debate in the House of Lords as to whether Cranfield should be deprived of all his offices, 1624 160
7 Justice Whitelocke complains about the behaviour of Lord Treasurer Marlborough, 1627 160
8 An order in the Court of Requests, January 26, 1629 162
9 Richard Chambers opposes the seizure of his goods, 1629 163
10 Charles I consults the judges with respect to the Petition of Right and parliamentary privilege, 1628 and 1629 164
11 Charles I, in his 'Declaration Shewing the Causes of the late Dissolution', denounces attempts by the House of Commons to interfere with Councillors and judges, March 10, 1629 169
12 The plea and demurrer exhibited by Sir John Eliot in the Court of Star Chamber, May 22, 1629 171
13 Privy Council orders with respect to peers accused of contempt, 1629 173
14 'Considerations offered by Sir Henry Spelman, knight, touching the suppression of unjust fees': at the inner Star Chamber on Monday, May 3, 1630 175

15 Privy Council order, with assent of the judges, clarifying the privileges and limits of the Stannaries, February 18, 1632   177

16 An example of conditions in the Fleet, November 29, 1632   179

17 A complaint about practices in the courts of law, *circa* 1632   180

18 Opinion of the judges to the effect that 'liberty may not be given to prisoners by force of a *habeas corpus*', 1636   182

19 Lord Keeper Coventrye instructs the judges to encourage ship money payments, 1635 and 1637   183

20 George Croke on *Hampden's Case*, 1638   186

21 Extension of the limits of the honor of Peveril, May 31, 1639   188

22 A Star Chamber fine, 1640   188

23 The case of Francis Freeman, December 1, 1640   189

24 Lord Keeper Finch speaks to the House of Commons, December 21, 1640   190

25 Mr Rigby speaks against Finch, December 21, 1640   196

26 The House of Lords confirms the right of peers, December 31, 1640   197

27 The activities of Mr Hyde during the early months of the Long Parliament, 1640–1   198

28 The charges against Justice Berkeley, 1641   199

29 William Pierrepont speaks against Berkeley, July 6, 1641   209

30 Denzil Holles speaks against the judges, July 6, 1641   214

31 Edmund Waller speaks against the judges, July 6, 1641   215

32 Extracts from *Leviathan*   216

INDEX   219

INTRODUCTION

Introduction

'They begin to say in the town that the judges have overthrown the law, and the bishops the gospel.'[1]

IN the early months of the Long Parliament, a number of the central Justices were impeached. However, the basic charge of treason was not proved in a single case, and condemnations for crimes and misdemeanours were only obtained before a rump House of Lords during the abnormal circumstances of civil war. Less deadly than the attack upon Laud and Strafford, the affair none the less deserves attention because it symbolizes the fate of an authority which carried reliance upon its legal rights, as demonstrated before the courts, to a level which was politically unacceptable. Contemporaries, however, did not think very far along these lines. Individual judges were criticized rather than the law which they supervised, the procedures within which they operated, or the royal rights which they affirmed. Ship money and other measures were treated as illegal, rather than as legal but repulsive. Accusation was thus based upon the comfortable assumption that only individuals had failed. This enabled continued belief in the virtues of English law and partially accounts for the largely unchanged survival of the Justices of the central courts of common law.

The men elected in autumn 1640 at first tried desperately to conform with existing patterns of constitutional thought. They found inspiration in the example of Sir John Eliot, whose death in 1632 remained an angry memory. Eliot had conceived of a faultless ruler surrounded by advisers who were both good and bad. He believed that Parliament must denounce those men and policies which were harmful to King and kingdom.[2] Charles, however, construed the supposedly loyal denunciations of Parliament as obstreperous criticism of his royal self, and he once said that the Commons resented dutiful obedience to the King (Doc. 11). Traditional attitudes can still be seen in Edmund Waller's speech of July 6, 1641 (Doc. 31), but on the same day William Pierrepont's attempt to avoid criticizing the King was almost embarrassingly

[1] November 1640; cited S. R. Gardiner, *History of England from the Accession of James I to the Outbreak of the Civil War, 1603–1642*, London, 1887–1904, ix. 224.
[2] H. Hulme, *The Life of Sir John Eliot, 1592–1632*, London, 1957, p. 106.

tortuous. Nevertheless he could conclude with confidence that men like Strafford had conspired against Charles because they were no longer afraid of the judges. 'Thus hath His Majesty now got our hearts, and will for ever have them. This judge [Berkeley] is to answer for what His Majesty and for what we have suffered' (Doc. 29). Denzil Holles called down curses upon the judges, but his references to acts of power, and to might being right, implied that they were as much the puppets of an unnamed superior authority as they were the misleaders of that authority (Doc. 30). However, the attempt to live with conventional ideas continued. Gardiner was probably right when he pictured Hampden and Pym as men who regarded the existing system as admirable but damaged by hindrances and defective organization.[3] It followed that when things went wrong, the responsibility was laid to an excessive extent at the door of the King's principal servants. There is nothing novel in this, but a distinctive feature of Charles's reign is the comprehensive nature of the attack. The judges sitting in Common Pleas, Exchequer and King's Bench were popularly condemned in advance. Only the aged George Croke and very recent appointees were excused from impeachment. Professor Judson has described the instinct of the parliamentary leaders as sound: King and ministers 'had used the law as their ally, and they had done it openly – by decisions in the law courts'.[4] The enthusiasm to mete out punishment, however, was greater than the ability to frame feasible accusations. The charge of treason was born out of political emotion. At the best there was little hope of establishing anything more than incompetence, prejudice, weakness of character, and other aspects deemed unfitting in a judge. Holdsworth felt that the appeal to law in the 1630s rings increasingly false – my own impression is that there was too much conviction – but one should certainly keep in mind his argument that ministers and critics were really appealing to political creeds elaborated in legal terms.[5]

It was normal for the government to indicate a conventional legal basis for its position and for dissenters to react in kind. Thus in the reign of James I, it was the Crown which forced the legal pace over impositions. Critical lawyers subsequently spent years searching the records to build up a case which they hoped would outflank and undermine the decision of the Barons of the Exchequer.[6] In the Parliaments of the 1620s, lawyer M.P.s made a unique impact, but before that decade

---

[3] Gardiner, ix. 370.

[4] Margaret A. Judson, *The Crisis of the Constitution*, New Brunswick, N.J., 1949, p. 144.

[5] W. S. Holdsworth, *A History of English Law*, London, 1903–26, vi. 30.

[6] *Proceedings in Parliament, 1610*, ed. Elizabeth R. Foster, New Haven, 1966, i. p. xvi.

ended – and certainly in the 1630s – the Crown was making an even more dramatic argument in terms of traditional legal right. Professor Judson, coupling Councillors and judges as persons who exalted the 'absolute power' of the King, has written of the 'legal absolutism' advocated by these agents as being an understandable position based upon the accepted practices and modes of English common law. It had little or nothing to do with higher forms of theory or more abstruse laws: 'royalist judges preferred legal arguments based on English precedents to those based on the general nature of monarchy and to those involving divine and natural law or the law of reason.'[7] The difficulty, as perhaps *Hampden's Case* reveals best, was that established law and statute were also conceived to cover and maintain both the King's power and the subject's property. Hence it was the way in which the law was exercised, and thus the persons of the judges not the law itself, which became the enemy. Certainly, many criticisms can be made of these men, and there was an unduly intimate association between their work and government policies. Yet they were also the victims of developments – institutional, political, religious – which were quite beyond their control.

Many fundamental points in constitutional and legal development will have to be passed over, for example the relationship between common law and acts of Parliament, or the themes raised in *Bonham's Case*.[8] McIlwain's argument[9] that the 'antithesis between legislation and adjudication' so often assumed by later writers did not exist has many valid points but it is not, I think, tenable for this period as a whole. Contemporaries generally assumed that there was such a distinction and they became very agitated when, as in the ship money affair, they feared not merely that it was being erased but that the judges were actually usurping a legislative role. Their fears were exaggerated because they were only groping towards an understanding of the other side of the coin: what in modern times might be described as the distinction between adjudication and administration. In 1640, the judges were

---

[7] Judson, pp. 141, 349, and chap. 4 generally.

[8] 8 Co. Rep., 114–21 (77 *English Reports*). For an initial bibliography, see the works cited by T. F. T. Plucknett, *A Concise History of the Common Law*, London, 1956, p. 51 n. 2. Attention should be paid to S. E. Thorne's introduction to *A Discourse upon the Exposicion & Understandinge of Statutes*, San Marino, 1942.

[9] C. H. McIlwain, *The High Court of Parliament and its Supremacy*, New Haven, 1910. For comment and criticism see Judson, and J. W. Gough, *Fundamental Law in English Constitutional History*, Oxford, 1961. Note may be taken of J. P. Cooper, 'Differences between English and Continental Governments in the Early Seventeenth Century', *Britain and the Netherlands*, ed. J. Bromley and E. Kossman, Oxford, 1960, p. 65. For the development of theories of mixed monarchy, see Corinne C. Weston, *English Constitutional Theory and the House of Lords, 1556–1832*, New York, 1965.

decried because they had not stood aloof from politics, in short because they had not observed a separation of powers which the men of Parliament were only on the point of discovering. Subsequent historians likewise have all too often assumed that the judges should have been persons distinct from the administration of the day. This had been aided by the ease of seeing a fallen Master of the Wards and Lord Treasurer, such as Cranfield, more as a financial administrator than as a judge; or a fallen Chancellor, such as Bacon, as representative of a legal approach which is somehow conceived to be alien; or a fallen Chief Justice, notably Coke, as virtuously a judge and curiously not a politician.

Professor Hurstfield has pointed out that 'corruption in law and in politics are two separate but related things'.[10] In what might otherwise be a maze this is an invaluable distinction, but the difficulty is that most major officials were judges, and most judges were administrators. It was understood that there was some kind of distinction, certainly with respect to function, but in practice it was difficult to draw those clear lines of demarcation which are often innocently implied by our modern terminology. The Lord Treasurer, the Master of the Wards, the Lord Privy Seal, the Presidents of provincial Councils, the Lord Admiral, the Earl Marshal, and so on – all were judges. The Secretaries of State appear as outstanding examples of men who were not, but by virtue of being Privy Councillors they could sit on the Star Chamber bench and they were, of course, J.P.s. A Lord Treasurer, such as Weston, would play a crucial policy role in promoting taxes, and then he could sit legitimately on the Exchequer bench when these taxes were challenged. Early in the reign of Charles, a committee was appointed to prevent frauds in the collection of various kinds of customs duties; apart from the Lord Treasurer, the Chancellor of the Exchequer, and the Attorney General, it included the Chief Baron, two other Barons of the Exchequer, and all the Justices of the Common Pleas. Yet they were men before whom such matters might come judicially.[11] Men who formulated proclamations were judges in Star Chamber. The confusion was enhanced by personal interests. A Master of the Wards might benefit from the sale of a wardship; then litigation concerning the ward and his lands might be commenced in his court. After Cranfield was condemned, he was told to his face how heinous it was for a judge to be corrupt through extortion even though, as Lord Keeper Williams said, there was

[10] J. Hurstfield, 'Political Corruption in Modern England: the Historian's Problem', *History*, 1967, lii, no. 174, p. 21. For an attempt to grapple with some problems, especially the 'rudimentary distinction' between 'political' and 'non-political' officers which did not exist in Charles I's time, see G. E. Aylmer, *The King's Servants*, London, 1961, pp. 8–11, and *passim*.

[11] C[alendar of] S[tate] P[apers] Dom[estic] 1625–6, p. 12.

no question of 'his judicature' having been influenced by bribery (Doc. 6). Institutions and their chiefs were constructed upon a firm alliance of official policy, judicial activity, and private vested interest. If the first two were disliked, it was possible to seek explanation in the last element. An extreme example of all this is provided by the Lord Admiral and the Admiralty, so well described by Dr K. R. Andrews. The Admiralty was 'at once a department of state under the authority of the Crown and a private province or liberty of the Lord Admiral. . . . The High Court of Admiralty was his court, and the judge, like all other officers, was his servant The organization and personnel were entirely his responsibility, and to him accrued the profits of justice and the perquisites of wreck, piracy confiscations, tenths of prizes and the rest. Consequently his authority was coolly disregarded by powerful men and local powers, and contemptuously dismissed for what, in large measure, it really was – a private concern making a profit out of the public.'[12] Officials and institutions could not easily be compartmented into tidy groups labelled administrative and judicial, or public and private.

Holdsworth described the early county and hundred courts as 'governing bodies quite as much as courts of law', and he saw the Council of Wales as 'both a court of law and an instrument of government'.[13] This choice of phrase is rather clumsy but perhaps unavoidable, and indeed the point is difficult to discuss without appearing to go to the opposite extreme. We really need a different terminology, and perhaps it is to be found in Coke who often wrote that an official or an institution had 'power of judicature'. In *Auditor Curle's Case*, he put his finger upon a related aspect: 'this office is partly ministerial and partly judicial . . . it is by Act of Parliament so entire that the ministerial part cannot be divided from the judicial.'[14] To early Stuart men, the distinctions implied by Holdsworth would have been rather obscure. The provincial Councils, for example, united what would now be called administrative and judicial duties within the single concept of controlling geographical areas. These were indivisible aspects of government. Yet, as has been suggested with respect to the responsibility of judges in general, theorists were beginning to make distinctions, and one of the features of the reign of Charles I centres upon a growing feeling that some kind of demarcation could and should be made.[15]

In most institutions, legal proceedings were an adjunct of well-staffed

[12] K. R. Andrews, *Elizabethan Privateering*, Cambridge, 1964, p. 30.
[13] Holdsworth, i. 69, 126.
[14] 11 Co. Rep. 2b (77 *English Reports*).
[15] It may have been inevitable once it was established that *mandamus* could be used to make royal officers answerable for their actions. See generally, Edith G. Henderson, *Foundations of English Administrative Law*, Cambridge, Mass., 1963, chap. 2.

B

administrative machines subsisting upon records, rolls, and secretarial devices which were at the heart of the political organization of society. The Chancery, wrote Holdsworth, was 'a branch of the civil service as well as a judicial court'.[16] The point doubtless applies more to Chancery than to any other institution, but it is one that in varying degrees can be applied to many courts. In a period when, despite the eccentricities of the 1620s, Parliament met infrequently and briefly, and when it was not supposed to meet on anything approaching a regular basis, the core of political activity is to be found in the institutions of central and regional government: Westminster courts, provincial Councils, Palatinates, counties, boroughs, and smaller units. A list would include almost every category: the Admiralty, the Chancery, the Exchequer, the Cinque Ports, the Duchy of Lancaster, the Exchequer court at Chester, the courts of the city of London, the courts of Southampton, the Chancery at Monmouth, or the web of manor courts at Taunton. All these edifices entertained legal proceedings, and these proceedings represented a vital part of government and the organization of society. A point which can be made is obvious, if unhistorical: this society lacked sufficient civil servants and alternative procedures. As it is, the interests of the Chancery, the Council in the Marches of Wales, or of the borough, were far greater and more varied than would be guessed if only legal proceedings in the conventional sense were examined.[17] King's Bench and Common Pleas may seem somewhat different, as indeed they were, but noting the function of their rolls and especially the latter court's position as an artery of land conveyancing, it is hard even to accept an amendment of this kind. The point is most obvious when attention is directed to the Duchy of Lancaster or the court of Wards. Both administered royal rights and revenue, and it may be appropriate that a well-known picture of the Wards looks more like a committee meeting than a modern court. On the other hand, some courts did not fit into this pattern. Requests and Star Chamber lacked involvement with administrative records. Both expired in the 1640s, one by lapse and one by statute. Of course, Star Chamber was connected through the personnel of its bench with the Privy Council, but this need not have been disastrous. Kings and ministers recognized the distinctive importance of legal proceedings but they also, and very naturally, assumed them to be a part of government. It could not be otherwise. Star Chamber, condemned by posterity for its governmental aura, was just one of many.

The executive of the day had reason to assume that institutions, which now are too often concentrated upon as 'courts of law', were

---

[16] Holdsworth, v. 245.

[17] A good example is provided by P. Williams, *The Council in the Marches of Wales under Elizabeth I*, Cardiff, 1958.

part of that executive. It was not perverse to suppose that judges should play an important role in the regulation of society. James I ordered those going on circuit to punish and prevent offences and also 'to take care for the good government in general of the parts where you travel'.[18] They were expected to report upon men and matters of interest, to use their influence in support of official policy, and to intervene when necessary (Doc. 19). Justices Jones and Winch summoned the clothiers of Gloucestershire in 1622 and ordered them to employ their workers despite the slump. Later in this reign, the circuit judges along with sheriffs and J.P.s were ordered to levy contributions for a drainage project in Lincolnshire. In 1629, the ostensible reason for seeking Chief Baron Walter's resignation or removal was that he had been lax in enforcing the obligation to attend musters. More and more was expected and in 1635, to give just one example, the judges were required by proclamation to assist in enforcing rules about saltpetre manufacture. In the words of Professor Barnes, 'it is difficult to imagine county government by local gentlemen without the judges of assize . . . the King's stewards, overseeing the governance of his realm'.[19] The format was old, but political circumstances were changing. Previous normality ceased to be a justification once the political classes – the parliamentary gentry – decided that the policies being enforced should have been rejected as illegal.

Litigants directed their suits towards institutions of government which were animated and influenced by political struggles, departments which were served by judges and lawyers who had an unavoidable political role and often political careers to make. The consequences were threatening to become apparent when in 1629 the House of Commons and the Barons of the Exchequer found themselves at loggerheads. Common-law judges upheld the King's right to impositions, to the taking of tunnage and poundage, and to imprison without showing cause; they imprisoned Eliot, incarcerated him until death, and overthrew the arguments of Hampden. In the 1630s, devices which aroused most opposition were not overthrown in the courts. The King's Bench, wrote Gardiner, was the 'great prop' of Charles's government.[20] In the Exchequer Chamber, the judges had begun to claim an overwhelming authority for their decisions. Their opinions were solicited by the King to clarify the strands of policy, and as such used for propaganda in a fashion which was intended to nullify, but in fact compelled,

---

[18] Holdsworth, vi. 57–8.

[19] *CSP DOM.* 1619–23, p. 358; 1623–5, p. 138. Gardiner, vii. 112. R. Steele, *Tudor and Stuart Proclamations*, Oxford, 1910, i. No. 1693. T. G. Barnes, *Somerset, 1625–1640 : A County's Government During the Personal Rule*, Cambridge, Mass., 1961, p. 91.

[20] Gardiner, ix. 161.

resentment. Some, including George Croke and Richard Hutton, were members of the High Commission.[21] Gardiner found difficulty in understanding that men could really think of Berkeley and Finch as endangering the foundations of the state – he wondered if it did not require very strong imagination[22] – but this is almost certainly how they were seen by contemporaries. More than anything else, the judges' promotion of ship money was resented. It was this which snapped the thread and caused them to be accused of perverting the proper function of the law. Falkland, speaking in the Long Parliament, asserted that their extra-judicial behaviour over ship money was their 'greatest crime', and he argued that it 'came not within their cognizance, they being judges, and neither philosophers nor politicians'.[23] Ideas like these had been around before in a modified form: the assertions of M.P.s in 1614 that kings could not make impositions because they could not make laws inevitably reflected upon the performance of the Barons of the Exchequer.[24]

Confident in the past, Charles and his judges tried to use this authority to isolate immediate issues from the general political picture. They were almost certainly sincere, but they were contributing to the picture which was being built around them. Hobbes argued that the legislator is not he by whose authority a law is first made, but he by whose authority it continues to be law (Doc. 32). A modern commentator has rejected this idea with sympathy,[25] but it remains relevant to the 1630s. Waller said that the judges had tried to usurp the right of Parliament to grant supply, and he spoke of 'this parliament of judges' (Doc. 31). It was as though men had come to fear that a novel concept, that of King and judiciary, was on the threshold of replacing that older understanding of King and Parliament.

In the Long Parliament, angry M.P.s, as in the attack on Laud and Strafford, levelled charges of subverting the fundamental laws and government (Doc. 28 [1]). Earlier, when Lord Keeper Finch protested that the judges by their oath had a duty to advise the King (Doc. 24), he was enunciating a truth that no one attempted to deny. Instead, it was insisted that they had deliberately betrayed their trust by proffering pernicious advice (Docs 29, 30). The affair brought embarrassment to Parliament and chaos to the courts, but it is the fact of accusation and not the nature and course of subsequent proceedings which is important.

[21] R. G. Usher, *The Rise and Fall of the High Commission*, ed. P. Tyler, Oxford, 1968, pp. 345–61. This does not seem to have been important in the attack upon the judges.
[22] Gardiner, ix. 306.
[23] J. Rushworth, *Historical Collections of Private Passages of State*, London, 1659–1701, iii. Appendix, p. 247.
[24] *Commons Journals*, i. 481–2.
[25] H. L. A. Hart, *The Concept of Law*, Oxford, 1961, pp. 62–4.

In sketching the background to these accusations almost the whole range of political existence is really relevant and thus, quite apart from the policies of Charles, economic development and fiscal stringency would have involved the Crown in difficult legal problems as it tried to adapt its creaking, out-dated weapons of law and machinery to immediate needs. The eventual lists of charges are important, but not all the accusations need be accorded the same significance. All available examples of alleged improper behaviour were trotted out, but clearly some of these were little more than supporting points (Doc. 28). Ship money and imprisonment were among the most momentous issues, and the judges were really accused of being mainstays of a distrusted and discredited regime. At the same time, the venom of the attack owed something to broader doubts about the structure and operations of the English legal system, its practitioners, and the law itself. Common lawyers in the House of Commons were prominent, but many of them were increasingly unhelpful in pushing matters to a conclusion, and they may have thought that some denunciations by fellow M.P.s really went beyond the specific accusations and might rebound. In any case, they recognized the near impossibility of proving all the charges, notably that of treason.

The Grand Remonstrance would rank the imprisonment and impeachment of Sir Robert Berkeley, Justice of the King's Bench, with that of Archbishop Laud,[26] but this expression of confidence marks a time when the futility of the affair was growing more apparent and the House of Commons was disintegrating. The House of Lords, increasingly anxious, was pressing for proceedings against the judges to begin, and was probably aware that the House of Commons was not in a position to do this. In any case, many thought that enough had been done: the death of Strafford, the fall of Laud, the flight of Finch and Windebank, and the acceptance of important legislation. At first, it had been possible to pretend that the King was revered but that he had been surrounded by evil bishops, Councillors and judges. Laud, Strafford, and Berkeley – as substitutes for the escaped Finch – represented the three categories. It could not even be said that Parliament took serious exception to the *form* of government as it had existed during the years 1629–40. This attitude was never lost, even during the first civil war, but it was increasingly hard to maintain.

Blackstone said that it was subversive of good government to set the judicial power above the legislature, but the sense of distinction which this statement assumes had taken some time to develop into its eighteenth-century form. The judiciary had still been considered an integral

---

[26] The Grand Remonstrance can be found in S. R. Gardiner, *Constitutional Documents of the Puritan Revolution, 1625–60*, Oxford, 1962, pp. 202–32. The immediate reference is on p. 222.

part of Charles II's administration.[27] Both judges and accusers were only groping towards a language of demarcation in 1640. It was believed that the judges had gone beyond their bounds, but it was difficult to articulate this feeling. Pierrepont slashed against discretion and suggested that the law was a certain thing which could not be touched by the individual opinions of judges. 'As often as a judge's reason changes, or judges change, our laws change also. Our liberties are in our laws, where a subject may read, or hear read, this is his, this he may do and be safe' (Doc. 29). In fact, the judges had often been called upon to decide matters which were not illuminated by legislation, and this was unfortunate for them since the gentry of the early Stuart period placed an increasing emphasis on statute rather than on the customary practices of common law and courts. Faced by arguments for the call of Parliament, as in *Hampden's Case*, some of the judges might have reason to suppose that they were being asked to give serious consideration to a mirage. Was there really any chance, in the light of past experience, that Parliament would grant the King adequate supply? But the judges never denied Parliament, and so their enemies were forced to try and establish that they had broken what Parliament had enacted. Although some possible examples could be produced – notably a case concerning corn (Doc. 28 [2]) – this was where the accusations were most feeble, and it helps to explain why it proved so difficult to press the impeachment proceedings to a conclusion. Ideas and convictions were legion – Coke and his generation had seen to that – but there was a shortage not so much of established definition, which we would hardly expect, but rather of generally accepted conventions. Yet both the King and the members of the Long Parliament exhibited a moral virtue which implied that this was not so.

Crown and Parliament, at least in any traditional sense, underwent severe strains in the first six decades of the seventeenth century, and for a time both ceased to exist. The place of Parliament in the 'constitution' was not always the basic question, but it has rightly attracted the attention of subsequent generations. Without Parliament, the first two Stuarts could survive, but they could not secure those supplies of money and legislation which would enable them to surmount an emergency. Even with Parliament, there was little possibility of doing more than make ends meet. In the 1620s, both James I and Charles I irritated Parliaments, but even so there is little reason to suppose that harmony would have produced an abundant financial return. The Crown was compelled to turn to farmers, financiers and legal devices. Charles capitulated in 1640, but there was no experience to govern the

[27] W. Blackstone, *Commentaries on the Laws of England*, Oxford, 1773, i. 91. A. F. Havighurst, 'The Judiciary and Politics in the Reign of Charles II', *Law Quarterly Review*, 1950, lxvi. 62–78, 229–52.

situation. As the emergency remained, it was the structure of Parliament, notably the factions, groups and individuals in the House of Commons, which aided in transforming his unique surrender of initiative into a sudden and headlong rush into civil war. The House of Commons, at the very least, was half responsible for this catastrophe – 'nothing can ruin a Parliament but itself', warned Pierrepont (Doc. 29) – and subsequently it claimed a responsibility and power of decision which was almost meglomaniac in the light of realities. Yet whatever the curious shapes of civil war and republican 'Parliaments', the existence and the idea of this assembly provided a continuance of authority, just as the attack upon the judges as individuals served to protect belief in the existing structure of law and its institutions. Whig historians were not all that much in error when they wrote the history of this period in terms of Parliament. It was not the only vital element in political and social life, but it came to behave as though it had been.

Considerable stress will be laid upon the House of Lords, but it is not intended to deny the importance traditionally accorded to the House of Commons. Sir John Neale has revealed the growing width of public opinion which was often indicated by the alertness of the lower House and by the sharp appreciation of individual M.P.s. As this came about, there emerged disputes over the limitations of Parliament's power and the right of restraining interference by the Crown. Privilege became transformed. Once representative of normal, almost casual, procedural development and convenience, it became a bone of contention. Elizabeth appeared to triumph – no one can take away from her the political skill of the Golden Speech – but she avoided a crisis at the price of leaving some parliamentary claims outstanding. James was the victim, but he need not be pitied since his own tactics and personal idiosyncrasies contributed powerfully to the creation of that celebrated vicious circle of Parliaments, each failure increasing the sense of public grievance. Criticism of foreign policy, when associated with discussion of supply, represented a push towards that situation when Parliament would claim to control policy. Similar strains were cast upon the administration, another clear royal prerogative. Incessant attacks on fees and offices, particularly in Chancery, opened up the possibility of Parliament claiming to control this sector of government. The King could snuff out the threat so long as he held the life of a Parliament in his hands, and before 1641 few could conceive of a situation when control was actually out of his hands. Furthermore, it was often convenient for the King to adopt a policy apparently in accordance with the popular view. This was tried on a number of occasions: the attack on monopolists in 1621, the conduct of foreign policy in 1624, and generally with respect to the investigation of fees. In 1629, Charles decided not to compromise further. He had, after all, been born and bred in a system

which assumed that King and Council bore the responsibility of deciding whether or not a statute should be seriously enforced. Country
gentlemen and borough types sitting in Parliament could obstruct, but
they could not compel King and Council to enforce a statute if this was
not their wish. This is why there was so much anxious debate over the
enforcement of the recusancy laws. Both Commons and Lords, with
their diverse strands of power, were limited by lack of permanency.
In contrast the Privy Council, the great officers of state, and the judges
were permanently at work. These were the facts of political life.

The 1630s are often described as a decade of personal rule, but
personal monarchy had long been a concrete political institution, even
though the story of Scotland tells us that personal monarchy could
become a cipher. Favourites or ministers might lead the monarch, but
they rarely dominated him and they could never dominate others without
him. Clarendon understood this when he looked beyond Buckingham
to James I and Charles I and suggested that the source of the favourite's
corrupt ambition could be found in the way in which he was seated 'in
the hearts of two such masters'.[28] In the Tudor and early Stuart period,
there are only a few instances of men other than the King grasping the
essential aura of command. It happened in the minority of Edward
VI, but the young King was not a nonentity and both Somerset and
Northumberland were shackled and destroyed by their inability to be
King. It happened in 1624, when Prince Charles and Buckingham allied
to browbeat an ailing James. It happened in the revolutionary circumstances of the 1640s. But it was easier to remove effective control from
the King than it was to supplant him. Victory on the battlefield and the
expedient of the axe could not do this. The practical justification for
killing Charles – a settlement could not be made with him and it could
not be made without him – is itself a resounding illustration of the
power of personal monarchy. Commonwealth men and Cromwell found
that they could not master a system of authority, government and law
which was predicated upon this form of monarchy. Even under the
later Stuarts, rebellion in 1688–9 would succeed not because it removed James but because it replaced one personal monarch with
another.

This is not to say that the problems of one sovereign cannot be found
in the years of his predecessor. Nor is it to deny rival classifications of
period, although it may be argued that economic and social forces of
change cannot by their very nature be bound captive with precise dates
of beginning and end. It is just that, with all respect to other lines of
analysis, the personality, strengths and weaknesses of individual
sovereigns represent for this period a political reality, and historians are

[28] Edward, Earl of Clarendon, *The History of the Rebellion*, ed. W. D. Macray,
Oxford, 1888, i. 43.

justified in drawing lines of distinction between the reigns of Elizabeth I, James I, and Charles I, although it must be noted that 1625 has rarely been accorded the same emphasis as 1603. The events of 1640 and 1641 were not automatically implicit in the situation at James's death. There was not a single early Stuart constitutional crisis, but when the explosion came – and it emerged in stuttering confusion – it naturally fused with events of the previous reign. Rushworth, assuming that the causes of strife were immediate, originally meant to begin his account with November 3, 1640, but he found that so much 'bottomed' upon earlier dissolutions of Parliament.[29]

What then, from the aspect of this study, is the importance of James I? He was a sovereign who lacked the Tudor ability to defend his respect in the eyes of the populace, and he came to suffer from a romantic comparison with Elizabeth, a mood which elevated the memory of the Virgin Queen into an appreciation beyond reality and touched her shroud with a golden halo which may have been a little surprising to those who had witnessed her last years. James brought his own problems of family, expenditure and foreign policy. He could never achieve a major triumph, and peace robbed him of the best reason for asking money from his early Parliaments. Foreign policy and corresponding doubts over the government's treatment of Catholics were major themes which tie together all the Parliaments of the 1620s. Characteristics which distinguished James from Elizabeth, and which may have represented a damning inheritance to his son, were his realm of Scotland, his favourites, and his indulgence for scholarship and theory.

As a young King in Scotland,[30] James had struggled for personal independence and control of the Church, and for the rest of his life the two themes would be intimately related in his mind. The Black Acts of 1584 were relaxed in 1592, but James struck back when he prohibited assemblies without his consent, and in 1605 it was declared that those who came of their own volition were traitors. In 1610, a Scottish court of High Commission was set up, and Scottish bishops were consecrated by their English counterparts. In 1618, following the visit by James and Buckingham, the Five Articles of Perth, ratified in 1621, established Anglican characteristics. In 1619, a prayer book was introduced. He had gone far towards being Scotland's Henry VIII, and as with England much of his stress on royal supremacy was with

[29] Rushworth, i. Preface. Clarendon, claiming not to be so sharp sighted, placed most emphasis upon events in the Long Parliament. However, he began with the accession of Charles I and paid considerable attention to the emergence of Buckingham in the previous reign. Clarendon, i. 3.

[30] For Scotland generally, see J. D. Mackie, *A History of Scotland*, London, 1964; D. H. Willson, *King James VI and I*, London, 1956; W. C. Dickinson and G. S. Pryde, *A New History of Scotland*, London, 1965; D. Mathew, *Scotland under Charles I*, London, 1955.

reference to the royal supremacy over the Church. It was always something of a façade. He revisited the country only once and increasingly seemed to be a foreigner; the reality of personal monarchy was being lost. Charles visited his other realm twice – in 1633 and 1641 – but his advisers tried to turn façade into reality, and hence the attempt to impose discipline on the Scottish Church. Just as Ireland came to be feared as the model of what Charles wanted in England, so the regulation of the Scottish Church was seen as a design for the future. The reaction, however, was also a model: the Scottish Parliament moved to control the Lords of the Articles – comparable to leading English Councillors – and abolished the episcopacy.

James, whose hopes of union had been thwarted, and Charles were sovereigns of two countries which had a tradition of enmity. They concealed the problem by keeping away from Scotland, but this device collapsed with the Bishops' War. Strafford's idea that Irish troops might be used was twisted into the claim that he had suggested using them in England. This was damning in English eyes, but the probable truth was equally damning to Scotsmen, and the minister's head was demanded in both countries. The 1640s were dominated by the impact of Scotland and its army. Charles's government had collapsed when he looked to loyal England for help against rebellious Scots, and he lost his head when he appealed to loyal Scotland to salvage his position from rebellious English. His activities in 1648 were the last straw in duplicity for Cromwell and Ireton, yet the Parliamentary side had used Scottish troops in 1644 and 1645. There was no standard to say that the King of Scotland should not make peace with his subjects, any more than there was a standard which allowed the English to cut off the head of the King of Scotland. The dual monarchy, always a hazard, became a disaster.

There is reason to suppose that James, whose mind had been fashioned in Scotland, leant in England towards those advisers whose words sounded familiar. He was a foreigner, a doctrinaire, and an old King, although this could be put forward as an advantage. From the beginning there was a crusty weariness about him. It was obscured by his outbursts of interest – scholarship, hunting, witches, the responsibilities of kingship – and he might have been happier if he had lived with the enlightened monarchs of the next century. Even if he hardly produced an original addition to contemporary notions of the divine right of kings, the fact that he was a personal monarch added lustre to his utterances. Other characteristics – he would be schoolmaster to a nation – implied a positive extension of this doctrine to all society. He made speeches, and though he may not have departed from the Elizabethan position, Elizabeth did not make this kind of speech at all. James's health deteriorated, kingship was a drab routine, and he tried to transfer as many onerous duties as possible upon the shoulders of a man whom he deemed to be faithful, loyal and congenial. Whether or not there were homosexual elements, Buckingham cannot easily be compared to Somerset or to any previous man whom James had favoured. The Duke, as the King acknowledged in 1621, had to carry the most tedious burdens and handle the pesterings of courtiers and office seekers.[31] He shielded the monarch and had few aspirations to hold high ministerial office – the acquisition of the Lord Admiralship was almost a mistake. Perhaps it would have been better if he had never become a member of the Council in 1618. He was thus transformed from being a royal deputy into one who was concerned with policy.

Quarrels over policy and tactics, restrained under Elizabeth, became public during the reign of James. When the dissolution of Parliament in 1614 was made known, the Earl of Northampton made his satisfaction public. The subsequent fall of Somerset, a captive of the Howards, did not destroy the position of this group, and they were sustained for a time by quarrels of their opponents, one symbol of which can be seen in the fall of Coke. In 1618–19, the Howards were smashed by the forces of Bacon and Buckingham, but the favourite was one to control factions and not to be controlled by them. He dragged the Crown into this turmoil. Hence the embarrassments of 1621, the blundering reversal of policy in 1624, and the disastrous overtones of 1626. Buckingham poisoned the early years of Charles, for whom he was a friend rather than a favourite. The impact of this man cannot be discounted, and as Professor Trevor-Roper has observed, it was the moral and political characteristics of the court of James I rather than that of Charles I which aroused the strongest feelings in 1640.[32] The Caroline system, whatever its Tudor roots, was fashioned before James was dead. But with Buckingham's assassination there came a change. The King relied upon technicians – Cottington, Noy, Weston, and, for all his sense of magnificence, Laud – who were different from the colourful, at times flamboyant, men who in support or opposition dominated the reign of James I. This was in character, for the new King would place his faith in the law of the land, and he would make the mistake of assuming that the judges who interpreted that law were above popular reproach and immune to vulgar insinuations of prejudice. No other King in English history was so genuinely convinced of the virtue of the bench.

Judges were royal appointees, and the major courts can fairly be described as royal. In the King's Bench cases were said to be heard before the King himself, *coram rege ipso*, bills of complaint in the

---

[31] 'The Hastings Journal of the Parliament of 1621', ed. Lady Elizabeth de Villiers, *Camden Miscellany xx*, 1953, pp. 28–9.

[32] H. R. Trevor-Roper, 'Oliver Cromwell and his Parliaments', in *Religion, the Reformation, and Social Change*, London, 1967, pp. 347–8.

Requests were addressed to the King – if the *subpoena* failed to secure the defendant's appearance it could be followed by another charging him to his allegiance – and the Marshalsea court was supposed to follow him on progress. Lambarde described the King as, under God, the only judge of his people. Necessity required him to delegate the task to others, but this did not discharge the responsibility.[33] All this was understood as having a special meaning. The possibility of a physical appearance by the sovereign was assumed to be more or less out of the question, largely because evolution in the second half of the sixteenth century had taken its course, with the minority of Edward and the rule of two Queens, without the point being seriously considered. Hence James I was being a nuisance when he raised the question of his right to decide cases in the King's Bench. Since it was difficult to produce precedents showing that James was wrong, Coke's rebuttal had to be so much a matter of stating the obvious that it sounded offensive. The King could not delegate judicial power and yet exercise it himself on occasion. In any case, Coke pointed out, James 'was not learned in the laws of his realm of England, and causes which concern the life or inheritance or goods or fortunes of his subjects are not to be decided by natural reason but by the artificial reason and judgment of law, which law is an act which requires long study and experience before that a man can attain to the cognizance of it.'[34] As a debating point, arguments could be made in favour of the King's interpretation, but Coke had circumvented theoretical niceties by pointing out the facts of life. It was fundamentally a matter of political common sense. The picture of James I sitting in Star Chamber and giving judgment in a libel action was not very edifying, and it might do harm to that court which, as Plucknett observes, was most damaged by its friends.[35] Coke did not deny the right of the King to sit, for example, in King's Bench, but he insisted that when this occurred power of judicature remained only with the judges.[36] Charles would be less concerned over this kind of thing, but even more than his father he was anxious to engage in practical affairs, and he could sit with a commission of Privy Councillors to review a Chancery decree.[37]

Coke's celebrated citation from Bracton was common currency and had been cited by Nicholas Fuller in the *Case of Monopolies*.[38] None the

[33] W. Lambarde, *Archeion*, ed. C. H. McIlwain and P. L. Ward, Cambridge, Mass., 1957, p. 56.

[34] 12 Co. Rep., 63–5 (77 *English Reports*).

[35] Plucknett, p. 192.

[36] E. Coke, *The Fourth Part of the Institutes of the Lawes of England*, London, 1669, p. 73. 12 Co. Rep., 63 (77 *English Reports*).

[37] Bodleian, Tanner MS. 447, ff. 49–52.

[38] Noy, 173–85 (74 *English Reports*). M. B. Donald, *Elizabethan Monopolies*, London, 1961, pp. 208–49.

less, the Crown was on an elevated level when it came to legal proceedings. Lord Keeper Egerton, speaking of monopolies at the close of
the 1597 Parliament, expressed Elizabeth's hope that her loving subjects
would not take away her prerogative, 'which is the chiefest flower in
her garland and the principal and head pearl in her crown and diadem'.[39]
In 1623, Hobart, Chief Justice of the Common Pleas, said: 'the prerogative laws are not the Exchequer law, but is the law of the realm for the
King, as the common law is the law of the realm for the subject. The
King's Bench is a court for the pleas of the Crown; the Common Pleas
is for pleas betwixt subject and subject; and the Exchequer is the proper
court for the King's revenues.'[40] It is possible that in later years Berkeley
really meant something like this when he made his disastrously inept
distinction between things justified by law and things justified by
government (Doc. 28 [8]). Bacon spoke of the 'garland of prerogatives'
as the sovereign's corpus of special rights, notably those before the
courts. Thus the Attorney and Solicitor Generals were unique in
their ability to combine the work of attorney and counsel. On the King's
behalf they could sue in any court, and they could reply in criminal
cases even though the accused had not called witnesses. In cases
between party and party, they could intervene or request adjournment
if the King's interest was possibly involved. The claim that the sovereign,
by the writ *de non procedendo rege inconsulto,* could stop proceedings
in any common law court was probably justified.[41] Even supposed
weaknesses were really a distinction: 'everything for the benefit of the
King shall be taken largely, as everything against the King shall be
taken strictly; and the reason why they shall be taken for his benefit
is because the King cannot so nearly look to his particular, because he
is intended to consider *ardua regni pro bono publico.*'[42] In practice, all
this made it impossible to treat James's claims to act as arbitrator or
to sit in judgment as a serious practical possibility. The scales were
tilted in the sovereign's favour. Indeed, the courts might have to act
against undue care shown by laymen. Early in the reign of Charles I,
the Exchequer reacted appropriately against commissioners who had
refused to set down depositions because they 'were not beneficial for
the King'.[43]

The Crown had many powers, both in terms of substance and procedure, but – and this is partly the story of Charles I – it could be

[39] J. Hurstfield, *The Queen's Wards,* London, 1958, p. 333. See J. W. Gough,
'Flowers of the Crown', *EHR* 1962, lxxvii. 86–93.
[40] From Godbolt, cited J. P. Kenyon, *The Stuart Constitution,* Cambridge,
1966, p. 106.
[41] *The Works of Francis Bacon,* ed. J. Spedding, R. L. Ellis, and D. O. Heath,
London, 1859, vii. 687–725. 3 Bulstrode, 32–4 (81 *English Reports*).
[42] From Godbolt, cited Kenyon, p. 106.
[43] P[ublic] R[ecords] O[ffice], Exch. K. R. Entry Books, E. 125/4, f. 254.

dangerous to rely upon them to the point where they became a substitute for policy. James was more practical. Far more than Charles, he recognized that there were major limitations upon the prerogative in so far as the property of the subject was concerned. His doctrines belonged to the world of high political theory and not of necessity to his actual sense of government. He was neither unreasonable nor perenially foolish. In 1610, when he was making a particular effort to humour the House of Commons, he ordered the destruction of Cowell's *Interpreter*, which in some respects had come close to his own *Trew Law of Free Monarchies* in describing the unfettered powers of the King. Through Salisbury, he took the occasion to transmit an assurance that he was 'King by the common law of the land'. In an important speech in March, he made it clear that a monarch, in his situation, not the founder of a realm but the ruler of an ordered state, would be answerable to God if he exercised his option of not respecting the rights and customs of his subjects. This was not a retreat but merely an attempt to present his opinions in the most palatable light. The difficulty was to determine what these rights and customs were, and this question could not be flinched from when it was necessary to know precisely what the Crown's rights were. In 1610, the King was after money not rights, but since the attempt to fashion a compact with Parliament failed the dilemma remained.[44]

The kind of point that arose is illustrated by the furore over impositions. They had never been declared illegal, but on the other hand it could not be said before 1606 that they had ever been declared legal. Mr Hall has demonstrated that a law case about impositions was no new thing in 1606, but the direct point of legality had not been raised as a central issue in these cases.[45] There were two kinds of argument in justification: the force of previous practice and the King's legal right or prerogative. The topic raised the whole issue of the King's position vis-à-vis the law – and the same was later true of tunnage and poundage – when in an inflationary situation dwindling hereditary revenues compelled the King to push harder, while spasms of depression, as in the 1620s, made the subject more unwilling to pay. People who are unwilling are difficult to convince on the subject of legal right, or rather another issue of right can become involved. Who had the right to decide? Some said the courts, but these more often than not decided for the Crown. Others said Parliament, which in the language of the times represented the body of the kingdom. This is one of the pitfalls. It is true that James never levied money 'without authorization from Parliament or the

---

[44] Kenyon, p. 12. *The Political Works of James I*, ed. C. H. McIlwain, New York, 1965, pp. 306–25.

[45] G. D. G. Hall, 'Impositions and the Courts, 1554–1606', *LQR* 1953, lxix. 200–18.

courts of common law',[46] but the great financial issues of the two early Stuarts arose because they did not have *both* kinds of authorization. Instead they opposed decisions from the courts, however legally correct, to the political reality of dissent as expressed in Parliament.

That there could be a gulf between the role of the courts and the role of Parliament indicates that the contemporary framework of political understanding was at fault. As over impositions, it was assumed that the question lay between the sovereign's prerogative and the subjects' rights. This was the hallmark of the 'ancient constitution', and it was believed that if either side encroached the entire social balance would tilt dangerously. Those who simply did not want to pay certain taxes, and who saw the Crown gaining legal verdicts, assumed that this tilt was taking place. In reality, it was their concept of 'constitution' which was at death's door. Few saw it. Wentworth, in his first speech as Lord President of the North, spoke of 'the joint individual well-being of sovereignty and subjection'. Charles, in his speech of January 25, 1641, when he announced that he would 'concur' with Parliament in discovering and reforming all innovations in Church and Commonwealth, warned Parliament to distinguish between reformation and alteration of government. On the latter he would never give way, and in perverse fashion events would keep him to his word. He expressed the inadequacy of the entire generation: 'my intention being to reduce all matters of religion and government to what they were in the purest times of Queen Elizabeth's days.' In the 1620s and 1630s, the enquiries into fees had adopted the same standard, that most useless of all yardsticks. As Professor Kenyon has written, 'everyone spoke the same language', and the point was illustrated again by the speeches of Pym and Strafford at the latter's trial.[47]

[46] Kenyon, p. 8.
[47] *Ibid.*, pp. 10, 18–19.

2

Judges and Lawyers

'God doth assist the judge in his judgment seat but not in his chamber.'

Sir Edward Coke, 1605.[1]

IN selecting themes which explain the predicament of the judges in 1640, it must be remembered that many aspects of the legal system attracted hostility. Rigby's speech against Finch (Doc. 25) was not alone in its appeal to a popular sentiment which contained elements of distaste for the mechanics, if not the fundamentals, of the system of law over which the bench presided. This kind of criticism, however, was only of subsidiary importance during the early months of the Long Parliament. Attention should rather be paid to such matters as the government's faith in extra-judicial opinions and the use it had made of the Exchequer Chamber for debate. This forum – it can hardly be described as an institution – had developed most of its characteristics by the time James I came to the throne, and it was not seriously threatened by the aggrieved reformers of 1640–2 even though it had been the instrument of Hampden's defeat. Instead the integrity of individual judges was assailed. The Exchequer Chamber could be valued if the judges were respected men.

The legal world was a mosaic of practice and privilege. After the judges came the serjeants, leaders of the ordinary ranks in the profession. Then note must be taken of the benchers, the readers and, on a lower scale, of the utter barristers, those who had been called. Beneath this level swarmed a number of inner barristers or students, who had not been called, and a mass of attorneys, clerks, conveyancers, solicitors, and others important in the life of the courts and in the conduct of litigation. There were to be subtle clarifications in the century and a half after 1550. 'At the lower end, we see a growing distinctness in the profession of the attorney, a growing separation between the attorneys and the barristers, and the rise of three new classes in the legal profession – pleaders, conveyancers and solicitors – the first two of which approximate to the profession of the barrister, and the third to that of the attorney. At the upper end, the commanding position of the serjeants

[1] J. Hawarde, *Les Reportes del Cases in Camera Stellata*, ed. W. P. Baildon, London, 1894, p. 250.

was modified by the growth of the pre-eminence of the law-officers of the Crown, and the rise of the new class of king's counsel.'[2]

English literature provides rich evidence of hostility towards persons involved in the operations of the law. Many criticisms common to the early seventeenth century were later voiced by Swift in the second volume of *Gulliver's Travels*. On the other hand, lawyers were often portrayed as grave and worthy. Appreciation is as common as depreciation; if it were otherwise the profession could not have survived. Merchants habitually complained about lawyers and legal procedures, but Thomas Mun described the legal profession as 'noble' and necessary; he rejected notions that lawyers were responsible for tedious and unnecessary litigation and denied that even the worst aspects of going to law seriously damaged the national economy.[3] Ben Jonson, who dedicated *Every Man Out of His Humour* to the legal profession, included a glorious parody of canon lawyers and theologians in his *Silent Woman*. It may be that some popular satire was directed less against common lawyers as such than against pretentious experts who confused and cheated laymen. Financiers, merchants and physicians were not spared. Bravado, ignorance and simplicity were also targets: the boastful soldier and the common man in all his aspects were lampooned across the stage. Early Stuart Parliaments debated the fees of clerks rather than the fees of counsel. Even so, the temptation to play down popular hostility must be tempered with caution. In the House of Commons the barrister, unlike the attorney or clerk, was protected in that he had a kinship and place.

Lawyers were regarded as business men whose immediate purpose was profit. Some became considerable landowners. This was acceptable so long as they did their job of providing the litigant with what he wanted. All too often this did not happen, and then clients might complain: 'for what one saith to be true law, the other by and by confuteth the same, so that one knoweth not to whom to trust.'[4] Similar sentiments have often been expressed about the medical profession, but perhaps there is a different sentiment with those who go to law. The litigant generally feels morally justified – at the very least he wants to come out on top – and yet he is made aware, often correctly, that legal and moral justice are separate entities.

Judges and counsel did their best, but they must often have felt undermined in high quarters. In 1615, Cambridge undergraduates amused James I with the comedy, *Ignoramus*, which ridiculed the dullness and mendacity of lawyers. The lampoon of the central character

[2] Holdsworth, vi. 432.
[3] T. Mun, *England's Treasure by Forraign Trade*, ed. of 1664, Oxford, 1959, pp. 59–60.
[4] National Library of Wales MS. 9051, no. 95.

was savage (Doc. 2), although it was stressed that the faults of individuals should not condemn all the profession. The King was seen to revel in the fun, and he bestowed the advowson of Barton upon the creator of the title role. He praised judges but likened common lawyers to wind instruments (Doc. 3), and he made it clear that in appointing Williams as Lord Keeper he was sick of their ways, being men bred and trained in corruption. 'Most of our lawyers and judges,' wrote Salisbury in 1610, 'though learned in their profession, yet, not having other learning, they upon a question demanded, bluntly answer it, and can go no further, having no vehiculum to carry it by discourse or insinuation to the understanding of others.' A Master of Requests could describe some lawyers as 'peevish', and when Lord Chancellors told new serjeants not to bring unjust and vexatious suits, it could be believed that this was what some serjeants were doing. In assessing costs, Masters of Chancery were told to ignore 'what either the sumptuous client will give, or the greedy lawyer will take'.[5]

The attack upon Bacon, aided by a litigant who was annoyed that the Lord Chancellor had not been influenced, is symbolic. Most judges accepted gifts, and the proffer of sugar loaves was almost a ritual. In 1620, when the borough charter was in question, the Mayor of Lyme Regis was allowed discretion by his colleagues as to what 'gratuity' should be given to the Chief Baron at the assizes.[6] It is almost impossible to pin-point clear instances of judgments being affected, and it is probable that this happened rarely, if at all. However, going to law was not always a simple matter of moving from initiation of a suit in one court to judgment in the same court. Indeed, even if litigation was confined to one court, judgment might not be achieved. Often there were many suits around the same dispute, several courts could be involved, and the atmosphere might be that of a war of attrition. James Harrington's case against the Warden of his college is typical (Doc. 8). The very names of the parties should have raised the possibility that another jurisdiction might have claims. Sometimes the delay was a device, sometimes the parties were hoping to force discovery of evidence, and often it was just incompetence. Proceedings in a particular court might have no more than a tactical purpose. Even when there was only one set of proceedings, the end might well be some settlement or interim order. Every stage in procedure could be a subject of contest. Litigants hoped that gifts or letters from powerful friends would thrust the fact of their existence upon the judge's mind, and thus distinguish

---

[5] T. Birch, *The Court and Times of James the First*, London, 1849, ii. 292. *The Letters of John Chamberlain*, ed. N. E. McClure, Philadelphia, 1939, ii. 383. *Archaeologia*, 1806, xv. 51–2. T. Wilson, *A Discourse upon Usury*, ed. R. H. Tawney, London, 1925, p. 13. BM, Additional MS. 20,700, f. 13.

[6] *Diary of Walter Yonge*, ed. G. Roberts, Camden Old Series 1848, xli. 37n.

them from the faceless mass. Procedural advantage was so important that we cannot reject the notion that this common practice could be viewed as an abuse.

It was generally agreed that there were too many law suits, that many of these were duplicated and vexatious, and that delays and costs were intolerable. Recrimination was mutual, but attorneys, clerks, prothonotaries and solicitors were assumed to be largely responsible. Sir John Davies, writing about delays, asked 'who are they that make this objection?' He pointed to litigants, full of spleen and wilfulness, and to the corruption of 'needy' solicitors, 'loath to quench the fire that maketh them warm'.[7] If laymen despised the law in so far as they saw litigation as a game, judges and lawyers could respond in good measure and feel that too many litigants were gamesters. A litigant in Chancery was accused of threatening a witness outside the Examiners' office and of starting vexatious proceedings against him in King's Bench. 'Art thou there? It might and were better for thee to go and see what I have laid against thee in the King's Bench. I think that I have hooded thee. Before I have done with thee, I will break thy back. I will make thee weary of this place or of any other place wherein thy being or doing concerneth me.'[8] There are plenty of examples like this; many were fabricated, but the general tenor is convincing. Laymen were certainly abandoned and often vicious in their employment of legal proceedings, but the methods lay to hand. No layman ever invented a technical point with which to torment his opponent.

The period is often described as litigious. It is impossible to give comparative figures, but it would seem that practically everyone over the rank of yeoman was likely during the course of his life to be involved at law in suits before the major courts which were single or multitudinous. Yeomen and lesser persons were constantly appearing before the courts, especially quarter and petty sessions or borough and manorial tribunals. Contemporaries feared that the great, the wealthy and the vexatious were favoured by a system which allowed disputes to range from court to court. A Chancery Master recommended retention of a bill 'or else the plaintiff to be left remedyless as over-matched with mightier than himself, as much sued and threatened with multiplicity of suits, either to be undone or to be urged to relinquish his right'. Laymen condemned barristers who rushed from bar to bar in pursuance of their business, a well-known habit which was supposed to induce delays, extra costs and the need to hire several counsel. In 1585, Francis Alford suggested that counsel should be limited in their practice to one court. Sir John Davies was conventional in his utterances

---

[7] J. Davies, 'A Discourse of Law and Lawyers', *Works*, ed. A. B. Grosart, privately printed 1869–76, ii. 264–5.

[8] PRO, Chan. Reports and Certificates, C. 38/3, Pashew v. Rushworth, 1599.

about covetousness and malice creating force and fraud. He also thought that one of the most significant features was the increase in the statute book since Henry VIII. Society, he argued, was suffering from an expansion of wealth which brought in its train more contracts, real and personal. Wealth by itself would entail technical complications, but it also created luxury and excess 'which breedeth unthrifts, bankrupts and bad debtors'.[9]

There were few simple lines of conflict. Attorneys, clerks, counsel, judges, litigants and solicitors engaged in a desultory cross-fire. The judges tried to remain aloof, but this was impossible. Lawyers might be criticized, but judges were drawn from their ranks and were presumed to exercise much authority over courts and Inns. Attorneys, solicitors and others might be assailed, but once again the judges were held responsible for what went on in their courts. Despite moral strictures and efforts at counter-attack, they could not escape being tarred by the brush. Incidents did not help, as when in 1592 Chief Baron Manwood disappeared from the bench and died in an odour of disgrace and scandal.[10] The things said about Coke in 1616 were no less damaging than the attack upon Bacon. The sacking of Justices, however few, damaged the bench as a whole, and the same is true of the affairs of Cranfield and Knollys. The 1620s and the 1630s swirled with implications of financial and political corruption, even of incompetence, which were alien to the reign of Elizabeth even if the historian can argue that things were not all that different.

That doubt should exist over common practices is not unusual, and charges of corruption conformed pretty well with customary behaviour. It was said that Cranfield had allowed his secretaries to take fees for forwarding suits. An Elizabethan Attorney of the Wards was described as 'partial' and his accuser, Lord Sheffield, affirmed that it was 'a thing, God knows, too ordinary in this time'. Judges of assize were confronted with the suggestion that they and Privy Councillors were financially corrupt. At Norwich, Mr Justice Harvey retorted: 'it seems by the sermon that we are corrupt but know that we can use conscience in our places, as well as the best clergyman of all.' The fundamental suspicion was that men moved to the bench while encumbered with obligations. An Elizabethan merchant lent forty pounds without interest to Peter Mutton, a future Welsh judge, on condition that 'for the interest he giveth counsel in all my causes'. It was feared that judges might help their friends and relatives, and this had been one of the major issues in the disgrace of Manwood. The implications were more dramatic when it was widely supposed that Buckingham had influenced the

[9] PRO, C. 38/3, South v. Meere, 1599. BM, Lansdowne MS. 44, f.2. Davies, ii. 266.

[10] Holdsworth, i. 505.

promotion of George Croke, Nicholas Hyde and Richardson, but suspicions of this kind were not disastrous. Far more serious was the growing notion that judges – whose indebtedness to the government for promotion was taken for granted – could corrupt the King by providing self-interested advice.[11]

Career Judges and Lawyers

The twelve principal judges and all the serjeants were said by Thomas Wilson at the end of Elizabeth's reign to be men worth £20,000 to £30,000 a year. Coke, once a nobody, had risen during a decade to be an Attorney General who could annually dispense £12,000 or more. Indeed it was rumoured that he had made as much as £100,000 in twelve months. Bacon, evidently speaking of direct income, once told King James that his place as Attorney General was 'honestly' worth £6,000 per annum. Positions on the bench were also very valuable. Ley, who has been described as fabulously wealthy, was worth less than those other Somerset men, Sir John Popham and Sir Edward Phelips. The Chancellor had enormous opportunities, and therefore the greatest difficulty in convincing others of the separation between judicial integrity and patronage or personal interest. Fees are not a sufficient guide. The Chief Justice of the Common Pleas – Clarendon said he had the best office of the law – probably received more than his colleague in the King's Bench, who had the larger fee. On the other hand, many of the *puisnes* experienced financial anxiety. Whitelocke, who had a private estate, put his total income as a King's Bench Justice as £974 10s 10d after expenses. Almost a third of this came from going on circuit. Official salaries were sometimes in arrears, and in 1627 Doddridge, Jones and Whitelocke were only just restrained by Lord Keeper Coventrye from suing out writs of *liberate* in respect of the non-payment of their wages. The whole episode suggests that some of the judges were in a dangerous mood of revolt, and Whitelocke's scathing comments on that 'old dissembler', the Lord Treasurer – the former Chief Justice Ley, now Earl of Marlborough – is a striking indication of bad blood and dubious practices in high quarters (Doc. 7). Payment of fees was again in arrears during April 1635: £120 1s 10d was owed to Chief Justice Bramston, and £97 9s 10½d to Chief Justice Finch; £94 3s 2d was due to each of the *puisnes* of King's Bench and Common Pleas. Arrears owing to Chief Baron Davenport amounted to £94 3s 3d, and each of the three ordinary Barons of the Exchequer were owed

[11] H. E. Bell, *An Introduction to the History and Records of the Court of Wards and Liveries*, Cambridge, 1953, pp. 36–7. E. Foss, *Judges of England*, London, 1848–64, vi. 209. A. H. Dodd, 'Mr Myddleton, the Merchant of Tower Street', *Elizabethan Government and Society*, ed. S. T. Bindoff, J. Hurstfield, and C. H. Williams, London, 1961, p. 274.

£56 13s 4d. Furthermore, the remuneration for going on circuit and other tasks had not been fully met. Others also suffered: Secretaries Coke and Windebank were each owed £25 out of their basic fee of £100. It is evident, however, that the judges as well as ministers could survive on sources of revenue outside their official fees.[12]

Although the practice was common, it was considered improper to make suit for public offices of trust. Others, who may not have openly solicited promotion, reached into their pockets when advancement was gained. The morality of this was also open to question. This particularly affected the position of a judge, but it also applied to the Attorney and Solicitor Generals and to the serjeants, ranks from which judges were drawn. It was usual to give £500 to £600 for being called to the order of the coif, a sum which George Croke apparently refused to pay. Something like £7,500 must have been handed over when fifteen serjeants were called in 1623. When Whitelocke became a serjeant, his expenses – purchase money, robes, feasts, rings – exceeded his income from a year's practice. It was rumoured that Ley offered £10,000 for the Attorney Generalship, and when Yelverton received the post he paid over £4,000 on the grounds of convention although he had refused to strike a bargain beforehand. Less tangible, but more damaging, were rumours about appointments to the bench. In 1582, it was thought that someone was trying to buy the Chief Justiceship of the King's Bench. It was said in 1626 that Richardson disbursed £17,000 and married a relative of Buckingham. Whitelocke frowned on George Vernon who he believed had paid money to become a Baron of the Exchequer. Montagu certainly paid to become Chief Justice, and later Lord Treasurer, and Sir Charles Caesar apparently paid to become Master of the Rolls in 1639. Laymen, lawyers and even fellow judges could surmise that money explained the appointment of men deemed to be incompetent. It was an attractive idea because it supported the pretence that the system of law was being abused. It was thus possible to avoid the proposition that the legal system was at fault or that existing interpretations of law were to be condemned not because they were wrong but because they were unpalatable. The first two Stuarts sustained this attitude whenever they made clear their dislike of a judge.[13]

[12] T. Wilson, 'The State of England', ed. F. J. Fisher, *Camden Miscellany* xvi, 1936, pp. 24–5. C. Wilson, *England's Apprenticeship, 1603–1763*, London, 1965, p. 10. Foss, vi. 28. Barnes, p. 20. Clarendon, ii. 110. J. Whitelocke, *Liber Famelicus*, ed. J. Bruce, Camden Old Ser. 1858, lxx. 106. PRO, State Papers Domestic, Charles I, S.P. 16/301, no. 9.

[13] Foss, vi. 3. J. Bramston, *The Autobiography of Sir John Bramston*, ed. Lord Braybrooke, Camden Old Ser. 1845, xxxii. 6. Whitelocke, pp. 44, 84, 108. J. Strype, *Annals of the Reformation*, Oxford, 1824, III, i. 198–200. Yonge, pp. 97–8. M. Prestwich, *Cranfield: Politics and Profits under the Early Stuarts*, Oxford, 1966, pp. 287–8. Holdsworth, v. 353.

Tenure of most offices was potentially unstable: one has only to look at the varieties of fortune experienced by Lord Treasurers, Lord Chamberlains, Masters of the Wards, or Secretaries of State. Prior to the appointment of Davenport in 1631, the Chief Baron and Barons of the Exchequer, in some ways the most recent members of the club of senior judges, were appointed *quam diu se bene gesserint*, but the Justices of King's Bench and Common Pleas were normally appointed *durante bene placito*. Appointment of the Lord Chancellor centred on the ceremony whereby he was given custody of the Great Seal, and the sovereign could remove him by recalling the Seal. Certainly the judges were under a strain, but appointment during good behaviour might not have made much difference. It is true that Chief Justices Crewe and Heath were dismissed, as was Coke – whose removal should probably be considered as rather different in character – and George Croke retired when he was very old. The affair of Chief Baron Walter, suspended from 1629 until his death in 1631, does not really suggest that appointment during good behaviour provided adequate protection. Walter was able to resist dismissal – although his writ of *scire facias* demanding that the King show cause was denied – and this meant that he could not easily be replaced, although an offer was made to James Whitelocke. On the other hand, Walter's activity as a judge was over, and presumably this was the King's principal intent. The affair was embarrassing because Charles had recently adopted a virtuous stance, that of protecting his Barons of the Exchequer from interference by the House of Commons (Doc. 11). All dismissals under the first two Stuarts are deservedly celebrated, but they are only striking in comparison with the calmer years of Elizabeth. In the 1550s, the Chief Justiceship of the King's Bench had passed hands like a hot potato, and the later Stuart period was to see more dismissals than the early part of the century.[14]

The bench was associated both with the bar from which it was sprung and with the men who made government policy. Elizabeth had been distinguished by her restraint in keeping Justices off the Privy Council, although she admitted Popham. Even under the Stuarts, judges were never all that important as Privy Councillors. Nor did it follow that judges who were Councillors were automatically creatures

[14] Coke, *Fourth Institute*, p. 117. Gardiner, vii. 112–13. Havighurst, p. 64. Aylmer, pp. 111–13, rightly stresses the element of protection evident in Walter's case, but it depends on whether retention of the office or exercise of its functions is the main concern. The reader should consider this historian's suggestion that 'judicial' officers may have been supposed to be more answerable for what they did than 'ministerial' officers and therefore should be more easily removable. On the other hand, he writes that Chief Justice Heath's post was considered to be 'political' and that on dismissal no attempt was made to impugn his professional competence. *Ibid.*, pp. 109, 112. See above, chap. 1, n. 10.

of royal policy. Coke was a Privy Councillor and a weighty one at the time of his troubles, 1615–16. His dismissal may provide a clue. The few who became Privy Councillors could not but be involved in faction. It is not all that important a theme, but it was an unfortunate one. If the presence of Justices at Council meetings has sometimes been interpreted as renewing the tie between Star Chamber and Privy Council, it could also be seen as doing the same for other courts. The Lord Chancellor, traditionally accepted as a leader in Council business, occupied a different position. In March 1629, Coventrye's name headed three of the five principal Council committees. These were those concerning knighthood, trade and trained bands; and the first two were certainly pregnant with legal and political implications. He was not on the committee for foreign affairs, and his name was cancelled from that for Ireland.[15]

Although some association with the Privy Council, and more generally methods of appointment and perhaps remuneration, emerge as major points, one may still doubt if it all adds up to very much. Rather we must look at the ambitions and experience of the men who became judges.

Elizabeth had confirmed the importance of the Attorney and Solicitor Generals, law officers of the Crown who provided a bridge between the practising legal profession and the executive. They were selected from the double readers, that is from the upper ranks of the profession, but they were not serjeants. Although conditions had changed, the serjeants still pretended professional superiority to the King's Attorney and Solicitor, originally clerical men. The Attorney General was still classified as an officer of the King's Bench, although he was hardly treated as such by that court. A serjeant accepting the office of Attorney or Solicitor General would first relinquish the coif. However, judges still had to be serjeants, and so law officers promoted to the bench would first be admitted to the coif.[16]

The Attorney and Solicitor Generals did not theoretically represent the King since the sovereign was always supposed to be present in court. They supervised the preparation and preliminary stages of proceedings, as well as conducting the case in court, whereas a private litigant would rely on attorneys and other officials for much of this work. They frequently intervened in cases between party and party when it was thought that the sovereign's interest might be prejudiced. Godfrey Goodman later described the Attorney as 'ever the rod and instrument to give the lash to those whom the King will cast down'. There was plenty of work, and this was underlined by the existence of King's

[15] A[cts of the] P[rivy] C[ouncil], July 1628–April 1629, pp. 276–7.
[16] A. Pulling, The Order of the Coif, London, 1897, p. 171 n 5. Holdsworth, vi. 468.

serjeants and by the development of King's counsel learned in the law. Although advice was taken from the Lord Chancellor and the Justices, the Attorney and Solicitor Generals also had to advise and assist the sovereign and the Privy Council. Their importance in this respect cannot be separated from the practice of promoting them to the bench.[17]

It was fairly common for the Solicitor General to be promoted to the Attorney Generalship, and for the Attorney General to be moved up as Lord Chancellor or as one of the two Chief Justices. The positions of *puisne* were usually filled by serjeants, and it was definitely advantageous to be a King's serjeant. Egerton, Francis Bacon and Coventrye were all made Lord Keeper after being Attorney General, but Puckering was a Queen's serjeant and Williams was from outside the profession. Coke, Heath and Hobart were made Chief Justice from the position of Attorney General, but Montagu, Crewe and Hyde were King's serjeants, the latter becoming one in order to make his subsequent elevation more respectable. Richardson and Bramston had also been King's serjeants, but both had previously been attorney general to the Queen. John Finch, another who had been attorney general to the Queen, only became a serjeant in order to become a *puisne*, and he was quickly advanced to be Chief Justice. Ley had been Attorney of the Court of Wards, and Littleton was Solicitor General.

It is clear that not much significance can be read into the habit of promoting the Attorney General. Coke's career requires no comment, and Heath was soon sacked. Lack of administrative connection may, however, have contributed to the difficulties of Crewe. The main point was that men were moving into commanding positions on the bench from a previous experience in government, or work associated with government, rather than from mere legal practice. It should not be assumed that previous experience or political antecedents would determine the attitudes of a judge, but the suspicion was there. Solicitor General Fleming was made Chief Baron in time to preside over *Bate's Case*, and later became Chief Justice of the King's Bench. Subsequent insinuations about his performance are doubtless unjustified, as they are with respect to Hyde, who drew Buckingham's defence and was promoted in time to preside over the *Five Knights' Case*. Hyde preserved a reasonable reputation, as did George Croke, another who was supposed to be in debt to the favourite's patronage. The danger lay less in the rumours than in the facts. A career on the bench was becoming interwoven with a normal career in office. Thomas Trevor, who had been solicitor to the Prince, was quickly made serjeant, King's serjeant, and

---

[17] J. R. Tanner, *Constitutional Documents of the Reign of James I, 1603–1625*, Cambridge, 1930, p. 126. Francis Bacon is traditionally associated with the development of these counsel and with the establishment of their fee and precedence. Holdsworth, vi. 473–4.

Baron of the Exchequer after Charles's accession. It was fair reward for a competent servant and probably represented the summit of Trevor's ambitions. With others this could not be said. The possibility of Coke moving from his Chief Justiceship to become Lord Treasurer was at least a matter of discussion in 1616, and after his dismissal from the King's Bench he was almost certainly interested in this position. His replacement on the bench, Montagu, expressed his uneasiness at being Chief Justice, his dislike for sitting all morning in Westminster Hall, and his boredom with the inbred nature of conversation during dinner at Serjeant's Inn. He went on to become Lord Treasurer and subsequently Lord Privy Seal, as such making a considerable impact upon the court of Requests. Equally significant is the career of Sir James Ley, who was known as 'Volpone' (Doc. 7). After being Chief Justice of the Irish Bench, he moved to be Attorney of the Wards, and was made Chief Justice of the King's Bench in 1621. He became Lord Treasurer in 1624, and Lord President of Wales in 1628. Montagu and Ley may have been exceptional, but their careers suggest that a Chief Justiceship need not be the summit of an ambitious lawyer's career. Such a position might only be a stepping-stone.[18]

Coke and his generation were proven lawyers and government officials. It was not unreasonable to suppose that they were King's men, but in an age when it was anyhow impossible to separate judges from politics the distinction was becoming more blurred than ever, and it had a smack of novelty. Both the pitfalls and the real possibility of circumventing them – this is a central theme to Coke's career – are perhaps more easily understood in the United States than in Britain. There is evidence to suggest that even ordinary serjeants were expected to favour the official position in Parliament, and Bacon could assume that acceptance of this status meant future compliance in the Commons.[19]

One traditional distinction is that which lay between serjeants and non-serjeants. Ceremony accorded the serjeants a place of particular dignity. When John Croke was knighted by James I, it was decided that this honour did not enhance his precedence amongst his fellow serjeants. On taking the oath, which stressed loyalty to the client, they left the Inns of Court and resided at one of the two Serjeant's Inns. The Inn in Fleet Street was celebrated in Elizabeth's reign, and judges lived there. Judges subsequently moved into the Inn in Chancery Lane, and Houghton died in his chambers there. These were important places,

---

[18] B. Whitelock, *Memorials of English Affairs*, Oxford, 1853, i. 47. *The Fortescue Papers*, ed. S. R. Gardiner, Camden New Ser. 1871, i. 209. J. Campbell, *The Lives of the Chief Justices of England*, London, 1849, i. 358.

[19] D. H. Willson, *The Privy Councillors in the House of Commons, 1604–1629*, Minneapolis, 1940, p. 106.

frequently used for threshing out knotty points of law, and the collaboration of the judges and serjeants emphasized their standing
vis-à-vis the rest of the profession. But the separation of the serjeants
from the Inns of Court was of doubtful value, and their monopoly of
pleading in the Common Pleas represented a decreasing benefit. In
1604, it was established that a King's serjeant could not proceed by
information in the Star Chamber unless empowered by specific instructions. James I gave the Attorney General precedence over all but
the two most ancient serjeants, but Coke ruled that the Attorney
General could only precede the serjeants in giving motions if he was
moving on behalf of the King. It is too early to suggest that the serjeants were being definitively cut out of promotion to the bench, but
certainly their prominence was not what it had once been. A number
enhanced their careers by giving up the coif in order to become Attorney
or Solicitor General. Otherwise the emphasis was on becoming a King's
serjeant.[20]

The Inns of Court and the House of Commons

If one of the greatest symbols of prestige accorded to the English legal
profession was the coif – a tight white cap worn by judges and serjeants-
at-law and never doffed, not even in the presence of the King – most
common lawyers could be excused for seeing the Inns as the rock on
which their fortunes stood or fell. These were societies which provided
both organization and education. In comparison with other groups,
administrative or commercial, the common lawyers had a unique set
of arrangements. The civilians were few, and their organization was
small. The churchmen were many, and their institutional arrangements
were both too great and too loose. Unlike the colleges in the universities,
the Inns were hardly fettered by foundations and this, while it sometimes meant hard times, underlined their freedom of self-governance.
Public honours carried little weight. In May 1605, it was ordered at
the Inner Temple that knights called to the bench of the Inn should
take rank according to their 'anciency'. The Inns, possessed of a strength
which both created and perpetuated vested interests, were plagued with
problems: disputes between themselves, financial anxiety, arguments
over admission and call, disputes over curriculum and teaching methods,
and a current of resentment which on occasion burst forth into exhibi-
tions of what can fairly be described as student power. Traditional ways
survived because those who had been called to the bar were an entrenched group. Short of a revolution which would destroy the courts,
the Inns, and the law, it meant that the methods of these men and the

---

[20] Foss, v. 418–19; vi. 33–4, 133. A. Harding, *A Social History of English Law*,
London, 1966, p. 174. 12 Co. Rep., 121 (77 *English Reports*). Holdsworth, vi.
470. Pulling, pp. 188–9, 191. 3 Bulstrode, 32 (81 *English Reports*).

system of law to which they were accustomed were also entrenched. Despite variants and offshoots, the medieval land law, its exercise and protection, provided a bond between the barrister and men of landed fortune.[21]

It cannot be said that the Inns experienced improper intervention by the first two Stuart kings, although there were some well-known incidents. James I accepted the polite refusal of the two Temples to appoint a lecturer who had his recommendation. Whatever the circumstances, and the King's wish had been made known, it was Lincoln's Inn, which has been described both as 'cavalier' and 'puritan' in mood during the 1630s, which expelled Prynne in 1634 and, incidentally, brought him back in 1641. At the time of the original scandal, the four Inns tried to disassociate themselves from the affair. A masque by James Shirley of Gray's Inn had extolled their love for the King, and a play by the same author certainly pleased the royal couple. One incident at the Middle Temple attracted attention. In 1639 Edward Bagshaw, who would later join the King at Oxford, was ordered to stop his reading, apparently because his address questioned the activity of bishops in the House of Lords and on the commissions of the peace. He withdrew from the Hall, continued his reading in the kitchen, and eventually left with an escort estimated at from forty to fifty horse.[22]

The Inns were representative of a society which, often distrustful of Charles, had no real ill-will towards him. As lawyers, their members might at times have been equally distrustful of some events in Parliament, and they must often have resented the criticism of courts and of their profession. The fear of Catholic plots and the portent of Ireland also had their effect. On November 8, 1641, it was declared that recusants were not to be admitted at the Middle Temple, and on the following day the benchers of the Inns solicited a commission from the Lord Keeper to tender oaths of supremacy and allegiance to Irish students and other suspected persons. Expulsions followed. In December, they were willing to raise a regiment to fight in Ireland. Whether any political loyalty can be discerned in this is doubtful. Certainly the attempt to arrest the five M.P.s had an adverse effect upon Charles's reputation at the Inns; we must also assume that there were little eruptions. As late as

[21] Harding, p. 174. Foss, vi. 31. For legal education generally, begin with K. Charlton, *Education in Renaissance England*, London, 1965, and W. Prest, 'Legal Education of the Gentry at the Inns of Court, 1560–1640', *Past and Present*, 1967, no. 38, pp. 20–39.

[22] *A Calendar of the Inner Temple Records*, ed. F. A. Inderwick, London, 1896, 1898, ii. pp. xxxi–xxxii. G. Hurst, *A Short History of Lincoln's Inn*, London, 1946, pp. 17–18. M. F. Keeler, *The Long Parliament, 1640–1641*, Philadelphia, 1954, p. 27. A. Wigfall Green, *The Inns of Court and Early English Drama*, New York, 1965, pp. 123–4, 131. Gardiner, vii. 331. *The Middle Temple Bench Book*, ed. J. B. Williamson, London, 1937, p. xxii.

February 1642, the Middle Temple accepted the recommendation of the Archbishop of Armagh that they choose Hugh Paulinus Cresey as lecturer. Canon elect of Windsor, he later became a Benedictine, served with the royal army, and apparently never turned up at the Inn.[23]

Subsequent historians even more than contemporaries have stressed the role of common lawyers in Parliament. Certainly there were many debates dominated by lawyers when even an Eliot kept silent. Nor was the government particularly strong since its available talent was few in numbers and had to be split between the two Houses. The Attorney General received a writ of assistance to attend the Lords, and it was generally understood that he should not seek election to the Commons. There was uncertainty as to whether this was a principle, or whether it was a matter of priority as between writ of assistance and election, according to which came first in time. In 1606 Hobart, currently an M.P., was appointed to the position. The committee of privileges was inconclusive; he remained in the House and was again active as an M.P. in the sessions of 1610–11. In 1614, Bacon's right to sit in the House of Commons was questioned. It was decided that he might continue but that in future the Attorney General was not to be an M.P. The Solicitor General, on the other hand, was normally allowed in the House, and in 1566 he had been Speaker. Egerton sat twice while Solicitor General, but in 1589 the House of Commons noted that he was absent and attending the Lords. On two occasions, it was demanded that his presence in the upper chamber be explained and that he be returned. Both times it was replied that he had been called by writ of assistance before securing election to the Commons. It would seem that Egerton had created the problem, having been returned for Reading at a late date after the man originally chosen had opted to take another seat. In 1593, Coke was both Solicitor General and Speaker. Subsequently, Fleming served in the Commons while Solicitor General. It was probably appreciated that the attendance of one of the two law officers was an advantage to each of the Houses, and Coke's comments in 1614 do not merely represent antagonism to Bacon (Doc. 1). There was rarely hostility towards the Attorney and Solicitor Generals as such. In 1642, Sir Edward Herbert was impeached and imprisoned for his part in the attempt to arrest the five Members, but this was an isolated circumstance in an abnormal situation. The only other officials from this group who were political casualties during the period were Attorney General Yelverton, sacked in 1621, and Richard Sheldon, a victim of the King,

---

[23] *A Calendar of the Middle Temple Records*, ed. C. H. Hopwood, London, 1903, pp. 73, 97. *Pension Book of Gray's Inn*, ed. R. J. Fletcher, London, 1901–10, i. pp. xlv–xlvi. *CSP Dom.* 1641–43, p. 217. *Cal . . . Inner Temple Records*, ii. pp. cv–cvi.

who was removed as Solicitor General a few weeks after Heath's dismissal from the bench.[24]

Lawyers and those with legal education were important in the House of Commons, and appearance in that chamber was not without its advantages. Acquaintances and reputation developed in Parliament helped one's career either in official circles or with private clients. Of the lawyers in the Commons of 1597, twenty were subsequently promoted to legal office. In 1614, there were forty-eight lawyers. At the beginning of the Long Parliament, and including five Masters of Chancery and the Solicitor General, there were some seventy-five lawyers. Clarendon said of them that it was difficult to find eminent lawyers although many would become eminent, and he implied that lack of parliamentary experience was a bad thing. He instanced the choice of Lenthall, in his view an inferior man, as Speaker. When war came, forty-two lawyers sided with Parliament and thirty-three with the King. Those who failed to get elected must be remembered; they included Sir Thomas Gardiner, Recorder of London, the King's original choice as Speaker. A large number of M.P.s had experienced the Inns of Court without having been called. In 1593, 43 per cent could claim some such education. In 1621, 225 are known to have attended an Inn although only 64 of them had been called. The figures for the beginning of the Long Parliament vary, but at the very least it was 310, that is rather more than the figure for the two universities. One count breaks them into two groups at the outbreak of war: 184 for Parliament and 120 for the King. Charles was supported by a minority of M.P.s, but his percentage of support from those with some experience of the Inns was not unimpressive once the issue was that of war.[25]

The reliance of the House of Commons on its legal experts does not have to be stressed. It was not their numbers but their skill which counted. Of the twenty-five M.P.s who served on five or more out of ten major committees in 1621, eight were barristers and many of the remainder had attended the Inns of Court. It is an improvement on the general percentage of lawyers in the House, but even so the

[24] The Parliamentary Diary of Robert Bowyer, 1606–1607, ed. D. H. Willson, Minneapolis, 1931, pp. 188–9. Commons Journals, i. 459–60. Willson, Privy Councillors, pp. 215–17. Holdsworth, vi. 465. S. D'Ewes, The Journals of all the Parliaments during the Reign of Queen Elizabeth, London, 1682, pp. 424, 441–2. Aylmer, pp. 112–13.

[25] J. E. Neale, The Elizabethan House of Commons, London, 1949, pp. 151, 307–8. T. L. Moir, The Addled Parliament of 1614, Oxford, 1958, p. 57. Keeler, pp. 18, 23. D. Brunton and D. H. Pennington, Members of the Long Parliament, London, 1954, p. 5. Clarendon, i. 220–1. L. Stone, 'The Educational Revolution in England, 1560–1640', Past and Present, 1964, no. 28, pp. 57–68 and tables ii–iv, viii. There is a slight discrepancy over figures of M.P.s in the Long Parliament who had attended Inns of Court. Compare Keeler, p. 27 (331) with Brunton and Pennington, p. 6 (310).

point must not be pushed too far because the supply of lawyers was limited.[26]

The difficulty is that we know the number of M.P.s, but it is harder to be precise about the number of lawyers. In any case, these have to be divided into two categories: those called to the bar and those effectively practising. In 1574, at the four Inns of Court there were 51 benchers and 125 utter barristers. Counting all ranks, including students, another Elizabethan figure gives a total of 956 persons at the Inns in term time and 409 in the vacation. At the festivities for the creation of Charles as Prince of Wales on November 4,1616, an assessment for the Inner Temple gives 30 benchers, 66 barristers with over seven years' experience, and 42 with less. In addition to these – their total is 138 – there were 160 under the bar. For the years 1629–32, the number of communicants at the two Temples averaged just over 460. This figure would include students and some others. It is clear that the number of men called was never very large. Indeed if the serjeants are remembered and others excluded – judges, office holders, recusants, drunks and failures – it would seem that England suffered from a shortage of barristers. Furthermore, limitations restricted young barristers, notably with respect to pleading in the great courts of Westminster. The ratio between available counsel and the mass of litigation was never so great as to cause collapse, but it was wide enough to confirm the role of attorneys, propel forward solicitors (Doc. 17), cause delays, and irritate both the public and some students who might suspect that senior officers at the Inns were more interested in restrictive practices than in promoting education and professional standards.[27]

One conclusion is clear. It is important to count the number of lawyers in the House of Commons – the resulting figure is patently less than that for J.P.s – but it is even more necessary to count the number of M.P.s in the Inns of Court. The latter figure is far more emphatic than the first. Furthermore when Parliament was in session, the Inns would be a meeting ground not merely for lawyer M.P.s but also for those who had not been elected and for some who in various ways were associated with the government. House of Commons committees used the Inns as meeting places. They must have been very important political clubs.

A professional society provides its own bonds, but these can be tightened amid more personal relationships. Francis Bacon pointed out in 1617 that the Attorney and Solicitor Generals were both the sons of

[26] I am grateful to Mary Winch for information on the 1621 Parliament.

[27] Cal . . . Inner Temple Records, i. pp. lxxviii, 468 ff.; ii. pp. xliv, lxxxiv, 104. Foss, v. 427. The names of counsel across the reigns of Elizabeth (353) and James I (259) are listed, ibid., v. 421–3; vi. 35–7. These lists do not represent a yearly count or average and they include duplicated names and the names of judges.

judges and that he himself was the son of a Lord Keeper. Coventrye was the son of a Common Pleas Justice. The law is littered with great families, and one may note the names of Bromley, Croke, Finch, Hyde, Montagu, Yelverton, and others. Edward Bagshaw ascribed his education to the facts of being 'bred at the feet of a Gamaliel of the law [Judge Nicholls] that married my mother, and to my alliance to three judges more [Chief Baron Sanders, Judge Harvey, Judge Morgan], all of them Readers of the Middle Temple and all Northamptonshire men, where from my childhood I have lived.' Oliver Cromwell's grandfather, father and two uncles were members of Lincoln's Inn, where Richard Cromwell was entered as a student in 1647. Chamberlain informed Carleton about 'his old school fellows' who had come up to Parliament. Different generations found an association in the Inns, and they believed in the old school tie. Pym and so many others were together in these societies during the first years of the seventeenth century. Between 1616 and 1620, seventy-six future members of the Long Parliament were at the Inns either as students or as persons who kept chambers. Yet there may have been conflicts of loyalty. Strafford came from the Inner Temple as did Hampden and Selden. The ease of association can be overstressed.[28]

The lawyers of the early seventeenth century, judges and practitioners, became entangled in a situation of assumed prejudice which was not altogether of their making. If one looks at the early Parliaments of Charles I, for example, it is evident that the King honestly despised critical lawyers and their arguments, deeming both to be a perversion of legal veracity, a front to conceal mean, petty and provincial attitudes. Dissident M.P.s could develop a similar attitude towards those who spoke for the official position. Their disgust was less dramatic than that of Charles, however painfully he failed to conceal it, but this would be more than made up for by the Short and Long Parliaments.

Unanimous Decisions and Opinions

Legal men could not escape participation in political controversy, but a situation was reached when they seemed to be both participants and ammunition. Political society stumbled through a sequence constructed by rival statements of position. The danger of this kind of thing had become apparent in the 1570s when the nature of royal prerogatives with respect to House of Commons privileges had been defined. The target at which dissenters must aim had been clarified. The Apology of 1604, the fate of which is open to question, was a massive attempt to instruct the new monarch. In 1614 the House of Lords tried to

---

[28] *The Letters and the Life of Francis Bacon*, ed. J. Spedding, London, *1861–74*, vi. 192. E. Bagshaw, *A Just Vindication of the Questioned Part of the Reading of Edward Bagshaw, Esq.*, London, 1660, p. 115. Hurst, p. 23. *Chamberlain Letters*, i. 212, 243. Keeler, p. 28.

instruct the country. The Commons protestation of December 18, 1621, in contrast to their petition of December 3rd, was a forthright statement. James I dissolved this Parliament and then produced his own justification. Things had not become over-serious, and the petition remained a favourite form of Commons expression despite the emergencies of the 1620s which produced protestations and remonstrances. It was easy to appear factual in a petition. M.P.s were loyal men with a conventional sense of etiquette, and it was not customary to press argument in the face of a sovereign. This instinctive sense of proper behaviour was put under a strain by James's predilection for discoursing at length, but Charles, partly because of his impediment, proved withdrawn. James invited talk whereas his son chilled this possibility. After the dissolution of Parliament in 1629, his declaration was a recital of events and facts as he saw them (Doc. 11). The sweeping theoretical arguments of James had been replaced by a grey technical world. Charles would rely upon solemn opinions from the most distinguished members of the legal profession, the judges. For eleven years, he would try to utilize that high regard for the law which had been a thorn in the government's side during the Parliaments of the 1620s. But were all legal pronouncements of equal value? It began to seem that the authorities were trying to play two fields at once. On the one hand, they placed increasing propaganda emphasis upon the conclusions of the judges in Exchequer Chamber, while on the other they sought to make all possible capital out of extra-judicial opinions.

The Exchequer Chamber for debate, as it has sometimes been called, can be regarded as one of the most important elements in early modern English administrative, legal and political history. When great and complex matters of law arose, the point could be referred into the Exchequer Chamber for discussion by all the Justices of King's Bench and Common Pleas, together with the Barons of the Exchequer, and possibly the Lord Chancellor if it was appropriate. When a decision had been reached, it was pronounced in that court from which the case had originated. Thus in *Calvin's Case*, proceedings in Chancery were adjourned on the question as to whether the defendant's demurrer could or could not be upheld. The status of the *post-nati* was examined by the judges in Exchequer Chamber and their decision was announced in the Chancery. The value of this kind of proceeding had become evident in the fifteenth century. Reliance on this tribunal was probably muted for a while in the Tudor period but never discarded. The cases of Capel (1581) and Chudleigh (1589) were dissected by meetings of the judges in Exchequer Chamber.[29] In the next century, the cases con-

[29] For other 'courts' styled 'Exchequer Chamber', see Plucknett, pp. 162, 171-2. For an introduction to the Exchequer Chamber for debate, described as an 'informal assembly' or 'summit conference', see J. P. Dawson, *The Oracles of*

sidered included some of great fame, including those of Slade (1602), Calvin (1607) and Hampden (1637). Excepting Parliament, which was intermittent, this meeting of Westminster judges must surely have appeared to the layman as the most powerful expression of English law in action. And if we are looking for a novel power in the legal structure, this is precisely what the Exchequer Chamber was providing. In the celebrated case of *Godden v. Hales* (1686), which has its own niche in constitutional history, Justice Herbert stated that a decision of all the judges in Exchequer Chamber provided a binding precedent: 'we never suffer it to be disputed or drawn in question again.' He was not creating a rule; he was only describing what had happened.[30]

As early as 1483, the judges in Exchequer Chamber employed majority opinion in respect of a case transferred for consideration from the Common Pleas, and the Chief Justice of that court, who did not agree, accepted it. A basis had been laid for a system whereby the minority endorsed the opinion of the majority. Once a decision of the Chamber bound all the judges taking part, it was a short but pregnant step to thinking that it bound subsequent judges faced with a case, the principles of which had already been settled in Exchequer Chamber. In 1602, it was declared that a decision in the Exchequer Chamber was 'a resolution of all the Justices of England, and this to be a precedent for all subsequent cases'. Francis Bacon said in *Calvin's Case* that even the Lord Chancellor would yield his opinion to that of the judges. If the forum of Exchequer Chamber was used, it meant that a bare majority of judges – it was seven against five in *Hampden's Case* – could lay down a rule which would be binding (Doc. 20). If the opinion of the judges was favourable, and this increasingly seemed to be the case, the King could rely upon an awesome authority.[31]

However, it was not the Exchequer Chamber but the use made of pre-trial opinions which became the great grievance. The sovereign had many options. He could consult the Lord Chancellor, the two law officers, individual judges, or groups of judges. James, however, introduced complications. At times, this was because he hoped to circumvent Coke whom he suspected of exercising too much influence, and he sometimes had information which suggested very clearly that the Chief Justice did not represent the viewpoint of his colleagues. None the less,

---

[30] *State Trials*, xi. 1254–5.
[31] Plucknett, p. 347. 4 Co. Rep., 93 (76 *English Reports*). Yelverton, 21 (80 *English Reports*). *Works of Bacon*, vii. 642.

---

the Law, Ann Arbor, 1968, pp. 60–2, 68–73. For *Capel's Case* and *Chudleigh's Case*, see 1 Co. Rep., 61b–63, 120–40b (76 *English Reports*). *Shelley's Case* was decided by all the judges, but the procedure was different. Lord Chancellor Bromley summoned the judges first to his residence and subsequently to Serjeant's Inn in Fleet Street. 1 Co. Rep., 93b–106b (76 *English Reports*).

Coke was often consulted without difficulty and therefore without publicity at the hands of historians. Coke, for his part, was often offended. He argued in legal terms but his position was essentially political. He appreciated the curious complexity of faction politics which governed at court, and when the King tried to obtain separate opinions he feared that this might open the way to the judges being unduly influenced. This does not mean, as his own career and period of activity as a Privy Councillor indicate, that he imagined that judges could be divorced from politics and policy making. In a fashion, and partly as a result of his own disappearance from the bench, Coke won his point. In the 1620s and 1630s individuals, notably the two Chief Justices, would still be consulted but group opinions were standard. On the other hand, one wonders what he would have thought about the development of unanimous opinions which were then used as a bar against further argument in the courts. For Coke, who did not have to face the circumstances of the 1630s, had done much to build up the authority of judicial pronouncements. His *Reports* are laced with 'resolutions', many of them fanciful and only off-the-cuff remarks with which he agreed. He had affirmed that a resolution of all the judges was of the highest authority 'next unto the court of Parliament'. As Professor J. P. Dawson has written, 'contemporaries evidently did not find it strange that judges and lawyers, gathered in conclave, could be credited with issuing authoritative pronouncements on matters that were divorced from pending litigation. Other reporters beside Coke referred to judicial "resolutions", some as remote from the issues actually decided as those announced by him.'[32]

Many of these elements are to be found in the manoeuvres which preceded *Hampden's Case*. The second opinion could be seen as unnecessary – for the King already had an opinion – save in so far as it was required to undermine opposition. It was entered in the courts at Westminster, 'for this is a thing not fit to be kept in a corner', and the judges on circuit were ordered to give publicity to it (Doc. 19). Actually these opinions were not fully unanimous, although the second was signed by all, and the collapse of government in 1640 prevented the device from being perfected. Even so, it could be believed that serious wrongs had been perpetrated. Before the Petition of Right, the Crown solicited opinions as to its power to commit, and on March 3, 1629, the two Chief Justices and the Chief Baron were consulted on the extent of parliamentary privilege, particularly when it was alleged that crimes had been committed in the House of Commons. In April, questions were put to all the judges. From the beginning, the judges were thus involved in the campaign against Eliot, but they hesitated to answer

[32] E. Coke, *The Second Part of the Institutes of the Lawes of England*, London, 1671, p. 218. Dawson, p. 71.

points which might come before them judicially (Doc. 10). There were many other occasions. In 1623, their opinion was sought as to the nature of Parliament (Doc. 4); in 1628, they declared that the writs of summons for an Irish Parliament had been illegally issued;[33] in 1636, they limited the ability of prisoners to leave gaol during a time of plague (Doc. 18). They played a decisive part in the development of Charles's forest policy and in the extension of the boundaries of Stannary jurisdiction, the latter probably being an instance when the minority surrendered their will and conformed with the majority view and the will of the Privy Council (Doc. 15). In 1633, a Star Chamber decree followed an opinion of all twelve judges on a variety of subjects, including food prices, engrossing, and gambling in taverns.[34] In May 1640, all the judges 'asserted' the power of Convocation to make canons. In this matter, concluded Clarendon, the judges were 'at least as guilty' as the Councillors, the bishops and the clergy.[35]

Examples can be multiplied, and in most instances there was little ground for objection. It was the use to which some opinions were put, and the attempt to make them unanimous and binding, which aroused a storm of criticism. Coke's distinction – albeit made under different circumstances – between proper advice and the improper use of opinion in a dispute was forgotten (Doc. 1). At the dissolution of Parliament in 1629, Charles felt called upon to defend the independence of the judges (Doc. 11). They were increasingly involved in the approval and formulation of financial policies. Ship money represents the climax of this movement. Justice Berkeley, who was believed to have said that the judges were above an act of Parliament, was reputed to have maintained at the York assizes in March 1637 that all the judges were in agreement over ship money. It could not be otherwise, for 'it was a base and unworthy thing for any to give his hand contrary to his heart' (Doc. 28 [7]). Ironically, this was precisely the opinion of critics.

The judges were impeached in the Long Parliament and the practice of taking extra-judicial opinions was condemned. Charles I's belief that they should not be influenced by Parliament had come to be interpreted as meaning subservience to wicked ministers. The reaction can be seen in the argument of Hobbes that judges could err and that their decisions need not be binding upon the future: 'all the sentences of precedent judges that have ever been cannot all together make a law contrary to natural equity' (Doc. 32).

[33] Rushworth, ii. 19–21. Gardiner, viii. 18–19.
[34] Rushworth, ii. 196–201.
[35] Clarendon, i. 272–3.

3

The 1620s

'Parliaments never break with the King but that they meet with loss.'
Mr Mallet, August 9, 1625.[1]

THE accusers of November 1640 had not always been hostile to the administration, and the accused had not always been government types. Many persons who were prominent in official ranks during the 1630s had been notorious critics during the previous decade. Talk of apostacy is almost irrelevant, and discussion of transition between Court and Country – admittedly useful terms – is of little help. Men who made a choice in the late 1620s or early 1630s were not fighting the controversies of 1640. None the less, events during the ten years which span Charles's accession provide standard themes which, important at the time, were going to be crucial in later years. Aspects of revenue, parliamentary privilege, liberty of the subject – why did Eliot have to succumb? – are among the most important and well known. There were significant stirrings with respect to the place of the judges in constitutional society, and in this decade their collaboration with the House of Lords, itself experiencing a judicial renaissance, weakened as the possibility of some kind of collision with Parliament became more apparent. The attempt by the House of Commons in 1629 to get the Barons of the Exchequer to change their minds, followed by the King's insistence that judges should not be so approached (Doc. 11), was a fascinating climax to a great, if often fruitless, parliamentary decade.

Charles, who as Prince of Wales sat in the House of Lords in 1621 and 1624, believed that a consistent attempt was made in the Parliaments of the 1620s to take advantage of the Crown's financial predicament. He concluded that, at least for a time, the quest for parliamentary supply must be abandoned. Financial independence and a stable society could be sought through an effective enforcement of existing laws, and the country would be bombarded with evidence of the King's rights. This was less a new policy than an intensification of existing trends. Before Charles came to the throne there had been trouble over schemes of drainage, assessment of commissioners of sewers, methods of raising money for ships, and the structure of administrative office. Resentment

[1] *Debates in the House of Commons in 1625*, ed. S. R. Gardiner, Camden New Ser. 1873, vi. 105.

about these matters can be discerned under Elizabeth, and the same can be said of those old grievances, fiscal feudalism and purveyance.[2] Impositions, patents and monopolies were other standard items to which Charles merely provided a few new twists. After the wreckage of 1614, they overshadowed hopes for the Parliament of 1621.

Impositions, Patents and Monopolies

In the last years of Elizabeth, the tax on currants may have compensated the government in respect of a former annual payment which had been extinguished by the Levant Company's surrender of its charter. The principle behind impositions was old, but it had not been subjected to formal analysis. In any case, the impositions demanded by Elizabeth had not been many. Nor had there been any dramatic increase by 1606 when *Bate's Case* was heard in the Exchequer. The government was interested in having a questioned right vindicated, and Bate probably represented the Levant Company's wish to re-establish its former monopoly of Venetian trade. The bench found for the Crown: foreign policy and international relations were part of the prerogative, and foreign trade and its taxation were an intrinsic part of international relations. Bate was an importer of goods which at the relevant time belonged to Venetians and were not yet in England. The King's right to tax a subject or his goods was not therefore in question, and even if it had been the importer would suffer nothing since he passed on the impost to the consumer. In any case, all the ports in the kingdom belonged to the King.[3] A prerogative basis to impositions had been confirmed, the details of the judgment were reported to Parliament, and it was indicated that similar reasoning covered impositions upon tobacco. Hesitance became dissent when Salisbury chose to utilize this judgment in order to tax a broad array of commodities.

Some government supporters drifted towards the error of trying to intrepret the judgment in *Bate's Case* as a comprehensive authority, and so critics were seduced into commenting upon the value of this judgment. Not all fell into the trap, and an M.P. said in 1614 that something should be done if the fact of the tax was not to develop into a

---

[2] For purveyance, see: Allegra Woodworth, *Purveyance for the Royal Household in the Reign of Queen Elizabeth*, Trans. Am. Phil. Soc., new ser. xxxv, pt. 1, Philadelphia, 1945; G. E. Aylmer, 'The Last Years of Purveyance, 1610–1660', *Econ. Hist. Rev.* 1957, 2nd ser. x. 81–93.

[3] *State Trials*, ii. 371–94. Extracts in Kenyon, pp. 62–4, and G. W. Prothero, *Select Statutes and Other Constitutional Documents . . . 1558–1625*, Oxford, 1913, pp. 340–2. See G. D. H. Hall, *op. cit.*, and his 'Bate's Case and "Lane's" Reports: The Authenticity of a Seventeenth Century Legal Text', *Bulletin of the John Rylands Library* 1952–3, xxxv. 405–27. Only in later days did Coke reveal his disagreement, and his accounts vary. 12 Co. Rep., 33–5 (77 *English Reports*; cf. p. 1315, n.A). Coke, *Second Institute*, p. 63. Holdsworth, vi. 45 n. 3.

precedent. Sir John Davies was not greatly concerned with *Bate's Case*, which he acknowledged to be a particular decision. Coke probably agreed (Doc. 1). Davies, like other supporters of official policy, believed that the right to levy impositions could be found in a broad variety of precedents and arguments: 'that since the King hath absolute power to shut the ports and stop trade, it standeth with as good reason that he should have the like power to lay reasonable impositions upon merchandises for opening of the ports and for giving of freedom of trade again.' On the other hand, it was reasonable for critics to argue that goods were genuinely and not ficticiously owned by the importer before reaching England. The imposition upon coal – transported by coastal shipping – could be interpreted as being outside the decision of 1606 since the product was produced, consumed and owned in England. The Barons of the Exchequer had in fact suggested that the King could lay impositions on commodities produced in England, but this was not central to the case before them, and it cannot be said to have been established or fully discussed. Such impositions therefore fall 'within the dicta rather than the decision of the case'. This, of course, was precisely why the government did not wish to be committed to *Bate's Case* as its basic authority.[4]

An element in the situation was the suspicion that the consumer paid. As Noy said in 1629 of tunnage and poundage, 'the merchants pay it, so we pay them'. Merchants who complied, as did the majority of them, appeared to connive with officialdom. It did not help when it was supposed that Salisbury in 1608 had discussed the matter at a meeting in the Guildhall attended by a hundred merchants and the Barons of the Exchequer. Was this an attempt to evade Parliament's traditional role in respect of supply? In 1610, M.P.s were determined to press the matter. The King did not want discussion, but he was also amenable to Salisbury's hopes of securing a contract and therefore had to be tolerant. On May 11th he forbade discussion of the Crown's right, but he permitted discussion of grievances and details, for example the nature of merchant rate. However, the Commons rather ignored this limitation. James did not insist, and hence the great debate on impositions. At one time, it was more or less agreed that most should be remitted if Parliament would grant him the remaining ones. However, this was dependent on reaching an agreement with respect to feudal incidents. A number of impositions were in fact removed, but it was said in 1614 that the remaining three or four hundred were the most onerous.[5]

---

[4] Moir, p. 95. J. Davies, 'The Question Concerning Impositions, Tonnage, Poundage, Prizage, Cutoms, etc.," *Works*, iii. 52, 59. Kenyon, p. 75. *State Trials*, ii. 393–4. Holdsworth, vi. 44, 46–7.

[5] *Commons Debates for 1629*, ed. W. Notestein and F. H. Relf, Minneapolis, 1921, p. 142. Gardiner, ii. 12. *Proceedings in Parliament, 1610*, i. 130–1; ii. 82,

Impositions were largely responsible for the failure of Parliament in 1614, but in respect of collection the Crown does not appear to have been greatly hindered. Some mercantile complaints had been erased through adjusting the tax system more in favour of English merchants at the expense of foreign ones. In any case, many challenges centred not on the right but upon the amount of the tax, a point that had also been raised by Bate. In 1610, in response to parliamentary complaint, the government admitted a mistake in that Blyth and Sunderland had been wrongly grouped with Newcastle. The ministers of James employed a light hand, and Cranfield suggested the removal of impositions from over 240 commodities. Hostility towards impositions was not unlike that towards fiscal feudalism: there was the possibility of some sort of compromise through treaty. Hence impositions can appear to be of only secondary importance for most of the 1620s when Parliament was concerned with immediate wrongs. Eliot, against the background of trade crisis, would have liked debate in 1624 – he was particularly worried about the taxation on cloth exports – but he would not deny the necessity of this revenue. Taxes which bore too heavily on English trade should be done away with, and the remainder approved by Parliament. Serious controversy only broke out after the Petition of Right. Resentment was compounded by the judicial techniques employed, notably the ruling that the tax should be paid before the legal issue was heard. This was insisted upon even when good security was offered. In 1630 the Exchequer, on the authority of *Bate's Case*, ordered Samuel Vassall to pay the imposition on currants immediately. He refused and was imprisoned for contempt. By this time, as an M.P. in 1625 prophesied, argument about impositions had become inseparable from the debate over tunnage and poundage.[6]

The great issue of 1621 was provided by patents and monopolies.[7] Some grants are celebrated – ale-houses, inns, gold and silver thread – but the sense of grievance was broad and must be related to a multitude of patents which lack notoriety. Many of the complaints centred upon positions in the courts, and from an institutional point of view the attack upon patents was just part of the much broader criticism of the

[6] F. C. Dietz, *English Public Finance, 1558–1641*, London, 1964, p. 155. BM, Hargrave MS. 132, ff. 57v.–58. R. H. Tawney, *Business and Politics under James I*, Cambridge, 1958, pp. 132–3. Hulme, pp. 45–6. Rushworth, i. 641–2; ii. 73. Gardiner, v. 364–5; vii. 167–8. V. Pearl, *London and the Outbreak of the Puritan Revolution*, Oxford, 1964, pp. 77–8, gives an account of the opposition of Vassall and others.

[7] Impositions could benefit a patentee, and thus the two subjects became merged. Prestwich, p. 159, n. 3.

86, 102, 104. Tanner, p. 245. *Parliamentary Debates in 1610*, ed. S. R. Gardiner, Camden Old Ser. 1862, lxxxi. 162–3. *Common Journals*, i. 481.

structure of office and of fees. The weakness of Bacon, as Lord Chancellor and the man who wielded the Great Seal, was his exposure to all these angles of attack. Yet in some ways there was little novelty in the debate. In 1601 Elizabeth, faced by the greatest challenge to her prerogative, stooped to conquer, and critics of monopolies assumed a victory. Subsequent events, although disappointing, included a declaration of the judges that monopolies were illegal and a cautious proclamation during the first days of the new reign. Some patents were cancelled. However, it soon became apparent that royal lawyers were adept at translating imperfection into advantage. Sir Henry Brownker's patent of the issues of jurors who failed to appear was voided by the judges, but he received a new and more carefully worded grant. Objection was interpreted in clerical or legal rather than in political terms. Successful opposition became a lesson which would enable subsequent grants to be more circumspect in their wording. If anything, the system was strengthened. After the death of Salisbury, grants of patents and the inflation of honours drew the Crown more deeply into the political liabilities which surrounded the brokers of the patronage system, of which Buckingham became outstanding. While Ellesmere held the Seal there was some restraint, and it is more than probable that he dammed the tide by his obstinacy and refusal to seal grants without scrutiny. His death opened the way for Bacon who, while sounding reasonable, discarded the standards of his predecessor. It set the stamp upon Buckingham's rise to power, but the new Lord Chancellor would have to pay. Bacon had certified thirteen out of the nineteen patents condemned in 1621 and all, of course, had passed the Seal. James cancelled a number of patents, and in 1624 legislation confined the privilege of monopoly to inventions. Crown lawyers subsequently illustrated their ability to exploit loopholes in this statute. Patents and monopolies continued to arouse hostility in the 1630s. Sir John Culpeper, speaking of monopolies in the Short Parliament, said that they were a grievance 'which compriseth many: it is a nest of wasps, or swarm of vermin, which have over-crept the land'.[8]

The Rights of Peers
The emphasis of general histories is normally, and rightfully, placed upon the House of Commons, but the House of Lords has hardly received the treatment it deserves, although recent work has done much to restore the balance. The House of Lords, in retrospect, may not have

---

[8] Kenyon, pp. 65–6. W. J. Jones, 'Ellesmere and Politics, 1603–17', *Early Stuart Studies*, ed. H. J. Reinmuth, Minneapolis, 1970. pp. 11–63. C. Roberts, *The Growth of Responsible Government in Stuart England*, Cambridge, 1966, p. 27. 21 and 22 Jac. I c. 3; extract in Tanner, pp. 269–72. Rushworth, iii. 917.

the same significance as the House of Commons, but at the time it was
terribly important and exercised some peculiar strands of power and
responsibility which are central to any understanding of the early
Stuart story. This body will be treated as a chamber of Parliament, but
first it must be remembered as an assembly which was concerned to
maintain the rights of peers. It was and is common to refer to their
privileges, but the word can be misleading. The peers did not see the
attributes of their status as something exceptional accorded by grace.
They saw them as rights which formed part of the law and could not be
waived. When judges appeared to disagree, the body of peers assumed
that the law was being broken and not merely that a 'privilege' was
being denied or threatened.[9]

Noblemen, indicted by a grand jury for treason or felony, received
trial before their peers. If Parliament was in session, all the peers would
act as judges and the decision would be that of the majority. These
proceedings have been interpreted on the analogy of the manor: the
nobles sat as judges in their ancient capacity as vassals or suitors, the
presiding officer was the lord's steward, the Lord High Steward of
England, a position filled whenever the occasion arose. When Parliament
was not in session a special court, constructed in front of Chancery,
appeared in Westminster Hall. The peers were called to compose a
jury, and the Lord Steward appeared as a judge, with familiar responsibilities such as those of directing the jury. Each peer, after withdrawal
for consideration, gave his verdict individually but it was supposed to be
unanimous. The government could be selective in calling up a jury.
Some jurors might be enemies of the accused. In 1601, Essex tried to
introduce a challenge on this ground, but he was informed that peers
were subject neither to exception nor compulsion to take the oath.
On this occasion the two Chief Justices, the Chief Baron and other
Justices sat on the bench as advisers on the law, but this did not prevent
Popham from moving down and appearing as a witness. Not all cases
were political although with men of eminence, as in the trial of Somerset,
this could not but be an element. In 1631, Lord Audley, Earl of Castlehaven in Ireland, was found guilty of conniving at the rape of his
wife and executed.[10]

Peers had many rights in respect of commitment, examination and
pleading which, as Nottingham later stressed, had a legal basis. They
could not be imprisoned by ordinary course of law and, like judges, they
were not summoned to give evidence as witnesses. Instead they would
receive a polite letter begging that they certify the court concerned with

[9] Rushworth, ii. 94.
[10] Plucknett, pp. 203–4. Holdsworth, i. 388–90. G. R. Elton, *The Tudor
Constitution*, Cambridge, 1960, p. 80. C. D. Bowen, *The Lion and the Throne*,
London, 1957, pp. 121–33. *State Trials*, iii. 401–8.

their knowledge. This was on honour, and the same assumption applied if a peer was a defendant. The sixteenth and seventeenth centuries are littered with arguments over these procedures, and some peers were attached or even sent to prison for behaviour which could be construed as contempt of court. The initial case might be between party and party, but the peers were seized at the behest of the Crown, represented in the judge, even though the adverse party was probably responsible for urging such a course. In 1572, Lord Keeper Nicholas Bacon – not an hereditary peer – clashed with the Lords, of which body he was Speaker, when he argued that the rights of peers were a matter of grace. He was justifying the issue of an attachment against Lord Cromwell who had failed to answer a bill of complaint in Chancery. After the opinion of the judges had been taken, the House decided that the attachment must be quashed and it was declared that the privilege of the 'lords of this realm' was a matter of right. One is tempted to notice the arguments of the Wentworths in the lower chamber – the theory of grace was again under attack – but the peers could rely upon a double right. They had an ancient status in law and a temporary status with respect to their necessary attendance in Parliament. In 1621, Francis Bacon rebuked a clerk who had omitted some words in the writ of summons: 'noblemen's titles are incorporated into their honours, their honours into their blood . . . '. In practice the obvious opportunities for abuse were there, and among the judges it was the Lord Chancellor who pressed the issue. Indeed, Ellesmere denied the automatic right of peers to answer on honour.[11]

Between 1610 and 1621, the Addled Parliament being but a brief and unsatisfactory interlude, the courts could push against the rights of peers without being called to account by the House of Lords. In 1621, the judges irritated the House by refusing to give an opinion on the privilege of peers to testify on honour. They said that it was a prerogative matter and that therefore they needed royal consent. James calmed sensibilities, but the issue remained alive. In May 1628, the House of Lords debated the action of Star Chamber which, apparently following Chancery and Exchequer, had resolved with the approval of the judges that a peer was to answer on oath. The argument merged with that over the power of the courts to attach or arrest peers. The topic would certainly have been given greater consideration in 1629 had not Parliament been dissolved. On January 29th, the Lords referred the question as to whether a peer could be arrested by a serjeant-at-arms for contempt of a Chancery decree to the committee of privileges. The rights of peers were confirmed and ordered by the House, but it was recognized

[11] Lord Nottingham's Chancery Cases, ed. D. E. C. Yale, Selden Soc. 1961–62, ii. 893–4. D'Ewes, p. 203. Hastings Journal, 1621, p. 8. W. J. Jones, The Elizabethan Court of Chancery, Oxford, 1967, pp. 320–2.

that there might be justification for finding some agreeable form of compulsion. Some of the judges were invited to attend the committee to assist in consideration of this problem. Parliament collapsed, but the Privy Council took the opinion of the judges. They unanimously upheld not merely the right of Chancery, and by implication Star Chamber and similar courts, to proceed by attachment, but also of common law courts to proceed by *capias*: '. . . and it is agreeable to the course of the common law, for by the common law a *capias* doth lie against peers of the realm for contempts by them committed.' Ranging back beyond 1572, and making use of the cautionary provisos then noted, the judges of 1629 swept aside the doctrine enunciated by the House of Lords in *Cromwell's Case* (Doc. 13).[12]

In the central period of Charles's reign, Parliament was not called and hence the House of Lords was negated. Charles, despite the dissolution of 1629, had examined a grievance, but the judges had produced an opinion which displeased peers and which rejected an order of the House of Lords made in the reign of Elizabeth. The reaction came on December 31, 1640, when the upper chamber unanimously declared that peers need only answer on their honour as parties or as witnesses. The declaration was pointedly directed at all courts of justice, and the Lord Keeper was instructed to ensure obedience. Any order, constitution or custom to the contrary was abolished and void, and subsequent breach was to be punished with 'exemplary severity to deter others' (Doc. 26).[13] Prior to this there had been developments over other matters. On November 16, 1640, the House of Lords ordered the release of Bishop Williams, a former Lord Keeper imprisoned by Star Chamber, and an enquiry was instituted into the way in which the studies and papers of Lord Warwick and Lord Brooke had been searched at the end of the Short Parliament but within the time of privilege. Sir William Beecher was brought to the bar as a delinquent when he refused to answer or produce his warrants. He eventually submitted warrants signed by Windebank and Sir Henry Vane but was committed to the Fleet Prison.[14]

The House of Lords

James opened the way to the Commons' predominance because he allowed the search for supply to become his pre-eminent concern; but whether it was the debate of 1610, the shambles of 1614, or the

---

[12] Jessie L. Stoddart, 'Constitutional Crisis and the House of Lords, 1621–1629', unpub. Ph.D. thesis, University of California, Berkeley, 1966, p. 14. *Notes of the Debates in the House of Lords . . . 1621, 1625, 1628*, ed. F. H. Relf, Camden, 3rd Ser. 1929, xlii. 144. *Lords Journals*, iv. 16, 27.

[13] The order was entered into the Chancery entry book, and on the fly leaf of the court of Wards entry book. PRO, Wards 9/555.

[14] Campbell, *Lives of the Lord Chancellors*, ii. 566. *Lords Journals*, iv. 87–8.

witch-hunt of 1621, he kept to the fore both the possibility of a deal and the importance of other issues requiring legislation. Charles exaggerated what in his father had been an error of judgment. The Parliaments of 1625 and 1626 were squandered to one end, that of supply, and yet on the second occasion the prospect of success was thrown away in order that Buckingham might be protected.

Concentration upon supply meant concentration upon the Commons, but it did not mean that the House of Lords had to take a back seat, although in 1610 and 1614 this is the impression of their role. In the 1620s, great emphasis would be placed upon their abilities as a court, and from the beginning of the Stuart era it was appreciated that they might be used to control the Commons' exuberance.

The membership of the upper House had continuity and therefore experience. Furthermore, it is in the Lords that the notion of a government-controlled vote finds confirmation. Through the bishops, control of proxies by individuals such as Buckingham, and contacts with particular peers, a majority was normally assured. This power should have been enhanced by the inflation of titles – between 1603 and 1629 the number of peers more than doubled. The idea of influencing the Commons through the Lords was not intrinsically foolish. Control of the Lords only cracked in 1626, and this was due to revulsion against Buckingham and the stupidity of official tactics against Arundel and Bristol. In 1629, the Lords came near to an open split with the Commons, and in the early part of the Long Parliament there was often distrust, especially when it was supposed that Commons' proposals in respect of the bishops represented an attempt to tamper with the composition of the upper chamber. None the less for much of 1641, the majority of peers can be seen as standing with the majority in the Commons. They were able to apply some restraint. With the Triennial Act it was the Lords who reposed the power of summoning Parliament in the hands of the Lord Keeper and a committee of peers instead of the sheriffs, as originally proposed by the Commons. In 1642 they accepted the Militia Ordinance only after attempting to provide an alternative procedure.[15]

In 1610 – despite its use of a veto which occasioned the failure of several bills – and again in 1614, the House of Lords came near to futility. Despite an unfortunate initiative by Burghley in 1593, it was recognized that the House of Commons must take the lead in financial matters. Discussion of a Great Contract forced the Lords into a back seat. A handful of speakers, mostly official, dominated proceedings in

---

[15] C. S. R. Russell, 'The Authorship of the Bishop's Diary of the House of Lords in 1641', *BIHR*, 1968, xli. no. 104, p. 229. An important essay is Elizabeth R. Foster, 'Procedure in the House of Lords during the Early Stuart Period', *The Journal of British Studies*, 1966, v. no. 2, pp. 56–73.

1610. Lord Chancellor Ellesmere was unhappy about government tactics, and his gloom was increased as the value of joint committees was submerged amid the sense of the Commons' independence. He saw the two Houses as properly composing one body, the passivity of the peers was a disgrace, and it all amounted to an erosion of Parliament. If consideration of taxation belonged first and properly to the Commons, discussion of tenures concerned the peers just as much and perhaps more. It was also feared that the Commons' attack on the decision in *Bate's Case* represented an attempt to usurp the position of the House of Lords as a court of appeal.[16]

Parliament was traditionally the King's High Court at Westminster, but there was a habit of describing the chambers individually as courts of record. This dubious phrase was used with respect to the House of Commons in the Apology, and in 1610 an M.P. queried the rights of judges to consider prerogative matters if the Commons could not. There was a more valid base to the notion that the House of Lords was a court of record, but its ability was hampered as the judges became increasingly unwilling to co-operate when asked to produce opinions on contentious matters. In 1614, they declined to give the Lords an opinion on impositions, and Coke thanked those peers who had urged that the question should not be put (Doc. 1). A divided opinion would be damaging, but a unanimous one – which would probably have favoured the Crown – would have been used as a political weapon and would hardly have convinced opponents. Coke said that the judges should only be asked to give an opinion on questions of law after the debate. Ellesmere, who had hoped to extract an opinion and who did not want a conference with the Commons, failed to obtain sufficient support for the suggestion that a writ of error should be brought, thus enabling a test case before the House of Lords (Doc. 1). The judges would have paramount authority, for as he had stated in *Calvin's Case*, 'in all such writs of error, the Lords are to proceed according to the law; and for their judgment therein they are informed and guided by the judges; and do not follow their own opinions or discretions otherwise.'[17]

In 1614, the judicial capacities of the Lords had been stressed although nothing had been achieved. In future Parliaments significant

---

[16] *Proceedings in Parliament, 1610*, i. pp. xii, 38–9, 68, 276–83. J. E. Neale, *Elizabeth I and her Parliaments, 1584–1601*, London, 1957, pp. 301–3. Jones, 'Ellesmere and Politics', pp 34–40.

[17] *Proceedings in Parliament, 1610*, i. p. xvi. *The Speech of the Lord Chancellor of England, in the Eschequer Chamber, touching the Post-Nati*, London, 1609, p. 23. Legislation with respect to 'courts' of Exchequer Chamber, empowered to hear proceedings by writ of error, did not replace the House of Lords if litigants wished to make use of it. If anything, the importance of the House of Lords with respect to writ of error was confirmed. See generally, T. Beven, 'The Appellate Jurisdiction of the House of Lords', *LQR*, 1901, xix. 155–70, 357–71.

attention would be paid to these powers of the upper chamber, but their exploitation would be rather different from the procedures suggested by Ellesmere. At the same time, the value of the judges to the House would decline as their role as assistants to the King was increasingly emphasized.

The House of Commons had wanted to punish people before 1621, but its weakness had been illustrated in 1610 when it was urged that Sir Stephen Proctor should be punished for extortion 'in some other degree than such as by ordinary course of justice could be laid upon him'. It was desired that he be degraded from knighthood, disabled to bear arms, and – should further complaints be sustained – he was 'to be dealt with as a bankrupt, and his lands and goods to be subject to be sold, as in case he were declared a bankrupt by the laws and statutes of this realm'.[18] In 1621, when the Commons were desperately anxious to strike at Mitchell, Mompesson and others, Coke advised that their powers were limited and centred upon incidents of 'indignity' offered to the House. The Lords, however, could examine on oath and try and punish offenders; on petition from the Commons they could deal with the monopolists. Apart from the punishment of M.P.s and matters of privilege, it meant that the House of Lords was conceded to have a near exclusive judicial power in Parliament. However, the attack upon ministers and monopolists is only part of this story. Parliament was faced with a vast number of petitions, and many minor men of little renown were accused of malpractices. With over a decade since a 'real' Parliament, there must have been a will to restore the position of Parliament vis-à-vis the courts, notably those in Westminster Hall and those employing English bill procedure. Above all it was evident that the peers, although Coke had to spend much time explaining their jurisdiction to them, were not unwilling to make their presence felt in this manner.[19]

With respect to the famous criminal accusations, procedure in 1621 was relatively informal. The House of Commons committee of grievances met with a Lords committee to hand over evidence and name witnesses. Mompesson got away but was judged in the name of 'the Lords spiritual and temporal of this High Court of Parliament'. This was an important case in the establishment of the Lords' judicial role since he was a member of neither House. Mitchell was obviously guilty, and Bacon, who submitted, was judged in the name of 'this High Court'. Bacon, left to justify himself (Doc. 3), was expendable since the

[18] *Proceedings in Parliament, 1610*, ii. 412–14. For an account of this Parliament's frustrated dealings over Proctor, see Roberts, pp. 11–14.
[19] Relf, introd. *Notes of Debates*, pp. xii–xv. Kenyon, pp. 98–100, prints extracts from *Lords Journals*, iii. 33–72, covering arguments of Coke and others. Stoddart, p. 178.

King was mostly interested in obtaining supply. The investigation was initially suggested by Cranfield, a Buckingham supporter.[20]

The attack on Bacon must be looked at for its own sake and not merely tied in with that upon Mitchell and Mompesson. The tenure of senior offices had become unstable, and in 1614 the disgrace of Parry had illustrated the strength of the House of Commons. The pattern of assault against ministers had been confirmed in 1618 when Bacon and Buckingham overthrew the Howards, and the road of promotion was opened for Cranfield with the deposition of Sir William Knollys, Viscount Wallingford, as Master of the Wards. The victors had combined to secure power, but their alliance was uncomfortable. In 1620 when the council was split over the nature of preparations for a Parliament, Bacon solicited that his services should be rewarded after Parliament was concluded. He received a dusty answer from Buckingham: 'what the custom hath been for rewarding Chancellors after the Parliament I never heard, but it seems by your letter the last claimed it not.' Already, and among supposed friends, Bacon was being confronted by the memory of Ellesmere's standards. He was seeking remuneration on a realistic scale for his expenses as Speaker of the House of Lords, but he received cold comfort: the King would be hurt 'if, while he is asking with one hand, he should be giving with the other'. When the attack came, Buckingham was willing to support the Lord Chancellor, but not at any cost. There was resentment over the cost and intricacy of the Chancery machine, and bills of conformity were a specific grievance. Bacon was not the easiest person to support whereas something might be gained by letting him go. Caught off guard and counted as a liability, Bacon would be compared to Actaeon who was worried to death by his own dogs. Williams was advising James and Buckingham to go with the tide. The King became titular leader of the campaign; indeed, once assured of Mompesson's escape – he was to return in 1623 – James outdid the Lords by extending punishment to perpetual banishment.[21]

A very different atmosphere prevailed in 1624 when Coke told the Lords that the House of Commons as the 'representative body of the realm' were 'inquisitors general' of grievances. Not only was the temper against Cranfield more savage than that against Bacon – Charles and Buckingham were vindictive (Doc. 6) – but the accused fought back and pleaded not guilty. The Attorney General prosecuted as assistant to the House of Lords, the trial lasted six days, and Cranfield was judged by 'this High Court of Parliament'. James made the best of things, although he appreciated that an indirect way of influencing ministers

[20] Kenyon, p. 94. Stoddart, p. 155.
[21] Moir, pp. 102–4. Bell, p. 19. *Fortescue Papers*, p. 150. *CSP Dom.* 1619–23, p. 238.

was being developed. In 1621 he had produced arguments to show that
judgment in Parliament belonged to the King and the Lords (Doc. 3),
and now in 1624 he treated the Lords as a jury to be instructed, the most
honourable in England. In 1626, however, it became apparent that
political trials before the House of Lords might become a two-edged
weapon. The attack on Bristol raised enough contention, but the arrest
of Arundel, while Parliament was sitting, raised a storm; the Lords,
as much concerned for their privileges as the Commons, suspended
sittings. On the other hand, there was the impeachment of Buckingham.
Charles was not prepared to act like his father, and so the very fact of
the trial became an assault upon the King's position and against overwhelming advice to the contrary, he dissolved Parliament.[22]

These celebrated cases caused a stir, but they represented only a
narrow aspect of House of Lords jurisdiction. This was varied – civil,
criminal, appeal, original – and the procedures available were the old
ones, writ of error and bill, and the novel one of direct petition which
was probably founded upon a large number of petitions which greeted
the 1621 Parliament. A committee for petitions, eight in number, was
set up and its chairman, Bridgewater, subsequently presented a report
which provided some basic principles: a petition to Parliament was not
to stop proceedings in court, counsel were to be heard on both sides
before decrees were reversed in Parliament, and review was to be allowed
if the judges found cause. At the end of the year, the size of the committee was increased to eleven, and they were given the assistance of
legal attendants. In 1624, the committee – now twelve in number – sat
every Friday. It could reject petitions by majority vote, thus acting on
behalf of the Lords without bringing the matter to the floor of the
House. There does not appear to have been a committee in 1625, but
that of 1626 had doubled in size, and with a quorum of five it could
divide. It had developed a timetable, procedure and powers, including
the ability to stay proceedings and call up documents. In 1628, when it
numbered twenty-nine, the committee formed three working groups.[23]

Many petitions to Parliament were concerned with the proceedings
and decisions of courts such as Wards, Requests and especially Chancery, which were not otherwise equipped with a formal line of appeal.
With respect to the Wards, abuses in the feudal system were alleged,
applications were made for suits to be transferred to other courts, and
for injunctions or decrees to be reversed. Complaints about the Requests
were less significant. Despite expanding business, litigants often found

[22] *Lords Journals*, iii. 307, 343–4. H. Elsynge, *The Ancient and Present Manner
of Holding Parliaments in England, with their Privileges*, London, 1663, pp. 151–
93. The articles of Buckingham's impeachment, with some other speeches and
proceedings, are given in Gardiner, *Docs.*, pp. 3–44.

[23] Stoddart, pp. 178–84.

E

their solution in ignoring the jurisdiction of the court and commencing proceedings elsewhere. Chancery, however, carried too many heavy guns for such a practice to be feasible. Well before the end of Elizabeth's reign, the absence of appeal or procedure through writ of error had occasioned anxiety with respect to the decrees of this court, especially those affecting land. The Queen was advised that on petition she could refer a decree to the judges. This idea was upheld, but it was a limited solution. Litigants continued to rely upon private bills, hoping to get acts of Parliament to void and sometimes to confirm decrees. However, the reign of James became an arid ground for legislation, and by 1621 there must have been a backlog of disgruntled suitors. Furthermore, Bacon had been more active than his predecessor in handing down formal decisions from the bench, and in so far as decrees were enrolled – many were not – it had been understood since the 1590s that this made it very costly and difficult to reopen proceedings in Chancery. Recent practices, notably over bills of conformity, had raised a storm of dissent, and this was very much to the fore in 1621 even though Bacon and Chancery were forced to back-track. In any case, it was always easy to claim that decrees were gained by fraudulent means, defective evidence, and improper proceedings. These claims were often dubious but they could be effective in moving the Lords to intervene, and they were doubtless encouraged by the attack upon Bacon. The next Lord Keeper, Williams, was not a lawyer, and although in practice he received all necessary aid – from the Master of the Rolls, the judges and Masters – it was easy to suggest that he lacked competence, an impression strengthened by Buckingham's allegations once Williams had quarrelled with the favourite. Before this, however, the difficulties of Williams illustrate the uneven expansion of the Lord's authority.[24]

In December 1621, in *Bourchier's Case*, the House of Lords considered a petition against a Chancery decree. The question was whether it was just an ordinary petition, though oddly worded, or whether it was a judicial appeal. It was decided that there was no precedent for the word 'appeal' to be included in a petition, but it was agreed to hear the case even though Williams pointed out how discouraging this could be to the judge concerned. The Lord Keeper was probably embarrassed – he and two Justices sitting on the Chancery bench appear to have been rather hasty – but the matter went against Bourchier, who had to apologize at the bar of the House for his accusations. By 1626 it was Williams, no longer Lord Keeper, who would have to apologize for having ignored in 1624 an order of the House of Lords that a petitioner should receive a new commission. His explanation – that he had clarified the situation but that this had not been entered by the clerk – was not

[24] Bell, p. 135. G. Spence, *The Equitable Jurisdiction of the Court of Chancery*, Philadelphia, 1846, i. 394–5. Jones, pp. 268 ff.

accepted, but if true it illustrates the unsatisfactory technical arrangements which contrasted with the high claims now assumed by the Lords.[25]

In 1621, the House of Lords had offered an attractive possibility: litigants wanted quick justice and they were exasperated, sometimes by the lack of finality in proceedings before the courts and sometimes by the opposite circumstance, the difficulty of reopening a case. By 1628, it was clear that the burden on the Lords was too great, and proceedings there were getting palpably slower. Of course, the House often ordered the court first concerned to take some further action or to reconsider. It could not unburden itself so easily of all the cases, and its paucity of legal talent became apparent. Reality demanded reliance upon the judges, but they were of diminishing value when proceedings before their courts were the subject of enquiry. Some of the difficulties were exposed in the sensational trial of Bristol. In May 1626, the Lords intended to consider Bristol's answer and the proofs before deciding whether it was a matter of treason. Cranfield had been allowed counsel, and it was argued that Bristol should also be permitted this assistance. The Lord Treasurer, the former Chief Justice Ley, pointed out that counsel could not be admitted by law for examination of witnesses to decide whether it was treason. The King agreed to allow counsel, but the judges were assembled by royal order to reiterate that the old rules remained in force and that this was only an exception. Some speakers in the House of Lords justified the King's concession because 'at the common law the judges are the party's counsel, to direct the law; whereas here they be not judges, but we, who have no experience of the law'. Some wondered if it was possible to override such 'a fundamental law of the kingdom'. Earlier there had been difficulties on the technical side. The Lord Keeper, on behalf of the Attorney General, had moved that the clerk of the Crown in King's Bench be allowed to attend at the reading of the charge against Bristol. A precedent was claimed but this was rejected. Some evidently feared that an attempt might be made to switch proceedings into the King's Bench. It was ruled that the cause was to remain in the House of Lords and stated that the clerk of the Crown in King's Bench was not a minister 'of this court'. In April 1621, an objection had been raised against the practice of not sitting on Star Chamber days, 'as if this supreme court were to attend any other inferior court'. A corollary was the growing estrangement of the judges. When they had declined to pronounce on the right of peers to answer on honour, a peer demanded that they should explain themselves, and it was argued that their writs specified a duty to give advice. The assumption of an independent right to hear cases must have added further strain to the relationship between the House and the judges.

[25] Stoddart, pp. 40, 169–70. Relf, introd. *Notes of Debates*, pp. xxii, xxv–xxvi. *Lords Journals*, iii. 189–92.

It also affected the House of Commons and the sovereign, whose atten-
tions were for the moment concentrated upon the great criminal
accusations in which the Commons prosecuted.[26]

James had opted to lead the critics in 1621. With Mompesson it only
meant that an offender was being attacked – not the authority by which
patents issued – and hence the prerogative was preserved. Likewise, it
was logical for the King to accept the necessity of exposing the referees.
This was not merely a shrewd decision to desert erstwhile friends.
When Yelverton was under attack, James followed his policy of leaving
it to the Lords and, as Lady de Villiers observes, 'was rewarded by a
judgment which could not have been improved upon had it been
delivered by himself'.[27] This was more than acquiescence, it was triumph.
The King had very good reason to concur in the idea that the House of
Lords was the proper body to try and punish the accused. Confirmation
of the judicial powers of the Lords suited the King because he assumed
that he could exercise a greater control there. He could look at the peers
and bishops of his own creation (Doc. 3), and doubtless supposed that
through this capacity he might control the Commons. Yet Coke, for
all his work in upholding and explaining the judicial authority of the
Lords, was an M.P. and as such symbolized the growing dependence
of the upper chamber on legal advice from below. James did accept
much of Coke's advice, but he wanted the House of Lords to be really
independent of the Commons (Doc. 3). These themes came to the fore
in the case of Edward Floyd, who was accused of scandalous speeches.
The situation was awkward because the House of Commons had already
acted. Some M.P.s were reluctant to admit an error; others were in-
spired to refight the old battle against Coke and justify the judicial
initiative of the lower chamber. Coke was concerned to maintain the
jurisdiction of the House of Lords, but he did not wish the Commons
to appear in the wrong. He was emphatic that justification of the Lords'
jurisdiction must not be read as a denial of the status of the House of
Commons as a court of record. He spoke with and against both sides.
'He that says this House is not a court of record, I would his tongue
might cleave to the roof of his mouth. He that thinks we have no
judicature speaks ignorantly, he that saith we have in all cases is
deceived much too. . . . We have power of judging our own members
and also him that justifies a fact done out of Parliament in the House. . . .
And I can show one hundred precedents of the Lords alone . . . so that

[26] Hutton, 133 (122 *English Reports*). *Notes of the Debates in the House of
Lords . . . 1624 and 1626*, ed. S. R. Gardiner, Camden Soc. 1879, new ser. xxiv.
171–2, 181–2. Gardiner, vi. 98, 112. Rushworth, i. 267 ff. *Notes of the Debates in
the House of Lords . . . 1621*, ed. S. R. Gardiner, Camden Soc. Old Ser. 1870,
ciii. 13. *Hastings Journal*, p. 22.
[27] *Hastings Journal*, p. x.

we may join or they judge alone.' Later, at a conference, Coke repeated his stand: 'the upper House absolute without the Commons. The Commons a court of record of themselves.' A peer reported that Coke's maintenance of the jurisdiction of the Lords was disliked by many in the Commons.[28] James, with rather a fine speech, had made his own intervention on the subject of patentees on March 10th. He affirmed both the jurisdiction and the independence of the Lords, but he rebuked them for the heed they paid to lawyers from the Commons and slashed at Coke and his choice of precedents. The Lords, he affirmed, could stand on their own two feet: they did not need precedents 'for there is no question' yours is a House and a court of record' (Doc. 3).

James doubtless saw the House of Lords as an instrument through which he could express his leadership. He did not have to worry about his judges being scrutinized, yet from the beginning this was a theoretical possibility. Petitions were presented to Parliament, in effect to the Lords, with respect to proceedings which, although perhaps decisive to the parties, were technically interim. It might be Chancery orders or injunctions from the court of Wards. Intervention by the Lords could be equated with traditional notions of error or novel notions of appeal. The peers were being asked to supervise proceedings which definitely were not final judgments. There was no apparent reason why the Lords should not be called upon to examine proceedings in King's Bench or Common Pleas. This happened in 1628. A direct confrontation was averted, but granted the survival of Parliament it could only be temporary. James's dream of controlling the Commons through the judicial supremacy of the Lords would inevitably backfire if the Lords used, or were compelled to use, their authority against the King's judges.

The Early Parliaments of Charles I
Charles thought his policies were appropriate for both monarchy and society. His 'sincerity' was real, and it aided powerfully in deceiving him as rot spread through his original intentions. Believing in his own virtue, he could give little credence either to the honesty or to the tactical skill of critics. Throughout his reign, Charles adhered to the hopeless belief that people were either for or against him.

Charles's initial problem of war and finance was partly of his own making. In 1624, the then Prince of Wales and Buckingham had bludgeoned James into a reversal of policies. It was Buckingham's greatest stroke to combine his established position with the reversionary interest. Charles wanted war, a land war, and England was not capable of conducting such an enterprise without the assistance of France. Those who wanted a naval war were equally obtuse. A naval war could

[28] Relf, introd. *Notes of Debates*, pp. xvi, xviii.

not help the Protestants in Europe or Stuart relatives unless England could blockade the Spanish coasts and shipping. This could only have been feasible with the aid of the Dutch, with whom relations were strained. Those who urged a maritime war were proposing something irrelevant to the continental situation, and they were succumbing to the hallucination – proved wrong in the past and to be proved wrong in the future – that the Spanish overseas empire and shipping routes would fall an easy prey to plunderers. Despite concessions, the supply granted in 1624 was insignificant. Intended for defence, the navy and the Dutch, it was to be paid to treasurers accountable to Parliament; recovery of the Palatinate was not mentioned. This early exercise in appropriation was disliked by the Lords and in the end ignored, but it represented a snub. None the less, Charles approached his first Parliament with an almost silly air of confidence. He rushed the elections, kept M.P.s waiting a month in London during a time of plague, and then had to transfer the session to Oxford. He did, however, obtain two subsidies. In 1626, with the next Parliament, he squandered the prospect of supply and adopted dissolution against most advice. He was left with an acute financial problem.[29]

Elizabeth had difficulty in extracting money, but she had managed to maintain the impression that repayment of forced loans under Privy Seal was a genuine intention. Her credit remained good whereas that of James was poor. Charles's credit was almost non-existent, especially since he sought loans after failing to obtain parliamentary supply. It was difficult to believe in the theory of repayment, and so the situation was transformed although the technicalities remained as before. In 1615, the judges had recognized the King's power to persuade his subjects to lend money, but Charles was trying to compel the loan of specific sums named by himself. In 1626, in any case, the loans were aligned too obviously with parliamentary taxes which had been hoped for but not passed. A proclamation of October 7th naïvely stated that the emergency was immediate but promised that a Parliament would be summoned as soon as possible. Resistance was magnified. The time was not propitious: two Parliaments had ended amidst acrimony, the hunters of Buckingham had been thwarted, and there was still a desire to enquire into the fate of supply granted in 1624. Sir Ranulph Crewe, Speaker in 1614 and now Chief Justice of the King's Bench, was dismissed. Other judges declined to declare the loans legal, and over seventy gentlemen who refused to pay were imprisoned. The *Five Knights' Case* arose when writs of *habeas corpus* were presented to the gaoler. If the cause of imprisonment had been stated the judges, without prejudice to the issue, would have declared it a misdemeanour and allowed bail. The

[29] Kenyon, pp. 76–80. Gardiner, v. 234–5. Gardiner, *Lords Debates, 1624 and 1626*, p. 232 n.a.

gaoler was accordingly instructed to reply that the prisoners were held by special command of the King, without the grounds of imprisonment being stated. Both the grant of the writs and this procedure had probably been advised in advance by some of the judges.[30]

Counsel for the prisoners, notably Bramston and Selden, made much play with Magna Carta and argued that 'the end of this writ is to return the cause of the imprisonment'. Noy said that the prisoners should be discharged or bailed if the cause was not shewn. Attorney General Heath also made use of Magna Carta, and his argument that the King had the right both to commit and to withhold the cause was accepted, particularly in respect of an Elizabethan precedent which was utilized to show that men committed by the sovereign or by the Council were not bailable. Coke, aided by Eliot, was later able to produce a text of this precedent at variance with that used by Heath: the cause of commitment should be certified but it did not follow, if imprisonment was at royal command, that bail would be allowed. On the other hand, Heath had repudiated any suggestion that the King claimed the right to imprison a person and never bring him to trial. That, he said, would indeed be unjust. He had merely insisted that in the particular case the King's Bench judges had no power to grant bail. Even so, some of the arguments were hard to swallow. As Noy said, it was absurd if the judges, despite the nature of their oath which bound them to keep the King's secrets, could not be told all the facts.[31]

The prisoners were released in time for the 1628 Parliament, and similar grace was accorded to Hugh Pyne, a loose-talking lawyer, who had used the chair of quarter sessions in Somerset in 1626 to attack Buckingham and royal policies. He was said to have asserted that Charles 'was stripped and governed by a company of upstarts' and that he was 'as unfit to rule as his shepherd, being an innocent'. Pyne was turned off the commission of the peace. Ensconced in prison, he was elected for Weymouth and released by the King's warrant.[32]

When Parliament met, it quickly became apparent that the Commons expected the House of Lords to examine the conduct of the King's Bench Justices. Justice Whitelocke acknowledged this when he advised the Lords that they had to act: 'the Commons present a grievance in point of law that the subject is wounded in point of liberty by a judgment given in the King's Bench. The Commons to present the fact, and you to judge.' He insisted, however, that there had not in fact been a

[30] *State Trials*, ii. 899. Holdsworth, vi. 41. Steele, i. no. 1492. Gardiner, vi. 149. F. H. Relf, *The Petition of Right*, Minneapolis, 1917, pp. 2–3.

[31] The King's Bench proceedings and some subsequent events in Parliament are in *State Trials*, iii. 1–234. Extracts are given in Gardiner, *Docs.*, pp. 57–64, and Kenyon, pp. 106–9. Cf. Holdsworth, i. 509; v. appendix I; vi. 32–7. Relf, *Petition of Right*, p. 21.

[32] Yonge, pp. 96, 110, 112, 114. Barnes, pp. 16, 34, 70.

judgment. Selden said at a conference: 'if that court, which is the highest for ordinary justice, cannot deliver him [the subject] *secundum legem*, what law is there (I beseech you, my Lords) that can be sought for in any inferior court for his delivery?' For much of the session, the peers were preoccupied with the complexities of this question. They were uncertain how to examine the action of the judges, and they wanted to know if there had been any intention of making a final judgment. The judges said that there had only been a rule. Hence there were no grounds for a writ of error, and there had been nothing to stop the parties from suing out new writs of *habeas corpus* the following day. After a long debate, the judges were ordered to declare what their 'judgment' had been and to give the grounds. Chief Justice Hyde replied that the judges were subject only to the command of the King. This, he professed, was not a delaying tactic, for all were present and ready to speak. He was defending the independence of the judges, and he sought assurance that if they spoke Charles would not be offended. Buckingham, on the basis of conversations with the King, was sure that no offence would be taken. Some peers were not willing to continue on this equivocal basis, and they scented an attempt to undermine the authority of the House. As Devon asserted, 'this concerns the honour and justice of this place'. He believed 'that we here in this court may call any judge whatsoever in matter of fact which they have formally made'. The Bishop of Lincoln, the ex-Lord Keeper Williams, chimed in with the observation that if Lord Chancellors could be called to account in respect of appeals from their court, then why should not judges be compelled to explain themselves. It may have been sardonic, but it was an acute commentary upon developments in recent years. The debate was pressed forward by those who wanted it clearly understood that it was not good enough if Hyde spoke only because he was assured that the King would not be offended. Buckingham tried to stop the trend by pointing out that 'the judges have but expressed their respect to the King', but although Whitelocke made his speech and explanation nothing was concluded. On the following day, Lord Say and Sele asserted that Hyde had refused to speak, but Dorset said that the Chief Justice had only raised a doubt. Strictly speaking Dorset was in the right, but many had reason to suspect Hyde's question when it was answered by the casual informality of Buckingham's personal assurance. Eventually Jones – 'no judgment at all given in the King's Bench' – and Doddridge gave accounts of their proceedings and the authorities on which they had based their opinions. Hyde did likewise, after explaining that he had never intended to decry the privileges of the House and had only sought their opinion as to whether it was proper to speak without formally obtaining the King's consent.[33]

[33] Relf, *Notes of Debates*, pp. 98–108. Relf, *Petition of Right*, pp. 4–5, 8.

The judges had become a cautious group aware first of their responsibility to the King. As it happened their explanations were satisfactory, they shewed that they had resisted some pressure from the Attorney General, and there was, of course, little reason at this time to regard them with political suspicion. Indeed in 1628, a number of M.P.s including Noy, Pym and Wentworth, advocated a *habeas corpus* bill which would have placed an enhanced responsibility upon the shoulders of the judges. The episode in which the judges were questioned is of great significance only in retrospect. It is our awareness of what was to happen in 1640 which indicates that the situation was fraught with danger. The Commons had moved the Lords to examine an action of the King's Bench judges. Had immediate events been different, and had a sizeable body of peers been dissatisfied, they would presumably have had to think of further proceedings. In any case, the Petition of Right intervened and the matter was more or less closed.[34]

The Petition of Right was not a statute, and the principle adapted was the old notion that the King, who could do no wrong and who could not be sued in his own courts, must avoid any action which might be deemed as a wrong and himself move to right faults. Realization of this was subsequently to mean both the impotence and the protection of the Crown, but in 1628 it only reflected the dilemma of the House of Commons. The House of Lords had suggested five propositions which among other things confirmed Magna Carta and the old laws supporting it, but this was not acceptable. A proposed bill of rights, which the King would have accepted, was rejected because it lacked that kind of explanation which the Commons desired. The idea of a petition was first suggested by Sir Dudley Digges, and subsequently taken up by Coke, Phelips and Wentworth. The assumptions and logic of the leaders of the Commons left much to be desired, largely because they stuck fast to the belief that only ministers, and not the King, could do wrong and that these were restricted by force of law. The famous document itself was brief. It was petitioned that forced loans, impositions, and other forms of taxation, mostly anachronistic, should cease; that imprisonment without cause should be discontinued; that a number of activities with respect to billeting and the martial law be done away with. All the clauses were directly related to immediate grievances. The simplicity of the document destroyed accord; and on both sides there may have been deliberate intentions to mislead or unwise ambitions to dowse controversy by circumventing knotty problems.[35]

---

[34] *Ibid.*, pp. 9, 31.
[35] Hulme, pp. 213–17, 224, 228. E. H. Adair, 'The Petition of Right', *History* 1921, new ser. v. 99–103. H. Hulme, 'Opinion in the House of Commons on the Proposal for a Petition of Right, 6 May 1628', *EHR* 1935, cxcviii. 302–6.

The disastrous dispute over tunnage and poundage is a classic among political errors and misunderstandings. This form of taxation was customarily granted to a sovereign for life by his first Parliament. Together with traditional customs on certain exports which belonged to the King by prerogative, it made up a significant item in the yearly accounts.[36] Yet the advantage of reconsidering aspects of taxation, acknowledged in the 1610 debates, had long been evident. In 1625, the brutal economic depression, following upon the slump in cloth exports of 1622, exposed commodities normally embraced by tunnage and poundage. Members from depressed localities, and the interest of the majority as consumers or producers, invited a reappraisal or at least a pretence of this ambition. The House of Commons was not really hostile, but it was frightened by the plague, worried by the arrangements at Oxford to which it adjourned, and inclined to confuse the subject with enquiries into the fate of supply voted in 1624. Tunnage and poundage was voted for twelve months, but this was rejected by the Lords. Official influence may have been strong in the upper chamber, but the device was novel and it was impertinent in so far as it seemed to imply that Charles would be compelled to meet with Parliament in twelve months time. The tax was already being collected, and Phelips declared this to be wrong, but although Parliament went home without passing a statute the practice continued. In 1626, a bill was proposed whereby the King might be indemnified, but the pursuit of Buckingham and dissolution intervened. In 1628, some merchants who refused to pay were imprisoned but released on entering bond to pay what 'shall thereupon be found due'. The Commons agreed that a statute should be passed, but nothing was done until after the Petition of Right. There was growing anxiety, M.P.s thinking about the legality of collection without statute, and the King suspecting that the matter was being manipulated as an assurance of future parliamentary meetings. Thus the compromise of 1628 was strangled at birth. Charles, who published the Petition with both his answer and his previous unsatisfactory reply, felt that agreement was enough, and he now expected the Commons to do their duty with respect to tunnage and poundage. Instead he witnessed Eliot and Pym brushing aside Coke and Wentworth with assaults upon Buckingham and Manwaring, who had preached that those who refused forced loans were damned. When the House did discuss tunnage and poundage, an enabling bill was proposed with the main matter put over to the next session. Once again it seemed as though the House of Commons was trying to impose a time-table upon the King. Charles, exasperated, declared that he did not need their grant, a doctrine which had been argued prior to his reign by Sir John Davies. If his gesture was foolish, the response was intemper-

[36] Cf. the 'budget' printed by Elton, pp. 46–7.

ate, but we must appreciate the anger aroused by a foreign policy which had led England into war against both France and Spain. In its remonstrance of June 25, 1628, the House of Commons declared that the taking of tunnage and poundage 'and other impositions not granted by Parliament' was in breach of the fundamental liberties of the kingdom and contrary to the Petition of Right. Tunnage and poundage depended upon statute, and since a statute had not been passed the exactions became a kind of imposition. However, unlike the remonstrance of June 25th, the Petition of Right did not spell out this assumption, and the phrase 'tunnage and poundage' was not mentioned. On the other hand, the King had constantly used these words as had the Commons when they considered indemnifying him. Debaters in 1629, including Rolle, frequently distinguished between the two categories of levy. There must be a possibility that the explanation in the remonstrance was engendered by the King's angry rejection of statutory relevance in this matter and the continued taking of impositions. Charles prorogued Parliament on June 26th before the remonstrance could be presented to him. There was an ominous note as, speaking directly to the judges, he said: 'to you only under me belongs the interpretation of laws; for none of the House of Commons, joint or separate (what new doctrine so ever may be raised), have any power either to make or declare a law without my consent.'[37]

The Petition of Right had glossed over important issues, and it had failed to provide a time-table or any procedure whereby the taxes mentioned should be given up or the vested interests of collectors be compensated. On the other hand, the King had reconnoitred his possibilities within the frame of the Petition through consultation with the judges (Doc. 10). A suggestion had in fact been made by the Bishop of Rochester that the judges' opinion should be taken and entered on the Parliament roll. However it was the King, not Parliament, who sought advice from the judges, and in modern terminology this exercise, contrary to the Bishop's hopes, can be described as 'partisan' and not 'public'.[38]

In the months between sessions, impositions and tunnage and poundage were taken. The goods of some merchants, one of whom was John Rolle, M.P., who refused to pay were confiscated, although they offered security for anything found due by Parliament or process of law. The Exchequer, with Lord Treasurer Weston sitting on the bench, declared that the money must be paid but acknowledged that the King's right could be determined by Parliament. This invitation was enough to

[37] Gardiner, *Commons Debates, 1625*, p. 81. *APC* Sept. 1627–June 1628, pp. 436–7. Stoddart, p. 58. Gardiner, vii. 30. Hulme, *Eliot*, pp. 265, 273–4. Davies, 'Impositions', p. 95. Gardiner, *Docs.*, pp. 73–4. *Commons Debates, 1629*, p. 166.
[38] Gardiner, vi. 287.

ensure that the 1629 session was a shambles. Two months had passed between the seizure of Rolle's goods and the meeting of Parliament, but since the original date set by the prorogation was within a month of the protested action it was decided that the privilege of the House of Commons applied. Rolle himself was not constrained, but it was declared that the privilege extended to his goods, something that was hotly, and not unreasonably, questioned by the government. Many M.P.s believed that the Petition of Right had been flouted, but Noy was careful to stress that in so far as privilege had been breached this was due to the customs officials who had acted 'without relation to any commission or command from the King'. Charles would not accept this distinction, and he made it clear that the officials had acted upon specific instructions from himself and the Privy Council. The King had tried to be conciliatory, but by this time he was dismayed at the course of events and convinced that compromise was futile.[39]

Parliamentary enquiry and legal proceedings were beginning to merge. Richard Chambers, having like others attempted to rescue his goods from the Customs House by force, was summoned before the Privy Council and put in the Marshalsea for insolent words: that English merchants were more 'screwed up' in England than in Turkey. He managed, after some difficulty, to obtain bail and was prosecuted in Star Chamber. He was one of those who attempted to free his wares through process of *replevin*, a procedure which was barred by the Barons of the Exchequer. This was on January 29th, and he was relying upon the effect of developments in the House of Commons to which he had delivered a petition on the previous day and on the basis of which he was declared to be privileged (Docs 9, 11). It was in the debate on this petition that Eliot asserted that 'the judges, the Council, sheriffs, customers, the Attorney and all conspire to trample on the spoils of the liberty of the subject', words which were immediately challenged by Secretary Coke and formed a basis for subsequent charges. From the King's point of view, serious financial discussion appeared to be getting increasingly remote. Since the start of the session, the House had proceeded slowly in the matter of tunnage and poundage, the bill for which, as one M.P. said, would be expedited 'in due time'. Despite promptings, they turned again and again to discussion of religion. The relevant committee had become entangled with impositions, the Petition of Right, and the individual law suits of merchants such as Chambers. As Noy said – when the committee made its report on February 12th – it was impossible to grant tunnage and poundage unless the proceedings in the Exchequer were nullified. He meant that there was nothing to grant if the Exchequer action

---

[39] Dietz, pp. 252–3. Rushworth, i. 658–9. On February 10th, Rolle was called out of a committee to be served with a *subpoena*. This created a bad impression although it was said to be a mistake and an apology was made. *Ibid.*, 653–4.

were valid. However while speaking as an M.P., he also happened to be counsel for Chambers. He was thus relating two different responsibilities to a degree which was uncomfortable, as he himself may have realized when the House, probably against his advice, decided to approach the Exchequer directly. Convinced that these writs of *replevin* were contrary to the Petition of Right, and believing that the Barons of the Exchequer had been misinformed about tunnage and poundage, the House required them to void their order and injunction. The reply was that further proceedings at law were available to anyone who considered himself wronged. A committee was appointed to enquire into the precedents of Exchequer proceedings, but those who hoped to be assisted by the Commons in their litigation were thwarted when Charles chose to dissolve. As for Chambers, the Exchequer decision that he should receive his goods after paying duty was confirmed when the same court rejected his suit against the customs officials and the Attorney General (Doc. 9). The Privy Council rubbed salt in the wound by ordering the goods to be held until he had paid a fine of £2,000 levied by the Star Chamber for insolent words.[40]

The attempt to dictate to the Exchequer, and the consignment of a sheriff of London to the Tower, had a decisive effect. Furthermore the King resented attempts to examine the judges and the Attorney General (Doc. 11). Charles was not prepared to endure this sort of thing much longer. The climax came on March 2nd when the Speaker was prevented from calling an adjournment, and resolutions were approved which condemned impositions, tunnage and poundage, and merchants who paid these duties. Charles dissolved Parliament and presented a powerful justification for his action (Doc. 11). With respect to the constraint of the Speaker and other events, he also made it known that 'we shall account it presumptuous for any to prescribe any time unto us for parliaments, the calling, continuing and dissolving of which is always in our power'. In the near future, the courts would provide the only public forum for consideration of the privileges claimed by M.P.s[41]

By 1604, it had seemed that the privilege of freedom from arrest had been clarified. During the session, and for thirty days before and after, M.P.s and their servants were not to be arrested unless charged with breach of the peace, felony or treason. *Shirley's Case* resulted in a statute which allowed creditors, whose prisoners had been freed on grounds of privilege, to sue out new writs when privilege expired, and it extended protection to officials who surrendered prisoners in response

---

[40] *State Trials*, iii. 380. Rushworth, i. 639–49, 654–5, 658–9, 662–91; ii. 9. Hulme, *Eliot*, pp. 289, 293–4. *Commons Debates, 1629*, pp. 73–4, 112. Gardiner, vii. 1–6, 28–9, 31, 33–4, 37, 60–1, 85–6. Bramston, pp. 55–6.

[41] Rushworth, i. 656. Kenyon, p. 86.

to a claim of privilege. However, there were still broad areas open to disagreement particularly with respect to things done or said in Parliament. Coke appreciated this, and in 1621 he advised the House not to stir up a discussion of privileges. He wished it to be assumed that they had freedom and that the King could be trusted. But some were afraid of reprisals at a later date: in 1614, after dissolution, four men who had been M.P.s were sent to the Tower. In 1621, during the recess, Sandys and Southampton were imprisoned. In 1622, after dissolution, three including Coke experienced the same fate, and Pym was confined to his London house.

None the less, the latitude allowed by existing understandings of privilege was valued. Coke said in 1625 that 'many men (and I myself) will speak in Parliament that which they dare not speak otherwise'. In 1626, Digges and Eliot were arrested in mid-session for seditious words uttered in Buckingham's impeachment. Digges was released after five days, but Charles tried to hold on to Eliot on the ground that he had engaged in activities outside the House which were designed to wreck Parliament. Elizabeth had utilized the charge of outside activities on the few occasions when M.P.s were arrested during her reign, but Charles's variation on this theme lacked credibility. The House of Commons refused to sit, and Eliot had to be freed. These incidents were to be thrown into the shade by the events of 1629.[42]

Eliot, who had remained in the background during the restraint of the Speaker, took the opportunity to present his propositions. The government was probably right in supposing that there was an anti-court group in existence which had been making plans in a fashion which could be described as revolutionary. Along with eight others, Eliot was consigned to prison before dissolution. The two Chief Justices and the Chief Baron, and later all twelve judges, gave their opinions as to the nature of both the King's rights and of parliamentary privilege. It was held, among other things, that responsibility devolved upon the judges to examine the precedents when privilege was claimed. An information was laid in Star Chamber, but this lapsed with the court undecided whether to accept jurisdiction. The King was advised that the points raised by the defence with respect to privilege made it too difficult to proceed in that court. None the less, Eliot's plea to the jurisdiction of that court is an outstanding argument for the unique importance of Parliament in the great affairs of the realm (Doc. 12).[43]

[42] Tanner, pp. 302–17. *1621 Debates*, ii. 56–8. Gardiner, ii. 249–50; iv. 133, 267. Prestwich, p. 325. Gardiner, *Commons Debates, 1625*, p. 71.

[43] I. H. C. Fraser, 'The Agitation in the Commons, 2 March 1629, and the Interrogation of the Anti-Court Group', *BIHR* 1957, xxx. 86–95. Holdsworth, vi. 38–40, 97–8. For *Eliot's Case* see Hulme, *Eliot*, pp. 316–38, and *State Trials*, iii. 293–336.

Before the expiry of proceedings in Star Chamber, it had become clear that the battle would be fought before King's Bench, for the prisoners had sued out writs of *habeas corpus*. The gaoler was instructed to reply that they were held for contempts against the King and for seditious words. This meant that the Petition of Right was not in question.[44] The judges advised the King that they would probably order bail and they suggested that it would be wise if he ordered this himself. Instead Long, Hobart and Strode were removed to the Tower, and they were not present in court when the King's Bench next sat on their applications for bail. Despite a promise to the contrary, Selden and Valentine were also prevented from appearing in court and term was soon over. Charles had gained his point, but at a terrible cost. Gardiner wrote of this episode: 'he had humiliated the judges, and if he humiliated the judges his subjects were not likely to respect them.' Chief Justice Hyde told the prisoners that bail would be forthcoming as an act of favour if they put in surety for good behaviour. The prisoners, however, were only interested in what to them was the traditional procedure of tendering bail for appearance. They certainly were not willing to accept bail, whatever the conditions, as a favour when they conceived it to be a right. In any case, as Selden put it, the claim of parliamentary privilege would then have been prejudiced. The King and the judges, wrote Professor Hulme, 'had shrunk to the level of tricksters'. Certainly the judges were embarrassed, and Hyde, apparently convinced that Charles and Attorney General Heath had reached the stage when they were creating problems, went close to suggesting perpetual imprisonment without trial. This was not what the King wanted, and Chief Baron Walter was suspended when he advised that because of privilege the accused could be imprisoned but not proceeded against. Rarely before had the King's Bench judges been so clearly set adrift in a political maelstrom. 'They were dragged forth to act as arbiters where arbitration was impossible. The Commons had spurned their decisions, and now the King . . . waved away their claims to measure his political authority by the standard of legal precedents and maxims.'[45]

The case opened towards the end of January 1630. The defence threw all their hopes into a plea against King's Bench jurisdiction grounded upon the claim that offences committed in Parliament were only punishable in Parliament. Mason, who was Eliot's counsel, urged that Parliament was a superior court to King's Bench and not therefore subject to its jurisdiction. The prosecution said that the alleged offences – sedition, conspiracy, and violence against the Speaker – were not

[44] Eliot did not at first join in this. For proceedings, see *State Trials*, iii. 235–94.
[45] Gardiner, vii. 94–7, 111–12. Bramston, pp. 57–9. Hulme, *Eliot*, p. 325.

covered by privilege, and full use was made of the opinions already given by the judges (Doc. 10). The supremacy of the High Court of Parliament was not denied, but it was insisted that the King's Bench had jurisdiction over offences committed and not punished in Parliament. The outstanding speech from the bench was probably that of Whitelocke who cut through the political sophistry of the defendants. However much they might deny it, they were in fact questioning the supreme authority of the King. A direct defence was not raised. The accused were sentenced to imprisonment at the King's pleasure with fines rated according to their capability. Eliot died in prison, almost certainly from consumption exacerbated by the nature of his lodgings. His death might be laid against the King, but it was the King's Bench judges who had put him in prison and kept him there. Holles escaped. Others submitted and were released. Valentine and Strode were freed in February 1640, in time for the Short Parliament.[46]

With the dissolution of the Short Parliament, Henry Bellasis and Sir John Hotham were sent to prison for giving undutiful answers to the Council, and the houses of several M.P.s and a couple of peers were searched for documents. John Crew, who had been chairman of the committee on religion, was sent to the Tower because he refused to surrender papers or to reveal the names of persons to whom he had given them. In July 1641, the proceedings against Eliot and his friends were condemned as a breach of privilege and damages were ordered. The nature of that privilege was not set out and this Parliament failed to put the privileges of M.P.s into any agreeable form. Even the action taken with respect to Eliot was no more than a declaration. Only in 1668 was the decision of 1630 reversed on writ of error, brought by Holles, by then a peer. Yet the case of Eliot and his friends had left a memory, how bitter was only to be appreciated in 1640 and 1641.[47]

The Judges and Parliament: An Incident
When Parliament was dissolved early in 1622, Walter Yonge noted that seventy laws which stood upon continuance had expired.[48] However, others believed that the statutes were still on the book and in force.

The problem of expiring statutes had often been pondered in the past, and it was the subject of a House of Commons committee in 1584. With few exceptions the Tudors handled their Parliaments successfully, and so they never had to face all the technicalities which lurked behind the established method of framing statutes. It was standard practice for a statute to be created on the understanding that it was to be in force until the end of the first session

[46] Gardiner, vii. 117–18. Hulme, *Eliot*, pp. 332–3.
[47] Gardiner, ix. 129–30. *CSP Dom.* 1640, pp. 141–2.
[48] Yonge, pp. 51–2.

of the next Parliament, the end of the next Parliament, or some such formula. Unless continued, some statutes would expire. This was the situation when the Addled Parliament was dissolved without producing legislation of any kind. In 1623, the judges were of the opinion that the meeting of 1614 was not a Parliament but a convention. It followed that the statutes remained in force. The judges at the time of this opinion (Doc. 4) were however being asked about the status of the 1621 Parliament during which two pieces of legislation – an act for two subsidies and an act confirming subsidies granted by Convocation – had been passed. This had been done in mid-session, or so it was hoped, since the Commons had been adjourned on the understanding that despite passage of the subsidy bill the session was not ended. Indeed a proviso about this had apparently been included. The King's proclamation of January 6, 1622, dissolving Parliament, stressed that the Commons had refused an extension of two weeks in the summer of 1621 and had failed to consider a continuance bill when they reassembled. It was proclaimed 'that the said convention of Parliament neither is, nor after the ceasing and breaking thereof shall be nor ought, to be esteemed, adjudged, or taken to be or make any session of Parliament'.[49]

The immediate result was confusion. At the sessions held at Aylesbury in May 1622, with uncertainty as to whether the statutes were to be considered as effective, their rehearsal was omitted and they were not acted on. There was particular concern about statutes dealing with rogues, vagabonds and maimed soldiers. Complaints were received from soldiers whose pensions had been suspended. Elsewhere, Sir Jerome Horsey continued to act on the statutes as best he could, but he complained at the way in which the judges evaded giving an opinion on the matter. The guidance desired by local administrators was not forthcoming. This was hardly surprising, since the judges were baffled. They were clear enough about 1614, but evidently the majority, including Hobart, felt that nothing could or should be done about 1621. The Chief Baron evaded giving an opinion, but Ley tried to argue in favour of treating the statutes as good, and he made play with the intention of Parliament at the time when the statutes were passed. There was uncertainty over the proviso in the subsidy act and over the King's actions. The judges met twice, and on the second occasion not all were present. This was a good excuse for deferring a matter on which, as was admitted, they could not agree (Doc. 4). In 1624, Parliament tried to sort out the mess. A massive statute continued a horde of previous statutes and repealed others. With respect to the immediate past, it was stated to 'be adjudged' by the authority of the present act that these

[49] Neale, *Parliaments, 1584–1601*, p. 89. Tanner, pp. 289–95. The two revenue statutes were not enrolled in the Chancery, and the texts are not included in *Statutes of the Realm*, iv. 1208.

F

statutes had been in force all the time. A separate act dealt with a statute concerning cloth manufacture which had been passed in 1607 and which was to have lasted until the first session of the ensuing Parliament. This was now continued in force, with the repeal of one clause, until the first session of the next Parliament. In 1625, Parliament continued the process of erasing the difficulty. An Act was passed declaring that the session would not be determined by the royal assent to this and other statutes. This was to take away all doubts 'whether his Majesty's royal assent unto one or more acts of Parliament will not be a determination of this present session'. All statutes needing continuance were to remain in force until the session was fully ended and determined. If the session ended in dissolution without further action having been taken, the statutes were to stand continued until the end of the first session of the next Parliament. Coke, in his *Fourth Institute*, tried to sum up and explain the many technicalities brought together in this episode (Doc. 5).[50]

The substance of this affair belongs to parliamentary history, and the crucial problems raised – definition of a session, of a Parliament – deserve to be fully studied. The Short Parliament could be described as a 'convention in Parliament' (Doc. 31). Mr Hinton has suggested that it may be very important for us to find out how far, if at all, the statutes were enforced in the interim.[51] As indicated, this is not too much of a problem with respect to 1614, although it would be nice to know whether the decision that it was only a convention was an after-thought. The judges in their opinion of 1623 implied otherwise, but this may not mean much (Doc. 4). The crucial time is that between January 1622 and the meeting of the 1624 Parliament. It could be argued that if statutes were enforced, although not on the book, then this was a revolutionary exercise in government. Certainly the point is of great significance in terms of law and political theory. However, as the legislation of 1624 seems to imply, ministers and judges, M.P.s and J.P.s, appear to have regarded the situation as one of embarrassment rather than conflict, and we must presume that there was no urge to see all these statutes killed. The episode never became a renowned constitutional crisis, although it contained all the elements that could have made it so. For the purposes of this study, it emphasizes how un-certain were many of the rules and definitions concerning the life of Parliament. Old precedents of behaviour could seem out of step once Parliament was playing an ever greater political role but was still a temporary institution. In a society which had permanent royal govern-ment and desired a permanent sense of order, the onus of decision fell

---

[50] *CSP Dom.* 1619–23, pp. 415, 423. 21 Jac. I, c. 18, 28. 1 Charles I, c. 7.

[51] R. W. K. Hinton, 'The Decline of Parliamentary Government under Elizabeth I and the Early Stuarts', *Camb. Hist. J.* 1957, xiii. 129–30.

on the judges. In this episode, however, their inability as well as their importance is apparent. They could not, through an opinion, give that kind of leadership which they were to offer so disastrously in the next decade. On the other hand, as in their clarity of opinion with respect to what may be called the Convention of 1614, they underlined their power. They had erased what was popularly considered to be, and has been so considered ever since, a Parliament.[52] That institution, however, could no longer be approached in such abstract legal terms for it was a living political organism.

[52] It should be noted that the language employed by the proclamation differs from that used by the judges. Whereas the proclamation appears to distinguish between a 'session of Parliament' and a 'convention of Parliament', the judges flatly described 1614 'as but a convention, and no Parliament, or session' (Doc. 4). Coke's language, while ambiguous, seems to conform more with the proclamation (Doc. 5). The proclamation had complicated matters since it opened the subject, and even made specific reference to the need for statutes to be continued, without making any point as to the fate of the statutes.

4

Projects and Extraordinary Courses

'In this court I am subject to the bench. In my own chamber I am subject only to the law of the land.'

Mr Chaffanbrass.[1]

BY 1629, the judges were being seen in an unfavourable political light. Yet despite the angry words attributed to Eliot, it would have been inconceivable for most contemporaries to imagine that in ten years time the judges would be impeached for treason. The judges would not in fact change their ways to any great extent, and the King's expectations of them remained unaltered. The explanation is, of course, that their role, initially only questioned, would be condemned in conjunction with government policies of the 1630s. An assortment of representative topics will be looked at, nearly all of which were related, intimately or generally, with matters of finance. In this decade, full advantage was to be taken of such 'historical research' as appeared to sustain the King's claims, and men like Noy and Selden would achieve the limelight. Among institutions, the Wards has been selected because it was a renowned financial agency and the Star Chamber because it was condemned as such. The Stannaries are noted in order to preserve the balance: their history illustrates aspects of provincial institutional difficulty which have little to do with the political crises of the early Stuart Kings. Much the same can be said of the system of fees and office, although this was a great grievance throughout the period. The judges were involved in all these topics.

From his accession in 1625, Charles's government was financed by hand-to-mouth devices. Dissolution of his first two Parliaments, wrote Clarendon, prompted projects which served to offend. There were outstanding debts from the previous reign, others would fall due, and fresh debts made. A loan from the city was secured by the mortgage of Crown lands. In order to meet war expenses, attention was given to ship moneys, county levies, forced loans, and so on. In the aftermath of the failure to secure parliamentary supply in 1626, a debasement of the coinage was discussed. Perhaps the most ill-considered scheme is represented by a draft proclamation which, on the basis of a promise to call Parliament as soon as possible, required sheriffs to assemble

[1] A. Trollope, *Phineas Redux.*

freeholders and take their votes on levying the supply which had been proposed in Parliament. The idea was dropped, but the demand for forced loans was only a more discreet device based upon the same kind of thinking. It was decided in 1627 to step up the taking of impositions, even though some merchants had refused in the previous year. Soon the Privy Council was contemplating arrears in impositions on both currants and wines, and telling merchants not to unload before payment. As on previous occasions, it was still standard to try and secure a reduction in the duty in preference to challenging it outright. This was the aim of a petition from the owners and masters of ships living at Neston in Cheshire when they appealed against the tax on seaborne coal. In February 1628, it was ordered that arrears of £6,000 on currants together with the residue of a loan of £5,000 – after being used for supplying Jersey and Guernsey – should be paid to the Treasurer of the Navy for wages. In July the King, attending the Privy Council, again declared his intention of having the imposition on currants and ordered merchants not to unload without paying. Yet he had previously accepted the Petition of Right and been granted five subsidies. These, although making it more difficult for the government to evade its creditors, amounted to only a fifth of anticipated expenditure, and collection was anyhow spread over several years. Some of this money had to be laid against existing debts in the hope of maintaining some credit and thus of raising further loans. Sir Anthony Fell, who had lent £7,000, was willing to forbear and lend a further £3,000 if he could get 8 per cent interest and assignments for repayment of the total sum. This was arranged at the end of March 1628, although it was admitted that he might have to wait a long time. The subsidy facilitated this kind of arrangement. At the end of July 1628, two London merchants lent £5,000 with interest for forbearance. This, plus more than £1,000 due for victualling royal ships, was to be repaid out of the third subsidy. A large sum – £22,000 – out of the subsidies was assigned to Burlamachi. Special instructions were sent to the subsidy commissioners exhorting them to make the collection as efficient as possible. This could not prevent exhaustion of the Navy magazine and depletion of the powder in the Tower. In these circumstances of arrears, anticipated loans, interest for forbearance, and imminent financial calamity, it is difficult to know who was the most captive: the Crown or its creditors. The Crown always managed to make ends meet and raise money, though it meant paying attention to detail. The Exchequer supported a previous declaration of the Privy Council when it was decided that sons of men who had been born aliens had to pay 'stranger's custom', that is double tax. The recusant rolls were sent to the commissioners for the subsidy, it being suggested that recusants were congregating in Middlesex and thus trying to escape assessment in their counties. The records of the Exchequer reveal how few stones were left unturned – improvements, forests, wastes and other items. From the beginning of 1628, suggestions were being considered: revaluation of benefices, purchase of impropriations, levy of fines for encroachment on highways, and so on. The whole reign prior to 1640 is marked by similar financial characteristics, and in this respect not too much emphasis should be placed on the eleven years after 1629.[2]

The 1620s had been remarkable for the number of parliamentary meetings. Parliament may not have fully represented the public mood, but by 1640 it would be supposed that it had done so. In truth, little had been achieved apart from the legislation of 1624. The condemnation of individuals had provided only a spurious triumph. James had dispensed with Bacon and Cranfield, but Charles's refusal to desert Buckingham exposed the feebleness of parliamentary attack. The King had side-stepped or won every major dispute. The price was in the loss of legislation and revenue, but he probably took this less seriously than have subsequent historians. Parliament had failed, and in 1629 the King might be excused for wondering just what the value of this occasional institution was supposed to be. His financial position was near calamitous, but perhaps much of this – including lack of co-operation from producers and merchants – could be attributed to war and economic depression. The times were bad, but if policy and the grace of God could remove these elements, might it not appear that the financial basis of the Crown was really solid?

Parliament, in the years since Elizabeth, had hardly been profuse with legislation and supply. In terms of weeks, the total figure for James is not much less than that for Elizabeth, but her Parliaments were more evenly spread and productive. Between 1614 and 1621, James had not called a Parliament and, more to the point, from 1611 to 1624 there was no legislation apart from the two financial statutes in 1621. This record deserves as much attention as that accorded to the 1630s, although Charles's endeavour must not be underestimated. There was still a sense, if now only fragmentary, that Parliament was extraordinary, an imposition upon the subjects' sense of duty. Elizabeth had claimed credit for calling few Parliaments, and the first two Stuarts had to live with the implication of this claim. Yet, because of the way in which Parliament had evolved in the previous decade, the situation during the 1630s was novel. The House of Lords had exercised a tremendously

[2] Clarendon, i. 32. Pearl, pp. 72ff. *APC* Jan–Aug. 1627, pp. 103–4; Sept. 1627–June 1628, pp. 24–9, 84–5, 263, 367, 455–63, 516–17, 519; July 1628–April 1629, pp. 31–2, 44–5, 64, 369–70, 377–8. Dietz, pp. 234, 236, 262. Steele, i. no. 1476. Cheshire R. O., Neston I (box xix). PRO, E. 125/4, ff. 262v.–263. For Crown finances and the decline of royal credit, see R. Ashton, *The Crown and the Money Market*, Oxford, 1960.

important judicial function, and the House of Commons had produced debates which, though fruitless, were important. These meetings, spread out as they were, represented a mosaic of national and provincial politics. At the least, Parliament provided a safety valve and a means of enlightening the government; at best it meant that when Parliament was sitting the nature of politics was exceptional. The Privy Council by itself could attain little of this quality. The suggestion made in 1610 that Parliament should be called at regular intervals if the Great Contract was agreed upon may have been improper, but it need not be interpreted entirely in a partisan sense. The significance, if not the achievement, of Parliament had developed radically. So it is that the most obvious feature of the 1630s is still that which traditionally has invited most comment.[3]

It is difficult to judge at what point the political gentry became convinced that Charles did not intend to call another Parliament. Merchants who briefly resisted tunnage and poundage after the dissolution of 1629 probably believed that another Parliament would soon be called and therefore feared reprisals if they paid. Possibly it was only ship money which made the situation clear. In December 1636 the Earl of Danby, claiming ship money to be illegal, had the temerity to write to Charles calling for the summons of a Parliament. It is difficult to judge the King's mind. Precisely because he held the initiative of summons his position was flexible, whatever his pronouncements. In 1626, through Dudley Carleton, he suggested that another Parliament would not be called unless behaviour improved. In 1629, he affirmed that he could call Parliament when he chose. Asserting that the recent frequency of meetings proved his love of Parliaments, Charles explained that he was disturbed by the ease with which people were misled. There would be no further meetings of Parliament until subjects came to 'a better understanding of us'. It was made an offence to repeat rumours about the likelihood of a Parliament being summoned. It may be assumed that Charles would think of calling a Parliament some day and this would probably be, as Wentworth once put it, when the debts were taken off. There was no convention that the King had to call Parliament, but in so far as the word can be used it may be thought that there was a convention that he should not express his intention not to do so.[4]

It was possible to think of Parliament once a state of peace had been

[3] Neale, *Commons*, p. 380. *Proceedings in Parliament, 1610*, i. xx.
[4] P. Zagorin, *The Court and the Country*, London, 1969, pp. 102–3. Kenyon, pp. 50–1, 86. Steele, i. no. 1578. In 1633, on the death of the clerk of the Commons, no successor was appointed and the Secretary of State confiscated his archives. S. Lambert, 'The Clerks and Records of the House of Commons, 1600–1640', *Bull. Inst. Hist. Research* 1970, xliii. 215 ff.. This would seem to be a fairly strong indication of the King's intent at the time.

established, since it might seem that foreign involvement had been largely responsible for the initiative grasped by the House of Commons in the 1620s. Rumours were rife when Noy was appointed Attorney General and Selden reconciled with officialdom.[5] In February 1634, after a Duchy of Lancaster decree arranging a composition in respect of a group of copyholders whose entry fines were uncertain, the King agreed that the decree should be confirmed by statute. Clearly the tenants supposed that Parliament would be called some day in the relevant future. Furthermore the King reacted, at least formally, against supposed critics of Parliament. In the aftermath of 1629, proceedings had been ordered against the Earls of Bedford, Clare, and Somerset, together with Sir Robert Cotton and others, in respect of a pamphlet which purported to show how the 'impertinency of Parliaments' could be bridled and the King's revenues increased. In a meeting of the Council, it was said that these proposals were more fit for a 'Turkish state' – recalling the words of Chambers – 'being contrary to the justice and mildness of His Majesty's government, and the sincerity of his intentions'. The pamphlet, apparently written in 1614 by the illegitimate son of Elizabeth's Leicester, was said to be circulated in order to damage the King's reputation, but in the end the matter was dropped.[6]

The achievement of peace and an improvement in the economic situation contributed to the government's relative success in the early 1630s, but whether or not Parliaments were summoned there were always some basic weaknesses: neither a standing army – even the last years of Elizabeth had been marked by recruiting failure – nor a paid bureaucracy in the country.[7] Nothing was done, and these inadequacies were even more painfully apparent in 1639–40 than they had been in the 1620s. It only needed a major crisis to push over Charles's house of cards. Even so, the collapse might not have come had not genuine policies been perverted; royal rights were affirmed so that they might be sold. The level of intensity varied but the trend could be seen in distraint of knighthood, upheld in the Exchequer, in the commissions into defective titles and forest encroachments, and in the largely normal operations of the Duchy Chamber. Laudian reforms of the Church and social welfare combined with financial interest, and it was easy to believe that the fines paid by offenders were the goal. In terms of repute the regime was left morally bankrupt.

With respect to compositions some parties, especially the powerful, might feel that they were gaining something, if only security. Fines

[5] PRO, State Papers Domestic, Charles I, S.P. 16/203, no. 108.
[6] PRO, Duchy of Lancaster, Entry Books, D.L. 5/31, ff. 508v.–512v. *APC* May 1629–May 1630, p. 177. *State Trials*, iii. 387–400.
[7] Kenyon, pp. 1–2.

levied by courts of law might be unpopular, but the strand of legality was clear and could be accepted up to that point when criticism became general rather than particular. Ship money never fitted into these circumstances, and it was not alone. Peculiar monopolies, such as the ridiculous soap patent, circumvented the 1624 statute under the guise of inventions. The disputed taxes on trade were still taken, and the method of collection, a continuation of previous practice, was that of customs farming. The customs were increasingly important and the farmers, themselves involved in the most intricate of political man-œuvres, became ever more important as long-term lenders to the Crown and as organizers of such loans from individuals as could still be raised. Not surprisingly, along with judges and ministers, they were among the first to suffer during the Long Parliament. Largely because of tunnage and poundage and impositions, they were held to have assisted in the denial and betrayal of Parliament. Their lease was sequestered and a bill prepared to confiscate their estates, but they were eventually allowed to compound by paying a fine.[8]

Many devices were unproductive in comparison with the trouble caused. Cranfield, appearing briefly upon the scene in 1637, pathetically urged the King to give up these 'projects and extraordinary courses'. Furthermore, ship money and the taxes on trade were regarded as in breach of the promise given to the Petition of Right. Yet the govern-ment was increasingly interested in demonstrating the legal validity of the anachronisms which it produced. In the end, judicial approval and political absurdity walked hand in hand. Charles never understood this. In 1628, he believed that the assurance of the judges about his freedom of action despite the Petition of Right had political weight (Doc. 10). He may really have believed in the legacy of the past. After the Short Parliament he called a Great Council of peers, and in long-dead terms of the military obligations of feudalism a proclamation of August 20, 1640, summoned all those who held of the King 'by grand serjeanty, escuage, or knights service to do their services against the Scots, according to their tenures'. They were to assemble at Newcastle on September 20th, but before this date those who wished might make composition. The Achilles heel of combining medieval legality with immediate finance was still there, but legality as seen from the bench had ceased to be the point.[9]

If the phrase 'the personal rule', has justification as a particular label for this period, it is to be found in Charles's direct involvement. In April 1629, it was reported that the Council sat every day for three or four hours with the King always present. He continued his close contact with Council meetings and his intervention in other spheres could

[8] Ashton, p. 111.
[9] Tawney, pp. 293–5. Steele, i. no. 223.

become a decided nuisance, as the commissioners into fees found out. A great deal of financial, legal and political expertise was expended, but the best description of the result can be found in that old English phrase, 'muddling through'. Clarendon, speaking of events at the end of 1640, said that 'the sinking and near desperate condition of monarchy in this kingdom can never be buoyed up but by a prudent and steady Council attending upon the virtue and vivacity of the King; nor be preserved and improved when it is up but by cherishing and preserving the wisdom, integrity, dignity, and reputation of that Council'. The Council numbered over forty and the steady increase in numbers since Elizabeth had exposed it to faction. Buckingham's predominance also had this effect, but by the late 1620s the King's faith in him was so great that faction within the Council was again muted. One was either with the favourite, or out of government and out of influence. His death again enabled a degree of faction to flourish.[10]

Professor Elton has described the outstanding feature of the Tudor Council as 'its all-pervasiveness: nothing that happened within the realm appeared to fall outside its competence'.[11] Leaving aside its position as a regular court of appeal for such places as the Isle of Man or the Channel Isles, it cannot fairly be described as a court of law in any normal sense but it was important in respect of judicial proceedings which it might direct or control. In 1605 King James, before taking a holiday, directed that in his absence no one was to seek remedy before the Privy Council in matters of justice – i.e. between party and party – and he pointed out that the courts were more qualified. However Councillors with special information, or if they received authority from the King, could make reference to the court where the case was pending. In 1615, over an affair of piracy, the Spanish Ambassador was informed that 'this Board takes no cognizance of their own authority, otherwise than to command that justice be done with expedition'. This might embody a fairly broad discretion, as when the Council wrote to the Barons of the Exchequer in 1623 ordering them to free Sir Thomas Wilson from a suit arising from service done for the King at the Council's command. At various times, notably before 1624, it was the initial means whereby creditors or persons with a normal legal right were restrained. In the early part of the reign of Charles, it was assuming a greater authority over affairs of prize. In 1631, Charles granted a commission to all Privy Council members to hear and determine controversies touching the jurisdiction of the courts of law, 'it being

[10] E. R. Turner, *The Privy Council of England in the Seventeenth and Eighteenth Centuries, 1603–1784*, Baltimore, 1927–8, i. 93. Clarendon, i. 261. From June 1, 1637 to Feb. 27, 1638, the King was present at Council meetings on at least twenty-six occasions. *Privy Council Registers*, I and II.

[11] Elton, p. 101.

manifest that our said justice . . . is originally and in sovereignty only and entirely in ourselves'. The notion had previously been apparent when James in 1622, as supreme judge of the jurisdiction of courts, called upon the Privy Councillors as his representatives to consider the jurisdiction of the Earl Marshal. However, Charles's commission was more comprehensive and permanent, and it fitted Wentworth's conception of how disputes should be handled. The new Lord President of the Council in the North had been outspoken about some of the writs issued by the Westminster judges, but problems – demaraction, jurisdiction, procedural ability – were commonplace and do not imply that there was a gulf between Wentworth and the judges on other matters. The idea that the King and his senior advisers should supervise the settlement of jurisdictional disputes both carried forward the ambitions of James and made sense in the context of the 1630s.[12]

The Council could be influential but, as Professor Dawson has indicated, King and Councillors were increasingly lukewarm about spending their time on private disputes: 'its work in private controversies . . . was intermingled with the multifarious actions and decisions required for general government. For the busy men who comprised the Privy Council the jurisdiction over private disputes was a distraction and nuisance of which they tried to relieve themselves.'[13] However, petitions were numerous, and the Council could not be protected from private controversy. Orders for conduct of Council business were much concerned with the handling of disputes and petitions.[14] The Council did not make judgments, but then so few of the institutions described as courts of law invariably made judgements in the proceedings before them.

The Privy Council was a collection of individuals who took an individual oath. A growing membership pushed forward the process whereby select groups were responsible for foreign affairs, religion, and other major matters. Through letters, instructions and exhortations, the Council deluged J.P.s, sheriffs and other local officials with demands and strictures. There was a strenuous effort to make existing legislation, and in particular the Tudor statute book, a reality. A comprehensive range of agrarian, industrial and social regulations was applied in earnest, and use was made of the courts to mete out direct punishments for disobedience. There was a determined effort to activate local officials and to place a greater supervisory responsibility upon the

---

[12] *CSP Dom.* 1603–10, p. 186; 1619–23, pp. 412, 589. *APC* 1615–16, p. 309. Turner, i. 168–9, 181. R. R. Reid, *The King's Council in the North*, London, 1921, pp. 408–10.

[13] J. P. Dawson, *A History of Lay Judges*, Cambridge, Mass., 1960, pp. 173–4.

[14] *APC* Sept. 1627–June 1628, pp. 331–2; June 1630–June 1631, pp. 105–7. Elton, pp. 104–5, prints an interesting memorandum of April 1600.

justices of assize. The Book of Orders issued in January 1631 demanding full enforcement of the law by J.P.s has been described as unprecedented.[15] Yet this activity is also an indication on what was not being done. The ability to enunciate policy was well ahead of administrative capacity. If all the rules had really been enforced, a revolution in society would have occurred. Instead the government was selective, and even so it could achieve no more than a glimmer of enforcement.

William Noy

William Noy, who was appointed Attorney General in October 1631 and died in August 1634, was subsequently condemned as a major architect of government policies. After his death he was lampooned: 'a hundred proclamations being found in his head, a bundle of moth-eaten records in his mouth, and a barrel of soap in his belly.'[16] He was prominent in notorious prosecutions, including those against Prynne, Sherfield, and the feoffees for impropriations. Along with Banks, Digges, Edward Herbert and Wentworth, he was reputed to be a turncoat. Many assumed that favour and office had proved too strong a lure. However, Clarendon, although uncharmed by Noy's character, believed that the wiles of court and courtiers had perverted his judgment after he had hesitantly agreed to become Attorney General.[17] Gardiner said that his brain was 'a mere storehouse of legal facts', and pictured Noy as a mechanic without any depth of constitutional analysis: 'it may have seemed as easy to quote precedents on one side as on the other.'[18]

Noy was lucid. Speaking in committee on May 18, 1610, he argued that, despite a restraining message from the King, Parliament might have a duty to discuss an issue. 'If we may not say this is our right, if we may not complain, because we are commanded not to complain; then we must bear any apparent wrong, if a commandment come to us not to dispute it. Therefore, I think it very convenient and behoveful for us to answer that we must of necessity dispute it, and cannot make

[15] T. G. Barnes, 'The Clerk of the Peace in Caroline Somerset', *Occasional Papers*, Dept. of English Local Hist., Univ. of Leicester 1961, xiv. 45.

[16] 'A Projector Lately Dead', cited *DNB*.

[17] Clarendon, i. 91–2.

[18] Gardiner, vii. 221. Attention should be paid to the career of Selden. Regarded as an 'opposition' lawyer in the 1620s, he was released in 1631 and came into favour, partly because of his *Mare Clausum* which was published in 1635 with a dedication to the King. Charles may even have considered him as a possible Lord Chancellor. In the Long Parliament he opposed both the attainder of Strafford and the Militia Ordinance, but he sided with Westminster when war began although virtually withdrawing from public life. His career is another illustration of the fact that different battles, fought at different times, should not be strung into a single pattern of opposition.

our petition until we have disputed it; for as the right is, so must our petition be grounded.' In 1621, when he was counted among the 'chiefest pilots' in the House, he was a prolific speaker and committee man. He made the first speech in the assault upon patents and monopolies – probably this was by arrangement with Coke who spoke next. In this, and in his association of exactions and the sale of office, Noy set the mood which was to dominate the last two Parliaments of James I. Patentees and referees had failed the Crown. The sovereign had been wronged and, far from wishing to clip the prerogative, the intent of the House of Commons was to 'extend' it. As Coke said of one list of referees, they were so respectable that no king in Christendom could have refused. The aim was to press the attack while absolving the King of blame.[19]

Noy was assumed to be a Commons man, and he was more concerned than Coke to stress the judicial independence of that House vis-à-vis the upper chamber. He served as counsel for Sir Walter Erle, imprisoned for refusing the loan, and strenuously opposed the King's right to levy tunnage and poundage. In 1629, his argument that parliamentary privilege was effective even when Parliament was prorogued apparently converted Hakewill. No wonder he was to be seen as a turncoat, even though two years passed between dissolution and his appointment. However, he was not all that inconsistent. We must remember the depressing effect of the 1629 affair, and the relatively promising impression made by the government in the next two years. Nor was Noy unknown to Charles. Around 1621 he had been of counsel to the then Prince of Wales, and with Walter had advised Charles about his rights in the Duchy of Cornwall. In the previous year he had served with Finch and Hakewill on Bacon's committee which sifted obsolete statutes. Perhaps he was already establishing himself as an authority on this kind of subject. In 1631, just before his appointment as Attorney General, he was busy together with Finch as counsel for a city of London syndicate which had purchased Duchy of Lancaster lands. Work of this nature and an extensive Exchequer practice appear to have been the mainstay of his professional career.[20]

In 1624, many critics believed that they had the sympathy of the Prince, but the sustained though recent attachment of Charles to Buckingham inevitably isolated men like Noy from office, although he was a member of the commission of enquiry into fees. The death of

---

[19] *Proceedings in Parliament, 1610*, ii. 93. *Commons Debates, 1621*, ii. 27, 108; iv. 78–9; vi. 249–51. Elizabeth R. Foster, 'The Procedure of the House of Commons against Patents and Monopolies, 1621–24', *Conflict in Stuart England*, ed. W. A. Aiken and B. D. Henning, London, 1960, p. 64.

[20] Aylmer, p. 352. *Commons Debates, 1621*, iv. 114. Prestwich, p. 294. PRO, D.L. 5/31, ff. 20, 23.

Buckingham and the uproar over Eliot altered the situation. The Attorney Generalship when it fell vacant was appropriate to Noy's position and talents. Other men were also amenable to improving their prospects. Dudley Digges had obtained a reversion of the Mastership of the Rolls – a position which he did not fill for some years – and Edward Littleton became Recorder of London.

For just under three years, Noy put his skill to work on behalf of the Crown and thus dominated a period in which the pursuit of legal right influenced the provision of revenue. The approach was not novel. Prior to 1629, Charles was 'probing the wall of law and custom which protected his subjects' money in the hope of finding the odd gap through which he could press'.[21] It had all been piecemeal, but Noy thought in terms of maintaining the law, not making it, and he set the tone for the 1630s as a decade of intense government by common lawyers.

Antiquarian scholarship was nothing new, and it had been very much in vogue since the last half of Elizabeth's reign. Many antiquarians were lawyers – Cotton, D'Ewes, Selden, Spelman, – but the habit of searching the past was suspect. In 1604, James closed down the Society of Antiquaries. This King, who disliked examples drawn from the reigns of such ill-fated monarchs as Richard II and Henry VI (Doc. 3), believed that if the Crown joined in the battle of precedents it might do so with the preponderant advantage. It was natural that those who sought recognition should apply antiquarian scholarship to the problems of the Crown. In order to honour and advise Prince Henry, Doddridge wrote a treatise, dedicated to James I, in which he stressed the decay of revenues properly belonging to the Prince of Wales and suggested some means of rectification. It was published in 1630. John Davies resorted to history when it was suggested that Charles, the second born, could not succeed Henry with respect to the Duchy of Cornwall. Noy put together a treatise describing the ways in which the King could support or increase his revenue. He argued that the Crown should receive much more from the Admiralty, Duchy of Lancaster and Wards. Incidental reference was made to abuses and errors established under Elizabeth, reform of which might be attained either through Parliament or through the Privy Council. This was a compact and arid little piece, but the flavour is that of an author who believes reform to be the object. The fifth chapter was devoted to 'abating and reforming the excess of gifts and rewards', and a warning was given of 'the mischief that the open hand of the sovereign might bring the state into'. Ship money presents Noy in a different light. He was undoubtedly crucial in placing a heavier emphasis on money rather than on ships, but his advice to start with both maritime counties and towns was overruled. This

[21] Kenyon, p. 59.

may suggest that he was not entirely responsible for the planned progression, or softening-up process, which had a reverse effect to that intended. Likewise, it was Finch who transformed the forest policy initiated in Noy's time: as Mr Hammersley has put it, 'the transition from the remarkable to the scandalous began with Noy's disappearance from the scene'. Even so, it is evident that he advised and approved of many things. The soap monopoly is a notorious example (Doc. 28 [3]), but this was really Weston's concern. Indeed there are grounds to suspect that Noy's death serves to draw a line between stratagems of restoration and their perversion. But by 1640, he was the most convenient scapegoat, and Finch's personal defence was in part an attempt to shift the line of enquiry on to Noy's activities (Doc. 24). [22]

Forests and Other Devices
The general picture is of royal rights being extended to the utmost that the law would allow. Subsequently, these rights were often sold or used as a means of raising money. The emphasis varied. There was activity in the Duchy of Lancaster – which got into most counties – especially in respect of forests and compositions for entry fines. This was not abnormal for that estate institution, but it is possible that the reign of Charles I was marked by a novel intensity. Although his words might be understandable, if delivered years before, it is difficult to swallow Attorney General Banks's argument on May 15, 1640, that an injunction should issue from the Duchy Chamber to restrain the defendant's proceedings at law, otherwise 'it may tend to the defeating of His Majesty and to the lessening of his revenue'.[23] The extension of the bounds, and thus the jurisdiction, of the Honor of Peveril rather catches the eye because it was admitted that this was an innovation (Doc. 21).

Distraint of knighthood provides an example of the Crown turning to ancient rights. Writs had gone out in January 1626 requiring sheriffs to summon all freeholders having £40 per annum to appear at London to receive the order of knighthood. However, the proclamation of July 1630 was particularly irritating in that it extended committees for compounding to all parts of the country and stated that those who did not attend would have to come to Whitehall at their own expense. Between 1630 and 1635, the government obtained considerable sums through

[22] J. Doddridge, *The History of the Ancient and Modern Estate of the Principality of Wales, Dutchy of Cornwall, and Earldome of Chester*, London, 1630. J. Davies, 'The Declaration of our Soveraigne Lord the King . . .', *Works*, ii. 359–96. W. Noy, *A Treatise of the Rights of the Crown*, London, 1715, pp. 21–4. *Ship Money Papers and Richard Grenville's Note-Book*, ed. Carol G. Bonsey and J. G. Jenkins, Bucks. Rec. Soc. 1965, p. xi. G. Hammersley, 'The Revival of the Forest Laws under Charles I', *History* 1960, xlv. 94. Dietz, p. 265.
[23] PRO, D.L. 5/33, f. 360. My remarks about the Duchy of Lancaster are based on an impression gained from reading the entry books of that court.

compounding with offenders. Sometimes an inducement appeared, as when in June 1638 the Privy Council advised reduction of a composition from £25 to £5 because of a J.P.'s services to the Crown. As already noted, most avenues of traditional royal right were investigated. A brief outline of the laws governing the royal game of swans was published in 1632. This was based upon an Elizabethan compilation and upon orders established by Baron Tanfield and others at a court at Burford during the reign of James. The author referred to the ancient customs for keeping swanherds' courts and indicated that misdemeanours should be punished. Many other examples could be instanced, from similar minor rights stressed by hopeful antiquarians to such major matters as defective titles and the forest laws. The agents of the Crown were not always successful in legal disputes, but the validity of these policies was grounded upon approval by the courts.[24]

Commissions to compound with tenants for defective titles had been issued since before the death of Elizabeth and frequently were the subject of unfavourable comment in Jacobean Parliaments. In 1624, an act was passed protecting Crown tenants who could prove possession for sixty years. Commissions of 1628, 1630 and 1635 were aimed at those outside this statute and also at people occupying reclaimed land, encroaching on forests, or breaking the laws with respect to enclosure on commons and waste lands. However from 1632, forest encroachments were also the subject of separate enquiries.[25]

The forest laws, never regarded as an automatic wrong, were not abolished by the Long Parliament, and their value was often stressed after the Restoration, notably with respect to the preservation of timber. Forest organization was highly complicated. The leading officials were two chief justices, one north and one south of the Trent, who presided over the forest eyre or justice seat. Manwood described the laws existing in Elizabeth's time as 'very mild, gentle and merciful'. In many places these rights had been forgotten, but although the laws were not taken very seriously the forest courts were by no means dead. The central courts upheld the forest jurisdiction by applying a set of rules, justifiable but narrow, which amounted to a stranglehold. The King's Bench was often content to hear cases transferred to it. Coke said that men imprisoned unlawfully could obtain *habeas corpus* from the King's Bench, and that proceedings could be moved by *certiorari* into that court if injustice was alleged. Conversely, if the justice seat refused a rightful claim, King's Bench might command it to hear and allow the

[24] Yonge, p. 89. Steele, i. no. 1614. Gardiner, vii. 167. Dietz, pp. 262–3. *Privy Council Registers*, III, March–Aug. 1638, p. 274. J. D'Oyley, *The Orders, Laws, and Ancient Customes of Swanns*, London, 1632. N. F. Ticehurst, *The Mute Swan in England*, London, 1957.

[25] 21 Jac. I, c. 2. Kenyon, p. 87.

claim, while it could also issue writs of error to the justice seat. The ordinary forest courts could do little beyond presenting criminals at the eyre, but the eyre was not being held at the end of Elizabeth's reign. None the less, the position of chief justice was not without value. It was one of the positions obtained by Buckingham, and Queen Anne appointed Sir Edward Coke as justice in eyre for all her forests. Decrepitude need not be overstressed, and it has been argued that the forest laws had become something of a benefit to the inhabitants of forest areas while being something of a restriction upon the Crown.[26]

The possibility of revival had always been there, and in 1604 the Commons had passed a bill protecting holders of certain lands taken from the forests by royal grants. Sir John Burroughs, in a memorandum of 1628 as to how Kings had previously raised money, discussed the possibilities of forests and parks. In the same year, after commissions surveyed the chase of Leicester in order to arrange disafforestation, quarrels and law suits followed. In the summer, the King was selling lands in fee farm within Rockingham Forest. Disafforestation and resulting enclosure was an issue of resentment in several places, notably between 1629 and 1631. It was still a piecemeal approach, but the surveys undertaken must have confirmed that a rich field of royal rights was being neglected. A fresh impetus was provided by the combination of Noy and the new chief justice south of the Trent, Henry, Earl of Holland. The intention appears to have been to restore royal rights and punish offenders without being so rigorous as to arouse serious resentment. A forest eyre held at Windsor and Bagshot in September 1632 was a success. Lengthy preparations were made for another, this time in the Forest of Dean. It met after Noy's death, and £130,000 in fines was levied, although many of these were subsequently reduced. Finch's energy on this occasion, partly a self-advertisement for promotion, would not be forgiven (Doc. 24). There had also been continued activity in the Duchy of Lancaster. In November 1633, the Earl of Newcastle and others were accused of intrusion into royal forests. An agreement was reached whereby one-third of the area in dispute was acknowledged to be the King's and the remainder was confirmed as common pasture.[27]

The Crown's rights were prosecuted relentlessly in the second half of the decade: areas long devoid of forest law were reclaimed – the bounds of Rockingham Forest were increased from six to sixty miles – and extensive amercements, compositions and fines were garnered, the

[26] Holdsworth, i. 104–6. J. Manwood, *A Briefe Collection of the Lawes of the Forest*, London, 1592. Coke, *Fourth Institute*, pp. 290, 294, 297. *HMC 9th Rep.*, App. pt. ii. 373. Hammersley, p. 87.

[27] Kenyon, pp. 87–8. BM, Additional MS. 34, 324, ff. 269–74. *APC* Sept. 1627–June 1628, pp. 475–7; July 1628–April 1629, pp. 11–12. Barnes, *Somerset*, pp. 156–60. Hammersley, pp. 87–99. PRO, D.L. 5/31, ff. 446–7, D. G. C. Allan, 'The Rising in the West, 1628–31', *Econ. Hist. Rev.* 1952–3, 2nd ser. v. 76–85.

victims sometimes being among the greatest in the land. There were growing complaints about the outrageous behaviour of Crown lawyers and the intimidation of juries. In 1638, Sir Ralph Hausby was ordered to pay £640 damages and a fine of 1,000 marks to the King for spoil and waste of royal woods in the Duchy of Lancaster. A further £200 was to be paid to the informer. Vigour and punishments might have been acceptable. The real cause of complaint was the new tone of the campaign. Only months after the eyre in the Forest of Dean, the Crown began to offer its freshly underlined rights for sale. This became the pattern. Eyres went out, shortly to be followed by commissions for disafforestation. Men, punished once, were offered the chance of composition whereby they bought the Crown's rights and thus saved themselves from the next round of enquiries. A vigorous restatement of royal right had assumed the character of a financial racket. None the less, it was almost impossible in conventional terms to argue against the legality of Charles's enforcement of the forest laws. The Long Parliament, mostly concerned with the area affected, fixed boundaries as they had been in the twentieth year of James I. In addition, and reflecting the legislation of 1624, places were held not to be forest unless a forest court had been held for sixty years before the first year of Charles I.[28]

The Stannaries

In studying the reign of Charles I, particular difficulties attract historians like flies to fly paper. The failure of his regime and the revolutionary circumstances of the 1640s are the magnet. Yet, if none of this had happened, there would still have been long-standing grievances and problems, such as those raised by the relationship between courts. It is even harder to draw the line when the two sets of circumstances, although joined, mingled in a muted and local atmosphere, as was the case with the Stannaries.

There were many franchise jurisdictions concerned with mines – in Cumberland, Derbyshire, the Mendips, and the Forest of Dean – but the Stannaries of Cornwall and Devon are best known. The stewards held courts of first instance twice a year, and appeal lay to the court of the vice-warden which also exercised an original equity jurisdiction. A further line of appeal lay to the Duchy of Cornwall, and early in the reign of Elizabeth it had been decided that writ of error did not lie against the Stannaries. But in the 1590s and early years of the seventeenth century, the Stannaries found themselves increasingly crowded by the central courts. Complaints were raised against the Chancery and the common law courts and against the Star Chamber with respect to 'appeals'. Most troubles stemmed from disputes over the geographical

[28] Hammersley, pp. 85–102. Holdsworth, i. 105. PRO, D.L. 5/32, ff. 446–8. 16 Charles I, c. 16. C. E. Hart, *Royal Forest*, Oxford, 1966, p. 131.

boundaries of the Stannaries and the definition of 'tinners'. In 1608, an opinion announced by Fleming and Coke tried to clarify some problems. Their definitions can be seen as part of the process of limitation being applied by the Westminster courts to all provincial jurisdictions. In 1627, the judges amplified part of this opinion, but disputes continued. In the following year, Eliot denounced the policies of the vice-warden. In 1632 the Privy Council, with the King and Noy present and in conjunction with the judges, apparently broadened the privileges of the tinners. It was implied that at least in Cornwall the limits of jurisdiction covered the whole county. Suggestions were made with respect to Devon (Doc. 15). There was an air of independence among Stannary officials, fostered by the powerful Lord Warden, Pembroke. On the other hand, it is difficult to believe that the Council order really represented the views of all the judges, despite their signatures. There was suspicion about the way in which the Stannary courts operated. A decision of the judges that the traditional jury of six in the courts of the stewards was illegal was apparently ignored. The King's Bench, following an argument by Noy, made it clear that the jurisdiction of the Stannaries only covered tin and tinners, and the lack of formal course in their proceedings was described as illegal. A few years later, there is evidence that the tin miners of Cornwall were again placing reliance upon the definitions of 1608. In 1637, there was comment on the great difference 'fallen out' between King's Bench and the Stannaries.[29]

Uncertainties of definition could have occurred without the problems and attitudes of Charles. Yet there is something uneasy about the Privy Council emphasis in 1632. The Stannaries were an area of royal patronage and revenue of some, if slight, importance. After the early years of James, most of his financial interests had been surrendered to a syndicate of farmers who handled the tin. All the themes are there – including the use of judicial opinion – but the note is provincial and low-keyed. The Stannaries did not escape the Long Parliament. The statute of 1641 cut the jurisdiction down to size and confined the privilege to 'working' tinners.[30]

The Court of Wards and Liveries

An important part of Charles's income was supplied by the court of Wards and Liveries. Unlike some other limited and specialized institutions, this court and the Duchy of Lancaster had survived the

[29] G. R. Lewis, *The Stannaries*, Cambridge, Mass., 1908, pp. 101, 245–8. Hulme, *Eliot*, pp. 239–40. Holdsworth, i. 157 n. 7. Cro. Car., 259, 333 (79 *English Reports*). Aylmer, p. 54. *Documents Relating to the Proceedings against William Prynne in 1634 and 1637*, ed. S. R. Gardiner, Camden New Ser. 1877, xviii. 81.

[30] 16 Charles I, c. 15. Greater latitude was allowed after the Restoration. Holdsworth, i. 162.

rearrangements of the mid-Tudor period to continue separate from the Exchequer. For extensive periods, however, the last being 1621–4, the Master of the Wards was also Lord Treasurer, and Cottington, Master from 1635 to 1641, was Chancellor of the Exchequer and Under-treasurer. The court of Wards was concerned with the administration and marketing of royal feudal rights in respect of infants and their estates, together with some responsibility over widows, fools and idiots. The system aroused persistent hostility. Clarendon wrote that rich families 'were exceedingly incensed, and even indevoted to the Crown, looking upon what the law had intended for their protection and preservation to be now applied for their destruction; and therefore resolved to take the first opportunity to ravish that jewel out of the royal diadem, though it was fastened there by the known law upon as un-questionable a right as the subject enjoyed any thing that was most his own'. In fact, although it may be fair to think of the court 'as an important subsidiary cause of the civil war', Parliament did nothing in 1641. Despite decades of complaint, the Wards survived for a time. Possibly this was because it had never pretended to be anything other than a revenue court.[31]

Tudor Masters of the Wards had been distinguished men. William Paulet (1540–54), William Cecil (1561–98), and Robert Cecil (1599–1612) had been administrators and politicians of outstanding importance. Others, Sir Francis Englefield (1554–8) and Sir Thomas Parry (1558–60), were able and had particularly close connections with their respect-ive sovereigns. But when James I in 1612 appointed Sir George Carew, a talented public servant, he seems to have made a deliberate change. Carew himself affirmed that the King 'meaneth to be as it were Master of the Wards himself'.[32] It meant, the Great Contract having failed that the King would keep a more serious eye on his revenues from fiscal feudalism, and part of the process might involve cutting into the takings of the Master. Carew died within a few months, and the court experienced several years of uncertainty during which the King's initial ambitions were hardly realized. Walter Cope died amid rumours of his impending dismissal, and William Knollys, Viscount Wallingford, was sacked for maladministration. Cranfield (1619–24) had a devious robustness; the revenues of the court improved but its reputation in-evitably suffered from his impeachment and fall. The next two Masters – Robert Naunton (1624–35) and Francis Cottington (1635–41) – were clever functionaries.

The need to increase the Crown's revenues had long been realized, but Salisbury and Walter Cope had also appreciated the advisability of restraining the unpopularity of the court. That both aims were in-

---

[31] Clarendon, i. 199. Bell, p. 149.
[32] Bell, p. 20.

compatible was understood. Naunton and Cottington, however, concentrated upon revenue: money was the prime object of the court rather than provision of justice within the terms of feudal law, whether or not that law was popular. Naunton was practically a cipher as a judge, leaving most responsibility to the Attorney of the court. This official was so important that the House of Lords associated him with the twelve judges when in January 1641 they requested the King to accord their places the tenure of good behaviour. Cottington was intimately involved in the financial schemes of the later 1630s, and that important official, Benjamin Rudyerd, Surveyor from 1618, although called to the bar, was clearly an administrator. The core of the drive was found in the feodaries (the local officers) who were energetic in increasing valuations in their surveys in comparison with those given in the inquisitions *post mortem*. There was indeed, stemming from Salisbury's initiative, a definite trend towards committing wards to relatives. This was often through advance arrangements, but at a time of rising valuations the court was held responsible by those who lacked sufficient money. Spelman said that a mother was thereby doubly bereaved, losing husband and child. Mothers and relatives were by no means trustworthy, but the reaction was less against making money out of children or exploiting their persons and estates than against this being done by parties outside the family. It would also seem that the Crown was able to secure a larger slice of the moneys being paid into the court. Cottington, for example, almost certainly made a tidy profit, but it is doubtful if his takings can be compared to those of the two Cecils. While politics, the passage of events, and biased assessment enter into it, there are indications that the Mastership, once among the six most valuable offices, no longer had anything like its former value. The grudge existing in society may not have been alleviated – the number of clerks increased in the Stuart period and this meant more fees and gratuities – but it is not impossible that a new resentment was created among lesser officials whose vested interests were at stake. They were a small number and they would be influenced by the way in which the wind was blowing, but in the crisis of the early 1640s only a small minority can be described as 'royalist'. However, from the Crown's point of view, the results of new policies can be described as astronomical. Even allowing for inflation, a vastly augmented revenue from the court of Wards was received in the 1630s, notably from sales of wardships and marriages. A peak of £83,085 was reached in 1639, and the impressive figures for 1640 (£76,274) and 1641 (£69,297), while representing a decline, outshone anything before 1639.[33]

As a court of law, the Wards sat in the White Hall of Westminster

[33] *Ibid.*, pp. 19, 32, 117, table A. *Lords Journals*, iv. 131. Aylmer, pp. 211–12, 405–6.

Palace, the office of its clerk was established in the Inner Temple, and those of its auditors in Holborn and in the City. It used English pleadings, written interrogatories, and so on. The procedure whereby traverse was only allowed by bill was hotly criticized on several occasions, notably by Coke who in the 1625 Parliament expressed his conviction that this constituted a restraint of the common law.[34] Apart from this old grievance, the 'due process' of the court was never greatly questioned. Decisions of the Wards were reported in the burgeoning Reports, judges-assistant aided the Master, the advice of Justices and serjeants was often sought, and common lawyers found satisfactory business before its bench. There appear to be several strands: hostility to the administrative, clerical and fee structure of the institution, and to some aspects of procedure, mostly the machinery of evidence, which in terms of cost and irrelevance was open to objection in other courts (Doc. 17); hostility to the law which was seen as a vicious anachronism; and, in so far as money reached the King and appeared to do so in increasing quantities, hostility to his general policies for the realm. Whatever else has to be said, the Wards was seen as an uncontrolled source of revenue helping to sustain a deeply distrusted regime.

A House of Commons committee to enquire into irregular proceedings and into abuses committed by feodaries, escheators and others was appointed in February 1641. In the Grand Remonstrance, the court was accused of exceeding its jurisdiction, but most of the points were practical: excessive fines, ancient leases, and devices used in forcing juries to find an office (enquiry) for the King were all condemned. It did not amount to much, and this raises the question of judgment. Mr Bell considered the Grand Remonstrance as 'disappointing' because it did not express major objections made over the years; he suggested that they could not all have been put into a single document. Yet as we learn more about other courts, it is clear that some of these objections dwindle when they are seen in context.[35]

Cottington was replaced in 1641 by William, Viscount Say and Sele, the court carried on, and entries in the court books were conventional. Normality is perhaps symbolized by an entry of April 27, 1642, that the court did not sit because it was a public day of fast. Clearly some reforms were being stressed – often cited were James I's instructions that sufficient warning must be given before inquisitions – and compositions appear to have been numerous. But there is little in the records to suggest a crisis in the affairs of the court during the critical months before and after the outbreak of war.[36]

[34] Bell, p. 146. *Commons Debates*, 1625, p. 17. W. J. Jones, 'An Introduction to Petty Bag Proceedings', *California Law Review*, 1963, li. 903.

[35] Gardiner, *Docs.*, p. 213. Bell, pp. 146–9.

[36] PRO, Wards Misc. Books, Wards 9/556, p. 1.

Clarendon was correct to stress the hostility felt against the fiscal feudal system, but it would seem that the operations of the court were not especially repugnant. Furthermore, Say and Sele was regarded as reliable. The principal factor, however, may have been the awareness of past attempts to do away with the system, and these, as Sir Thomas Edmondes put it in 1610, meant 'that the court of Wards be dissolved'. For forty years, the court had lived under a shadow, and there must have been an idea that previous attempts should be imitated. The House of Commons had offered composition in 1604, and there had been the possibility of a Great Contract in 1610, an agreement which in terms of recompense had ignored escheators, feodaries and other local officials. James had again been interested in discussing the matter of abolition in 1614 and 1621. The logical thing in 1641–2 was to think of securing an agreement on these lines, but obviously the opportunity and climate for this kind of negotiation did not exist. And so this court, traditionally the most threatened in England, survived. During the first civil war there were two rival courts, one at Westminster and one at Oxford, where Charles had reappointed Cottington. In the year ending Michaelmas 1643, the Westminster court collected £17,369 from wards' lands and £13,641 from sales of wardships, a far more impressive performance than that of the Oxford court. It would have been unwise to abolish it at this point and leave the Oxford court in undisputed if feeble control of the field. But the intention was there. When the Commons decided on abolition in September 1645, they significantly went back to the Great Contract and suggested a sum of £100,000 per annum for the King. The court was abolished by ordinance in February 1646, but this left many things to be wound up including suits. In July, in the peace proposals, the suggested compensation was reduced by half. The court and the feudal laws were finally abolished at the Restoration.[37]

Star Chamber and Some Others

This court,[38] one of the established great tribunals of Westminster Hall, played an important part in the exercise and development of the criminal law, notably in respect of conspiracy, defamation, forgery, fraud, perjury, riot, and sedition. Its jurisdiction was technically confined to misdemeanours – it occasionally handled and punished felonies as

[37] Bell, pp. 140, 145, 155, 158–9.
[38] The main works about Star Chamber are by T. G. Barnes: 'Star Chamber Mythology', *Am. Journal of Legal History*, 1961, v. 1–11; 'Due Process and Slow Process in the Late Elizabethan – Early Stuart Star Chamber', *ibid.*, 1962, vi. 221–49, 315–46; 'The Archives and Archival Problems of the Elizabethan and Early Stuart Star Chamber', *Journal of the Society of Archivists*, ii. no. 8. See also, H. E. I. Phillips, 'The Last Years of the Court of Star Chamber, 1603–1641', *Trans. R. Hist. Soc.*, 1939, 4th ser. xxi. 103–31.

misdemeanours – and like Chancery it spent most of its time on mundane business. It had experienced a process of definition and of technical complication in its procedures which, again like Chancery, involved deceleration in the pace at which litigation passed through the court. This irritated suitors but it cannot be said that Star Chamber lost popularity with them on these grounds. Indeed, the old Whig myths being shattered, a pretty problem is posed. In the eighty years before 1640 harsh comments were often made about Star Chamber, and a proposal to extend its jurisdiction in 1584–5 was thwarted by the House of Commons, the debate producing some strident comments. Yet criticism was little worse than that directed against other courts. Coke said it was 'the most honourable court (our Parliament excepted) that is in the Christian world, both in respect of the judges of the court, and of their honourable proceeding according to their just jurisdiction, and the ancient and just orders of the court'. Indeed, there is little in the court's previous history to provide a warning of its precipitous destruction. It cannot even be said that it was afflicted with administrative sins on the scale of Chancery or Common Pleas.[39]

The Long Parliament in the first ten months of its existence examined many ills, but it concentrated legislation against particular characteristics of Charles's government. Star Chamber, said Pym in April 1640, had become a court of revenue, 'informations there being put in against Sheriffs for not making returns of money upon the writs of ship money'. sheriffs had been made the lynchpin of collection and become trapped between county and Council. The point was repeated in the Grand Remonstrance. Association with ship money was enough to put the court in a predicament, and it is one of the links which bound together the institution, the judges, and the policies of Charles. This was also the court where London soapboilers had been prosecuted in 1633 (Doc. 28 [3]). In the ten years from 1631, the Attorney General brought more than one hundred and seventy-five actions which Professor Barnes describes as 'for essentially fiscal ends'. Of these, about forty reached trial and determination. Twenty-nine actions were for depopulating enclosures, and this encouraged or compelled gentry, fearful of prosecution, to compound with special commissioners. The court did not always find for the Attorney General, but Barnes has described the situation. 'The same end was intended and purpose served by the prosecutions of office holders for extorting fees, gentlemen remaining in London contrary to the proclamation directing them to return to their country seats, builders of tenements in the environs of London, deceitful manufacturers, infringers of patents of monopoly, exporters of pro-

[39] Neale, *Parliaments, 1584–1601*, pp. 84–8. Coke, *Fourth Institute*, p. 65 Coke's reference to 'honourable' applied to the eminence of the bench, and he warned that this was why great care must be taken not to exceed jurisdiction.

hibited commodities, cornhoarders in time of scarcity, sheriffs for misdemeanours in office, and victuallers for selling meat in Lent. These test
cases, brought for entitling judgments, were essential to the collection
of revenue by extraction of composition for pardon; by threat of
prosecution in Star Chamber, Charles raised much of the revenue that
funded the "Personal Rule".[40]

The government of the 1630s relied heavily upon proclamations, the
nature of which had been clarified by the judges after protests in the
Parliament of 1610. Some of the resulting limitations accepted at that
time had been ignored, both with respect to procedure and substance:
it is possibly significant that early complaints specified proclamations
dealing with buildings and starch. The reaffirmation that proclamations
could only be enforced in Star Chamber was agreeable, but one of the
objections in 1610 had been the way in which alleged offences were
covered by proclamation and thus brought before that court. In the reign
of Charles a vicious circle developed, as can be seen from the disputes
over soap manufacture, although it is fair to point out that Justice
Berkeley was seen as the principal culprit (Doc. 28 [3]). None the less,
Star Chamber enforced proclamations, and other proclamations ordered
all persons to obey the decrees of Star Chamber. Generally, with a
particular eye towards securing fines and compositions, there appears
to have been greater willingness to hit offenders the first time without
giving a second chance. When in 1641 Parliament wanted to restrict the
King's freedom in government, the easiest way of undermining the
value of proclamations was to remove the only court allowed in law to
enforce them directly.[41]

Star Chamber had been a hunting-ground for informers and
'common solicitors' suing privately under penal statutes. Suits of this
nature were barred from the court in 1632, but this only partly explains
a drop in the number of bills. In 1636, the court again began to entertain
actions for some offences, provided that they were 'declared' by statute
and actionable at common law. An example is the prosecution brought
by Henry Lort which resulted in a fine of £2,500, of which the relator
was to receive £450 on the grounds of his efforts and expenses. This
figure is not easy to accept, despite the Attorney General's support,
and it may tell us something about speculation in litigation (Doc. 22).
The Grand Remonstrance would assert that money intended for the
King had not reached him. This charge, which was also made about
some other institutions, should not be underestimated. Almost certainly
the original intention was to reform Star Chamber, but it proved easier,
and certainly swifter, to do away with the institution. The Grand

---

[40] Gardiner, *Docs.*, p. 220. Barnes, 'Due Process', pp. 335–6.
[41] 12 Co. Rep., 74–6 (77 *English Reports*). BM, Hargrave MS. 132, ff. 54–5.
Steele, i. nos. 1649, 1668, 1680, 1692.

Remonstrance asserted in justification that the whole proceedings of the court had been too intertwined with abuse to allow of any other solution.[42]

In comparison with the quarter century before the accession of Charles, there had been an unusual number of political trials – the suits and sentences against Bishop Williams, formerly Lord Keeper, must come under this category – and some punishment aroused offence, although these were hardly more unpleasant than those meted out by other courts. In the case of Leighton (1630), the two chief justices indicated that in another place he would have been convicted of treason. Although the fate of Bastwick, Burton and Prynne excited attention, we must turn to the ordinary gentry who were angry or humiliated by the fact or threat of Star Chamber punishment. The treatment of Sir Thomas Wiseman in 1638 breached contemporary standards of how a gentleman should be treated, but ears apart it was hardly more humiliating than the punishment proposed by the House of Commons for Sir Stephen Proctor in 1610.

Whatever the force of these emotions, the court died amid confusion. Its relation to proclamations and revenue was important but other factors were vital to its demise. Star Chamber, alone among the great courts, brought together on its bench, under the presidency of the Lord Chancellor, the three groups of men convicted beforehand in the minds of members of the Long Parliament. The bishops were there as were the Councillors, some like Secretary Coke being assiduous in their work. The presence of the two chief justices and other judges had once been vital to the court's development and acceptance, but now it was damaging both to themselves and to the court.[43]

The so-called 'Star Chamber' jurisdictions of the provincial courts were also swept away by the Long Parliament. Proceedings of this nature before the Welsh Council seem to have been plentiful if normal, but my impression is that these were few at Chester during the reign of Charles I, and possibly do not bear comparison with the number of suits in the two previous reigns.[44] It was not the amount of litigation but the association between government policy and prosecutions which was of interest. The two provincial Councils, for example, had always served to stress some particular aspect of administrative duty, and in the seventeenth century local unpopularity was compounded by the use of legal proceedings to enforce distasteful national policies.

The two Councils exercised wide power – administrative, legal and ecclesiastical – over the localities in their area. Unpopularity and accepted service mingled. The Council of the North entertained many

[42] Barnes, 'Due Process', pp. 331–3. Gardiner, *Docs.*, pp. 212–13, 226.
[43] *State Trials*, iii. 385. Rushworth, ii. 56. Kenyon, pp. 118–19.
[44] This is a partial conclusion, drawn from my reading of the County Palatine Entry Books, PRO, Chester 14.

civil suits, mostly small, which were appreciated by northern landowners and townsmen.[45] Yet in 1640 the entire concept, and not merely one aspect of jurisdiction, was in peril. The flavour of local resentment has been aptly described by Dr Williams's demonstration of the difficulties of the Council at Ludlow at the end of Elizabeth's reign: 'it lay in the factions and interests of the officials . . . disputes broke up the Council; and vested interests could not be overcome'.[46] The Council at York experienced similar stress but it had additional problems: the reputation of Strafford, who continued as President after 1633 although practical authority was in the hands of the Vice-President, Sir Edward Osborne, and the proximity of Scots arms. It may be significant that the families of Fairfax, Hotham and Vane came from Yorkshire. Even though only the 'Star Chamber' jurisdiction was officially abolished, it is not surprising that the Council of the North collapsed. Yet the King had truth on his side when he said at York in 1642 that he knew of no legal dissolution of the Council: 'it is rather shaken in pieces than dissolved'.[47]

Whatever particular hostility may have been aroused by the two Councils, the emphasis was on their conjoined functions. Although it was an old policy, announced by proclamation in 1627, the Council in the North attracted suspicion in the 1630s through its work in compounding with recusants. Fines and forfeitures were thus transformed into a source of income for the navy. In 1631, it was summoning those who refused to appear for knighthood. James Malever was tried in the Exchequer at Westminster but that court, led by the Chief Baron, refused to fine him, insisted that he must compound, and issued writs of distress amounting to £2,000, most of which he had to pay. This episode was an absurdity. Enforcement of the law and the taking of compositions were exposed as linked elements in government finance. The issue of compounding for knighthood in the north led to a heavy Star Chamber fine on Sir David Foulis. Opposition to royal enclosure in the Forest of Galtres led to a similar punishment on Sir John Bourchier. The activities of the Council were strengthened by the Instructions of March 1633 which, although they contained little novelty, were included in the articles of impeachment voted by the House of Commons against Strafford in January 1641. The nineteenth instruction directed the Council to deal with offences against law and good order according to the course of proceedings in Star Chamber. Both Councils subsequently enforced payment of ship money and punished offenders.[48]

[45] F. W. Brooks, *The Council of the North*, London, 1963, p. 21.

[46] Williams, p. 311.

[47] Brooks, p. 30.

[48] Reid, pp. 418, 423, 429, 439. Steele, i. no. 1514. Rushworth, ii. 135–6, 147. Brooks, p. 30. C. A. J. Skeel, *The Council in the Marches of Wales*, London, 1904, p. 156.

On national and local levels, it is easy to understand the hostility aroused by the two provincial Councils. Yet, as with other provincial courts, the early Long Parliament merely removed their Star Chamber powers and without recourse to statute it discouraged Ludlow's authority over the border counties. The Council in the North collapsed, and the Welsh Council expired with the Glorious Revolution of 1688–9. The Palatinate courts continued their existence until the nineteenth century. The survival, in degraded circumstances, of these jurisdictions is a most important theme in institutional history. For, whatever the initial quantity of their business, these were courts which in the seventeenth century were subjected to suffocating restriction. They only survived after the interregnum as ghosts of their former selves. Political reaction, as seen in the Long Parliament, is not without importance but the real theme of provincial decrepitude is to be found in institutional developments which stand apart from the story of Stuart constitutional crises.[49]

The Commissions of Enquiry into Fees

Fees, patronage and perquisites represent a crucial element in the un-folding drama of early Stuart England although few practices were novel. In the reign of Elizabeth, critics supposed that the sovereign and great officers created new positions for their own profit which the public paid to support. Maintenance of existing offices could also be questionable, as sometimes the Crown itself appreciated. In January 1619, a commission was issued to root out positions which garnered fees in the Duchy and County Palatine of Lancaster although, it was alleged, no work was done at all. In 1621, a selection of related issues – Bacon, Chancery, patents of monopoly – prompted Parliament to explode with argument and criticism. The Crown adapted to the tide of complaint and in 1624 Cranfield, suddenly seen as a figment of deceit (Doc. 6), was overwhelmed. Early in his reign, Charles I picked up an initiative of his father's and sanctioned sweeping enquiries into the structure of administration and fees. Ironically the judges would appear as men trying to thwart reform in defence of their vested interests. Accused in the end of too much complicity, some of their instances of opposition were not such as to restore a balance of credit.[50]

The pressure of the patronage system, mingled with the power of

---

[49] In a previous book, I suggested that we should explain the eighteenth and nineteenth century circumstances of the Palatinate courts. My belief was, and is, that this would help us to see that the events of the Long Parliament were not all that important in the history of provincial courts, whether or not they vanished in the seventeenth century. Jones, *Chancery*, p. 377.

[50] PRO, Duchy of Lancaster Miscellanea, D.L. 41/9/15.

appointment, enabled the Stuart Crown to assume some positions hitherto controlled by major officials such as the Master of the Rolls. Agreements were reached prior to appointment. Finch, selected to be Chief Justice, agreed not to make appointments to some offices without the King's consent. There had been an old battle involving both Somerset and Buckingham over the chief clerkship of the King's Bench – an office of disputed but exceptional value – but now this post was clearly a captive of royal patronage. By such means, office could be purchased indirectly, but the necessity of prior agreement confirmed that the sovereign was limited. Office was conceived as being inseparable from its traditional incidents, and some had even denied that these could be relinquished by the appointed officer. Vacancies had also caused trouble. Mary Tudor's appointment of an exigenter in the Common Pleas was overthrown by the next Chief Justice's appointment of his own nephew. When the Mastership of the Rolls was vacant, 1593–4, Elizabeth made a number of reversionary appointments to Chancery clerkships, but Egerton more or less re-established the authority of the Master of the Rolls. A harder struggle centred upon the Crown's habit of creating new offices, usually on the grounds that there was new work or that existing work was being performed without authority or competence. The administration became the hunting-ground of patent-seekers. More than anything else, it created a fusion between the vested interests of great officials – judges or otherwise – and their anxiety both for the efficiency and integrity of their institutions and for the welfare of their subordinates. The principal argument was that existing offices represented a freehold. In 1587, Elizabeth appointed Richard Cavendish to a new office of making and writing writs of *supersedeas* upon exigent in the Common Pleas. The judges, defending the freehold of existing officials, refused to admit him, but the Queen ordered that all profits should be sequestered to his use and that he was to be admitted at the first opportunity. She looked 'for some more dutiful regard to be had by you of your prerogative royal'. In any case, she argued, existing clerks, if they indeed had title, would be able to recover through law. However, she gave way. This doubtless encouraged Egerton in his obstinacy as Master of the Rolls, and early in James's reign Coke was arguing that the clerkship of the outlawries was inseparable from his freehold as Attorney General. But the position which Cavendish had failed to establish was given by James, with some limitations, to a groom of the bed chamber, and Bacon argued in favour of the sovereign's power to create such offices. Later, the judges of the Common Pleas utilized the doctrine of freehold against the proposals of Charles's commission into fees. Their understanding survived, and Blackstone described offices as 'a right to exercise a public or private employment; and to take the fees and emoluments thereunto

belonging are also incorporeal hereditaments'. It is probable that
the greatest endeavour of nineteenth-century reformers was to smash
this understanding but then, as always, new problems were being
born.[51]

As business increased it might be thought that there should have been
more officials, but at the higher levels this was difficult because of the
rights of existing officers. There were more and more junior subordinates in the offices of the Six Clerks of Chancery, but since an attorney's
office could act for only one side in a case the client still could chose
from only six avenues of attorney. Then there was the question of
sinecures. The Prothonotaries of the Common Pleas, even if they did
not enter pleas on the rolls, continued to collect fees. Such practices
explain how it was that petitioners could produce genuine arguments
against existing officials as part of their plea that new positions should
be created. Officials deeply resented the credence given to these plausible
utterances, and officers who imagined themselves to be 'old' or 'traditional'
added fuel to popular resentment by attacking others, sometimes
established for half a century or more, whom they judged to be 'new'.
Rival officials accused each other of improper practices, stealing work,
or representing novel creations. Their mutual accusations of damaging
the 'client' were easily believed. Subordinates resented the financial
and social superiority of their masters, perhaps sinecurists although
this was by no means always so, and were accordingly embarrassed
by the devices to which they themselves were driven to secure a livelihood. The themes can be seen in 1629–30 with the quarrel of George
Norbury, who had penned a masterly analysis of Chancery faults, and
the Six Clerks of Chancery. Norbury, a Cursitor who had given
evidence to the commission of fees, lost his job in a Six Clerk's office
some years before, possibly because of his treatise. He was a former
subordinate who might 'blow the gaff' and represented a group of
officials who were always disputing with the Six Clerks over some work.
Although his evidence does not appear to have been particularly
damaging, the Six Clerks were deeply offended and, after trying
to deter him with threats, they expelled his son from his job. One
of the oldest Six Clerks remarked that he might complain in Parliament if he could. Senior men were beginning to feel the pinch as the
commission on fees decided on a principle of responsibility: that
officials were responsible for the takings and practices of their subordinates. The internecine fighting, with inevitable leaks to the public,
went on. The Cursitors assailed the Six Clerks with the charge that

---

[51] *HMC 4th. Rep.* App., p. 22. Aylmer, *Servants*, pp. 214–15. Holdsworth, i.
260–1. Jones, *Chancery*, pp. 50ff. 1 Anderson, 152–8 (123 *English Reports*).
HMC Hatfield, xv. 368. Bacon, *Works*, vii. 683–6. *Collectanea Juridica*, London,
1791, 1792, i. 167–213. Blackstone, ii. 36.

they had usurped the making of some writs. The Six Clerks battled against the Examiners over the custody of depositions taken by commission.[52]

Most disputes had existed in Elizabeth's reign and the failure to solve recognized internal problems is striking. Chancery provides a good example. It was a large institution and an enquiry into fees, conducted in 1597–8, provides evidence which is not very different from that garnered in the early 1630s. Suggestions about hanging approved tables of fees in places where clients could see them were still ignored. The Six Clerks had continued to collect 3s 4d a term for suits which were sleeping and occasioned no work. They still took fees for enrolling decrees and dismissions although for the first six years of Charles's reign only 193 out of 1,431 such directives were enrolled. Critics seized upon this sort of thing while ignoring the subtle implications: it was not quite true to suggest that there was great prejudice to the subject's estate, and the charge that payment was being exacted for enrolment, whether or not performed, was poisoned by a half-truth. Irrespective of whether enrolment was desired by the suitor and ordered by the court, a division of the fee between drawing and enrolling had not been made. The structure of the fee was at fault.[53]

Threatened vested interests within institutions were incapable of forming alliances with what might have been natural allies. Established Chancery officials and the public mood were equally against patent seekers, but in Parliament criticism was hurled at both patentees and Six Clerks. In 1621 the Masters of Chancery, consistently under attack, petitioned the House of Commons committee of grievances: either they should be given a set schedule of fees or patents given to others covering work which the Masters' claimed should be revoked. They were told that their judicial work was unnecessary. In fact, their services were invaluable, but their enforced reliance upon 'gifts' called in question the virtue of their involvement in judicial proceedings. Bacon's attempt to establish set fees had already been revoked by the King under parliamentary pressure. Aid was not forthcoming, and the squabbles of officials fuelled the popular campaign with evidence. Office seekers, who might be regarded as parasites by the House of Commons, could be effective when they pointed to the shortcomings of existing officials. In the 1620s, as the King put himself forward as the leader of public criticism,

[52] Holdsworth, i. 258. PRO, Commission on Fees, E. 215/6/496; E.215/8/606. Aylmer, *Servants*, pp. 129, 181. G. W. Sanders, *Orders of the High Court of Chancery*, London, 1845, I. i. 171–2, 189–91, 201–2.
[53] PRO, E 215/2/147, ff. 2v.–7. For administrative aspects of the Elizabethan Chancery, see Jones, *Chancery*. An interesting exhibition of some other problems is provided by G. R. Elton, 'The Elizabethan Exchequer: War in the Receipt', in *Elizabethan Government and Society*, pp. 213–48.

officials of Chancery, Common Pleas and elsewhere found themselves trapped between court and Parliament.[54] Under Elizabeth, James I, and Charles I criticism was sustained but unimaginative. The easy culprit was always sought. Men bought positions and secured the creation of new offices, often delegating the work at a price to deputies or clerks. Almost half of Chancery officials, early in the reign of Charles, worked through deputies, and these in turn had their own chain of satellites. The complexity of responsibility in some offices, where miniscule clerks were responsible only to the immediate man above, is almost beyond description. It meant that lesser men were driven to solicit gratuities and to spin out work in any fashion that might increase their takings. Worthy contemporaries, with a blind faith in historical authority, obscured the presence of genuine extortion by making dramatic condemnations based upon the most absurd kind of antiquarianism. Since the proper standard was usually sought a few decades back – there was little understanding of inflation – it was easy to show that fees had risen, but absence of authorization did not of necessity mean extortion. Some approved fees were as ridiculous as any. Officials exposed themselves by turning divided fees into duplicated ones, and Cranfield was charged with taking money for a special livery hitherto only paid to the Surveyor.[55]

Even if their practices were similar to those of minor and provincial institutions, it was only natural that officials of the great courts at Westminster should attract most hostility. Criticism of the Common Pleas was expressed by a balladeer:

> The Common Pleas our great disease
> of law is grown very sickly
> But there is hope a twined rope
> will ease it very quickly.[56]

It was said that the Prothonotaries of this court and their clerks drew pleadings at 'an extraordinary length'. The price for the first three sheets was supposedly 8d a sheet and less for subsequent sheets, but it was alleged that 12d was being charged throughout. The sheets were described as small, the margins large, the lines few, and the number of words to a line even fewer. Complaints of this nature against a myriad of officials, such as those responsible for equity pleadings and enrolments in Chancery and other courts, are common across the decades. The relationship between administrative practice and legal proceedings was

---

[54] *Commons Debates*, 1621, vii. 519–26. *CSP Dom.* 1619–23, p. 613. Steele, i. no. 1314.
[55] Aylmer, *Servants*, p. 127. Bell, p. 36.
[56] In PRO, Chancery Masters' Exhibits, C. 108/63.

easiest to pin down and most open to attack. Most criticisms of Chancery and Common Pleas raised themes which were common to current methods of administration (Doc. 17). Spelman claimed that, because of vile writings and poor skins, a grant to the city of London consumed $155\frac{1}{2}$ skins of parchment whereas 90 would have sufficed in 1568–9. In consequence, he said, the cost was increased by £272 15s. Whether or not Spelman was right, and he probably was, the difference is staggering.[57]

The critics flailed against a fog. An Edwardian statute forbade the purchase and sale of judicial and revenue offices, but the definition of a 'judicial' office was debatable and the statute excluded positions held as estates of inheritance or in the gift of the two Chief Justices and the justices of assize. It was pointed out in 1610 that 'judicial' offices could not be granted in reversion, but this never carried clear authority although, with respect to appointments in general, there may have been a reduction in the number of reversions during the two decades before 1640. Coke believed that profit destroyed the incentive to acquire knowledge and experience, and he argued that it produced 'corruption in the officers and extortion from the subjects and other great inconveniences'. He suggested that a term of years should be imposed before offices could be transferred. Holdsworth, arguing that offices should not have been transferred at all, was not impressed. Yet if the abolition of transfer was the logical answer, it would have been against the mentality of the times and against some of those claims of freehold. Most attempts at reform collapsed on this obstacle. The worst and the best features of vested interest were at play: great officials who looked to their own pocket also looked to the interests of men from whom they drew part of their income and for whom they were responsible. Avarice, loyalty and necessity were intertwined, and few parliamentary debates came close to a serious consideration of the possibility of abolishing transfer. The entire generation failed, but Coke's modest idea would have had a reasonable chance of not offending contemporary *mores*, and it must be regarded as one of the few serious proposals put forward.[58]

Charles I himself appears to have disapproved of sales of office – indeed there are relatively few examples of sales by the Crown between 1629 and 1639 – but an obvious sale was not the only means of making profit. One suggestion, the date and authorship of which is not determined, was that the Crown should resume control of all appointments

[57] PRO, E 215/2/147. Jean S. Wilson, 'Sir Henry Spelman and the Royal Commission on Fees, 1622–1640', *Studies Presented to Sir Hilary Jenkinson*, ed. J. Conway Davies, London, 1957, p. 466.

[58] 5, 6 Ed. VI, c. 16. 9 Co. Rep., 97b; 11 Co. Rep., 2b (77 *English Reports*). J. C. Sainty, 'A Reform in the Tenure of Offices during the Reign of Charles II', *BIHR* 1968, xli. no. 104, pp. 150–71. Holdsworth, i. 251. For a comment on reversions, their extent and significance, see Aylmer, *Servants*, pp. 96–106.

and punish delinquents.[59] Doubtless this reflected what the Crown was purporting to do when it negotiated with men prior to their appointment, but the idea is important because it dared to suggest means of tackling the issue of offices and their sale. Spelman probably thought along similar lines, but in producing proposals which stand among the most practical of this period he dodged the central subject of transfer. None the less, his 'Considerations' of 1630 represent the one great official attempt to bridge the gulf between investigation and reform (Doc. 14).

The idea of investigating fees was old, but it had developed slowly. The late-Elizabethan enquiry into Chancery, conducted by officials of that court, had provided an opportunity for internal back-biting. In 1610, James appointed a commission to enquire into exacted fees. This was composed of Privy Councillors, the two chief justices and the Barons of the Exchequer. It spent most of its time on the Exchequer, and conditions in that court were again emphasized by debates during the 1614 Parliament. Agitation in 1621 helped to produce a new situation. Cranfield, as Lord Treasurer, could tell the Commons in November that since bills of conformity had been abolished and an example made of Bacon there only remained the matter of fees to be dealt with. Henceforth commissions of enquiry would be dominated by men who were not personally connected with the institutions under scrutiny.[60]

In 1622, a commission was appointed to investigate the increase of fees since 1587-8. Along with eleven Privy Councillors, twelve assistants were named including Sir Robert Cotton, Sir Ranulph Crewe, Sir Dudley Digges, William Noy, Sir Edwin Sandys, Sir Edward Sackville, who had been chairman of the Commons committee on courts, Sir Henry Spelman, and Sir Thomas Wentworth. The names indicate the possibility of collaboration between Councillors and a diverse group of critics, but the position of the assistants was unclear, the Councillors were often busy, and by March 1623 the commission was defunct. A new commission was issued on May 8th, and with two exceptions the earlier Councillors and assistants were all named as commissioners. Edward Ayscough, the sole new appointment, would be a great help to Spelman who was soon established despite his age as the leading and most energetic figure. Spelman later produced a memorandum attempting to establish a procedure, something never really attained.[61] At a

[59] G. E. Aylmer, 'Office Holding as a Factor in English History, 1625-42', *History* 1959, new ser. xliv. 228-40. Aylmer, *Servants*, pp. 234-6.

[60] A major treatment of the commission on fees is that by Jean Wilson, op. cit. A somewhat different view is given by G. E. Aylmer, 'Charles I's Commission on Fees, 1627-1640', *BIHR* 1958, xxxi. 58-67. For administration generally, see Aylmer, *Servants*.

[61] PRO, E. 215/2/134 pt. 2. For a discussion of Spelman's other interests and the feudal revolution in English historiography, see J. G. A. Pocock, *The Ancient Constitution and the Feudal Law*, Cambridge, 1957, pp. 91-123.

meeting, attended by representatives of the courts at Westminster on May 23rd, the commission requested reports on fees to be produced by the first day of the next term. Sub-commissioners were appointed to deal with the provinces but their claims to examine on oath and compel the production of documents lacked authority. The work was cut short by the death of James.

When Charles I appointed a fresh commission in 1627, it was clear that a new atmosphere prevailed. The most recent Parliament had not provided the same pressure as that of 1621, but the hunt for abuse was to be intensified. These considerations suggest that the commissioners were already trapped between reform and the raising of revenue by fines, but reform must still be regarded as a major objective. The commissioners were required to report directly to the King rather than to the Council. They were to enquire not merely into fees, as before, but also into new offices. The historical deadline was pushed back to 1568–9, roughly the same terminal deadline as had been employed by the 1597–8 enquiry into Chancery fees. Reports were made on the officials of customs, prisons, parishes, towns, livery companies, sheriffs, escheators, and so on. It was an impressive extension, but the household and some other vital departments were excluded. Sub-commissioners were now to be appointed under the Great Seal with all the powers of the parent body, and a proclamation stated that all complaints were to be brought before the commission. Even so, the Privy Council had to lend its support in January 1628 because many persons refused to appear or behaved contemptuously when they did so. Future commissions – in 1630, 1634 and 1637 – were occasioned by minor changes in personnel. Continuity was preserved for more than a decade, but nothing could counteract the implications of the terms of reference given in 1627.[62]

Widened powers meant a deluge of complaints and more work. A further difficulty was the King's active interest. The commission was bombarded with royal instructions, and when a summary of selected findings was presented in January 1630 it was Charles who insisted on more evidence being garnered because generalities abounded in the reports of Chancery and Common Pleas. He was probably right, but his enthusiasm was a hindrance. He often referred complaints and petitions for immediate consideration, thus disrupting work in progress. In November 1631, the commissioners noted that 'the examinations and proceedings upon the references from His Majesty have been a retarding of the general service of the commission for at least above two months'. Merchants from Exeter and Liverpool complained about customs fees and Vice-Admiralty judges. The Warden of the Fleet was accused of protecting the murderer of a prisoner. The Master and Wardens of the

[62] Aylmer, 'Charles I's Commission on Fees', pp. 58–67. Jean Wilson, pp. 460–1. Steele, i. no. 1519. APC Sept.–June 1628, p. 256.

Cutlers Company were charged with pawning plate and wasting assets on feasts and a country jaunt with their wives. It all serves to put the complaints against the law courts and departments of state into context. The burden on the commissioners was intolerable, but late in 1630 they presented reports on the Prothonotaries of the Common Pleas, the Six Clerks of Chancery, and the clerk of the Hanaper of Chancery. Other reports were forthcoming, and Spelman was able to produce his 'Considerations'. These, read out by Wentworth in May 1630, received general approval and were again discussed in 1635, but it was easier to murmur approval than to accept and implement. Spelman proposed a fixed limitation on the number of clerks, abolition of many gratuities, and the establishment of fixed percentages out of takings for the various grades of officials. Tables of fees and patterns illustrating the proper proportions of documents were to be exhibited publicly. Many of the suggestions had been made before, but that was not the point. The government was at last faced with an official recommendation after decades of complaint (Doc. 14).[63]

Implementation of Spelman's proposals would have required an administrative revolution in a society of administrators dedicated to avoid uncomfortable change. Nothing was done, although some ideas were experimented with in a half-hearted fashion. It had been suggested that in the interim unjust fees should be prohibited by writs of Privy Seal directed from the King to the responsible official. This device was tried on at least three occasions against officials of the Common Pleas, but the writs were ignored with the approval of at least one Justice, Yelverton. Further obstruction was provided by Chief Justice Heath's opposition to a new and more stringent oath required of witnesses examined by the commissioners. In 1620, James I had ostensibly placed upon the shoulders of the judges responsibility for approving the creation of new offices in the law courts. Now it might seem that, in so far as Charles could still be credited with serious intentions of reform, the failure of the judges to co-operate was highly suspicious. It could be noted that the two Chief Justices and their *puisnes* were charged by a presentment of jurors with taking fees that were not due. This claim was exaggerated, but certainly there was a basic truth, and anyhow stories of extortion were popularly believed. When Common Pleas Justices, in defence of lesser officials, blocked writs of Privy Seal it might be believed that they were defending their own ill-gotten gains. Another possibility was that of prosecutions in Star Chamber. The clerk of the Hanaper in Chancery, George Mynne, was condemned and fined £3,000, but despite suspension he retained some control and was restored to the privileges of a Chancery official. Other suits failed to make progress, and it became apparent that fiscal considerations were

[63] Jean Wilson, pp. 461–2.

strangling reform. The Six Clerks paid over £15,000 for a pardon, yielded future appointments to the Crown, and had their current fees and privileges confirmed. Digges, in an attempt to recover the patronage of the Master of the Rolls, argued that this composition was an effort to secure the Six Clerks from prosecution. As such, he suggested, it encouraged them to continue taking improper fees. Some reforms were introduced by Lord Keeper Coventrye, and tables of fees appear finally to have been established on a regular basis in the office of the Six Clerks. These were small concessions to popular expectation. It had become clear which way the wind was blowing. Officials solicited pardons, and the commissioners complained about pardons being granted before a report had been made. Even established punitive methods were frittered away. Since the accession of James I, feodaries had been prosecuted in Star Chamber for exceeding fees. A standard fee was established in 1634 – 40s for each enquiry – but there is subsequent evidence of feodaries, and also some escheators, seeking pardon.[64]

It was hopeless. At the beginning of the 1630s the commission had met about ninety times a year, but in late 1633 attendance dwindled. In January 1634 six out of nine meetings were fruitless for lack of a quorum. Issue of a new commission in February 1634 may have given a new lease of life, and discussion of Spelman's proposals in 1635 implied that all hope was not yet dead. Industry was still evident, but by 1638 and 1639 life was petering out. It may be speculated that this absence of activity suggests that the commissioners themselves still believed that reform and not revenue was the object of their existence. They were not meeting in 1640, but Charles probably had them in mind when he spoke on January 25, 1641, about reforming the courts of law. Once a response to popular complaint, their efforts had spawned a grievous set of fiscal devices, and they would be condemned by the Grand Remonstrance.[65]

The commissions into fees are a central episode of the 1620s and 30s. Their surviving papers are scattered, but the student can benefit greatly just by casting his eyes over the entries in a single Public Record Office index.[66] The amount and nature of the evidence was influenced by the complaints received, by the way in which the commission was able to

---

[64] Aylmer, *Servants*, pp. 72–3, 112, 118–21, 301–2. Jean Wilson, pp. 467–8. *CSP Dom.* 1619–23, p. 183. PRO, E. 215/2/147, ff. 7v.–8; E. 215/9/674, 676. Sanders, I. i. 184–8; I. ii. 1047–50. *A Perfect and Exact Description to all those that desire to know the true and just fees of these courts following* : . . ., London, 1641. Bell, p. 44.

[65] Gardiner, *Docs.*, p. 214. It should be noted that by the King's orders of October 1638, and parallel to the commissioners, juries of junior clerks and officials were required to report on fees in their respective courts. There is some evidence for their activity in the Exchequer. Aylmer, *Servants*, pp. 199–200.

[66] List and Index Society, vol. 3.

dispose of its time, and by its periods of inertia and activity. The biggest collection of papers concerns the Chancery, the largest institution. It comprehended common law and equity jurisdictions, was the source of most writs for other courts, the provider of letters patents and other enrolled instruments, and the parent of many commissions. There were normal, but not excessive complaints about jurisdiction, but from this point of view the real crisis had occurred in the reign of James I. The decisive moment had been not the quarrel between Coke and Ellesmere but Bacon's attempt to utilize the event of 1616 as a means to establishing bills of conformity. This was ended in 1621. The really offensive thing about Chancery was its structure, costs and delays. The institution and its officials invited an investigation which was as deep as it was extensive. With respect to the Common Pleas most attention was paid to standard complaints against the Prothonotaries, and some attempt was made to investigate the fees taken by the Justices. Enquiries into the King's Bench paid much attention to the clerk of the errors, and those into the Exchequer emphasized the clerk of the pipe. Comparatively little was produced on the Admiralty and the Star Chamber, but the documentation has to be measured by the nature of the commission's investigations and by the size of the institutions. The prisons, notably the Fleet and the Marshalsea, provided a lot of information, as did the ecclesiastical courts although the bulk of papers is not as great as might be expected. However, the commissioners never got round to a direct consideration of the touchy matter of ecclesiastical organization, and Spelman avoided it in his proposals (Doc. 14). On the other hand, the papers submitted by sub-commissioners reveal more complaints about ecclesiastical officials than any other category.[67]

To reach the bench was an arduous and expensive exercise, and for many the road had been exacerbated by the necessity of approaching the courts at Westminster. The mass of material, however, would seem to suggest that faults alleged of major institutions were not distinctive. The easy issue of *subpoenas* was criticized, as was the random allowance of process of outlawry (Doc. 17). When Coke had been Chief Justice of the Common Pleas, one of the main criticisms of prohibitions had been that they were given without sufficient consideration. Courts might have different procedures, but all could be accused of not exercising adequate supervision. The nature of administration rather than the law exercised from the bench was open to attack. Of course, there were a multitude of complaints about 'the law' and the about the jurisdictions of diverse courts. But the work of the commissioners suggests a broad similarity of complaint, whether directed against Chancery, Common Pleas, boroughs, customs officials, livery companies, manorial courts, or petty constables. Objection was levelled against the current nature of

[67] Jean Wilson, p. 465.

administration, great and small, royal and private. The Westminster courts, whether taken singly or as a group, are only distinguished by the sophistication of their procedures, complexity and expense. But they had established a claim which invited, indeed compelled, a flow of litigation which they could barely meet and which therefore exaggerated the faults of their administrative habits. An outstanding complaint of the 1621 Parliament had been over the costs and difficulty of litigation in Chancery. As Wentworth said, 'it were a kind of injustice to make justice too dear'.[68]

The commissions into fees received a mound of evidence some of which must have leaked out and influenced politically-minded contemporaries. Wentworth, Noy, and others are famed for their sudden ability to join Court ranks, but years before the Petition of Right they had joined with ministers in analysing the alleged faults of administration. Charles seemed to be an enthusiastic supporter of this endeavour. If things hung fire it could still be understandable, as when the King demanded more information. It was only in the later 1630s that the mirage collapsed.[69]

The commissioners lacked force because, whatever their terms of reference, it was easier to concentrate upon fees than upon office. Unless patronage and the sale of office was tackled there could not be much progress. The Crown might have done something, but Charles was a nuisance. Personal monarchy is a matter of mind and verbal decision or influence. By its very nature, it tends to escape the records. If we look at the ministers, men like Cottington, Juxon and Weston were functionaries. Laud was a theological mediocrity who was at his best in building up the material foundations of his church. Wentworth had greater calibre, but he was removed from England and even the years of his activity with the commission are those of the King's clearest intervention. In effort and in failure, in initiative towards reform and in its perversion, Charles set his stamp upon the epoch. Most of the features which damned his regime are to be found in the story of the commissions into fees. His activity in the hunt for abuse vanished amid the pursuit of money. Many officials lost their dubious rights of appointment, that is of sale, but it was only in order that the Crown might bargain. The rejection by the Common Pleas of writs of Privy Seal amounted to a flouting of any notion that the King might regulate fees. Suddenly, it was Charles who appeared not merely as a broker but as an insipid one. He had encouraged a discussion of abuses at all levels of administration, confirmed the existence of abuse by his pardons, and in

[68] Cited Jean Wilson, p. 457.
[69] Some people may from the beginning have conceived a relationship between the work of the commissioners and the raising of revenue. Thus the methods employed to raise loans in 1627 cannot be ignored. Aylmer, *Servants*, p. 193.

1639–40 raised considerable loans from office-holders.[70] The whole endeavour became adapted to the King's immediate end of financial survival, and yet the fiscal return was moderate. Charles encouraged the idea that the system was corrupt only to increase the element of his financial dependence upon it. It was political stupidity on the grandest scale.

Prisons

The prisons, institutions of constraint, represented an important aspect of the judicial and administrative system. Debtors were prominent – a late Elizabethan list for the Fleet shows that they represented over half of the inmates – and attempts to alleviate their situation were fraught with difficulty. Commissions which included Justices were challenged in Elizabeth's reign when they tried to hear the suits of prisoners or make arrangements with creditors. Direct intervention by the Privy Council, usually to secure some sort of composition, ran into constant opposition. A statute of 1624 undercut such action by making it, granted the conditions were otherwise appropriate, a ground for bankruptcy proceedings. Another possibility had been through exhibiting a bill in Chancery begging a *corpus cum causa*. If this was successful, bail would be put into court for the prisoner's daily appearance. It was only one of many procedures, but it was recommended as having helped many persons 'lying oftentimes in prison upon great actions surmised against them, without just cause and thereby not able to put in such bail as the common law doth require in such cases'. Whether it was the Archbishop of Canterbury or the Lord Admiral complaining about prohibitions, general critics castigating the ease whereby Chancery *subpoenas* or process of outlawry from the common law courts could be obtained (Doc. 17), or the shouts of imprisoned debtors, the complaint at all levels was that people suffered because the courts were willing to grant process upon surmise. To many people in England, and they belonged to every rank of society, the normal operations of the prison system represented a repulsive element. This may have been of greater concern than many celebrated constitutional cases. In the eventual attack upon the judges both the death of Eliot and prison conditions generally were pointed out (Doc. 29).[71]

The men in charge of prisons, a vital link in the legal and governmental chain, were harassed hoteliers trying to conform with the law. The prisoner's standard of living, food and accommodation, depended upon his purse. The gaolers made their living out of inmates who were often bled through the nose. There was a considerable amount of

[70] Aylmer, *Servants*, pp. 200–1.
[71] BM, Lansdowne MS. 80, ff. 99–100. W. West, *The Second Part of Symbolaeographie*: 'Of the Chancery', London, 1618, f. 286v. sect. 176.

freedom, unless close imprisonment had been specified. The Warden of the Fleet, endeavouring to treat his prisoners with the courtesy and deference appropriate to their rank, was not an awe-inspiring guardian because his prospects and the financial ability of his flock were inter-locked. A prisoner of means could live in luxury – some stayed twenty or thirty years – but he was being cheated. He knew it and so did poorer men. There were constant complaints and counter-accusations. After an enquiry into the Fleet in 1597 specific charges were not proved, but it was recommended that changes be made in the rules. In July 1618, the Privy Council directed the Master of the Rolls and Coke to enquire into 'great excesses, outrages and abuses' which, the Master of the Fleet asserted, had been perpetrated against him by prisoners. In December, he was bitterly complaining against a 'faction' of prisoners who had been persecuting him with law suits. Among the ring-leaders he named Sir George Saville, who with his wife and family had been lodged in five rooms of the Warden's own house. In the following year, the prisoners of the King's Bench mutinied and their leader, Robert Marston, was described as 'the prisoners' orator'. The Marshal of the prison was accused of charging exorbitant rates for provisions, and it was said that he had erected a barrier – which the prisoners had torn down – in an attempt to prevent friends from bringing food. The crudest of popular sentiment and the most sophisticated criticism of administrative practice combined to point an accusing finger at the prisons. The commissions into fees garnered a fascinating amount of evidence (Doc. 16). Nothing was done.[72]

Unless imprisoned close, it was possible to pay for the privilege of leaving the prison for a day, accompanied by a keeper. In November 1627, Wentworth was given six days leave to attend private affairs. In the early years of Charles I's reign, prisoners – or at least those 'of quality' – were allowed to go away during the plague, a temporary freedom often obtained through *habeas corpus*. Selden caused some trouble in 1630. Because of plague, the judges of the King's Bench moved a number of prisoners from the Marshalsea in Southwark to the Gate-house in Westminster. Selden only applied after the judges had left town. He was given a warrant by the Lord Treasurer, but the judges on their return declared this to be an inadequate authority. In 1636, the judges said that it was improper for prisoners to be given liberty during times of plague (Doc. 18). Although harsh comment was made about debtors, the political implications of imprisonment were clear. Yet the King, in seeking advice from the judges, had indicated his sympathy with prisoners who petitioned for release during time of plague. Several themes were combined: complaints about the prison system, denial of

[72] *Parlt. Papers*, 1830–1, viii. pt. i. *APC* 1618–19, pp. 235, 335; 1619–21, p. 243. *CSP Dom.* 1619–23, p. 168.

habeas corpus, political confinement, the employment of majority judicial opinion, and the notion that judges misled the sovereign.[73]

Prison conditions provide a splendid example of the fusion of social and particular grievance. Many men of standing ended up in prison at one time or another. Eliot, when vice-admiral of Devon, spent nearly six months in the Marshalsea during 1623. In 1627, he was confined to the Gatehouse because of his refusal to meet the forced loan. These escapades were experiences of political normality, but Eliot went on to grasp a greater fame. The nature of imprisonment was questioned on a social level, and its application in a few circumstances was included in the Petition of Right. Ship money proceedings produced a number who, either because of their opposition or lack of collaboration, were imprisoned or threatened with that fate (Doc. 23). On March 10, 1640, riots and uproar broke out in the Marshalsea, the prisoners using cudgels, paving stones, and staves, and the Privy Council called in the trained bands.[74]

[73] *APC* Sept. 1627–June 1628, p. 126. Rushworth, ii. 73. *CSP Dom.* 1635–6, p. 544.
[74] Hulme, *Eliot*, pp. 35, 40, 165. Rushworth, iii. 991.

5

Condemnation

'Let all men hereby take heed how they complain in words against any magistrate, for they are gods.'[1]

SHIP money bound together strands of objection and exposed the weakness of Charles's hold over the country. Richard Chambers, imprisoned for refusing the levy of 1635, brought a suit for trespass and false imprisonment against Sir Edward Bromfield, who had been Lord Mayor of London at the time. This was heard before the King's Bench in June 1636. Berkeley was supposed to have said 'that there was a rule of law and a rule of government, and that many things which might not be done by the rule of law might be done by the rule of government'. The judges 'would not suffer the point of legality of ship money to be argued' (Doc. 28 [8]). Hampden's lawyers, influenced by previous cases, would probe for avenues left open or unconsidered. The presentation of his case was not representative of all the grievances which ship money had raised. The crucial point in the proceedings was consideration of a demurrer. The defence conceded the facts[1a] but disputed the extent of the King's powers if it was assumed that a danger to the realm existed. This still enabled them to argue that the circumstances, as stated by the Crown, indicated the feasibility of calling Parliament. The government for its part was aware of dissent in society, and probably welcomed an opportunity to crush new lines of argument. Prosecution and defence assailed each other with constitutional and legal niceties, but the central issue, that of ship money, had electrified a mass of provincial prejudice which was a world apart from the sophistication of a Westminster court room.

Ship money, as Pym put it, was 'a grievance that all are grieved at'. Yet ships had often been levied in the past and sometimes the alternative of financial contribution had been allowed. In 1570, all ships of over thirty tons were ordered to be held ready for service. In 1588, the call for ships was met with protest. York and other towns had to be coerced into

---

[1] Hawarde, pp. 176–7.

[1a] This, although noted by prosecution counsel and judges who decided for the Crown, should not be viewed too simply. Demurrer, Croke argued, did not amount to a confession of the matter of fact 'but where the matter is legally set down; but if it be not a legal proceeding, then the demurrer is no confessing of the matter of fact'. *State Trials*, iii. 1144.

helping Hull with its contribution. In 1596, on the eve of the Cadiz expedition, inland towns again tried to evade assisting ports in the cost of putting forth ships. A continual difficulty was the weakness and limited operational capability of the official navy. London merchants planned to organize a fleet against the Dunkirkers in 1603 because 'the Queen's ships were not fittest to take them'. The government, deciding that London could not bear the full cost, called for contributions from coastal and inland districts. The scheme was largely abortive, but there is sufficient evidence of its unpopularity. Later, with respect to the fleet that eventually sailed against Algiers 'pirates' in 1621, James requested contributions, mostly from London companies, but the return was disappointing. York would not help Hull, and Weymouth declared that most of its trade belonged to inland merchants. Cinque ports spokesmen believed that it was just a device to subsidize the protection of London trade. In 1626, coastal towns and counties were required to provide ships for defence. Even in a state of war, it was apparent that there was a conflict of interest between towns and counties, between coastal and inland districts. London said that it could not bear the cost of five ships to guard the Thames, the defence of which was deemed to be 'regal work'. Subsequently, when fifty-six ships were sought from the nation, there were plenty of quarrels. Bristol was required to carry two-thirds of the cost of fitting out two ships, the remaining third to be levied on the counties of Gloucester and Somerset. Bristol considered this unfair: the two counties should contribute more, and aid should also be levied from Cardiff, Shrewsbury, Tewkesbury and Worcester. The contribution of the two counties was increased, and Somerset men objected. Bristol, they said, was a rich town, and the county had shouldered heavy expenses in respect of coat and conduct money. Partly because of protest, the general demand on the county of Buckingham in 1628 was withdrawn. Coastal communities wanted ship expenses to be shared by inland areas, but counties, coastal or inland, often felt that their military expenses were enough to bear. Communities were inclined to think of distant crises on a local level – as concerning some other locality – and when they accepted it as a national problem they said it was the responsibility of the Crown.[2]

By 1634, fishing and trading interests needed a greater show of support by English warships. There were also considerations of European diplomacy and the development of the doctrine of England's sovereignty over the narrow seas. In 1633, Sir John Burroughs's tract on sovereignty over the seas had encouraged the Admiralty commissioners to order Sir Henry Marten and Noy to produce a 'reglement' whereby the King's ancient power in the narrow seas might be preserved. Following their

---

[2] Rushworth, iii. 1134. Dietz, pp. 16, 58, 79, 98–9, 175–6, 189, 229–32. Brooks, p. 26. *CSP Dom.* 1619–23, pp. 21, 22, 25. Yonge, p. 93. *Ship Money Papers*, p. x.

report, a committee was set up headed by Coventrye, Banks and Winde-bank. Charles seems to have been genuinely enthusiastic. In 1634, the Council decided that the following year should see the publication of Selden's *Mare Clausum*, written in 1618, and also the putting forth of a fleet. Noy, before his death, prepared writs addressed only to the ports. London protested but provided, and the total assessment was not over large. Naval requirements were not met, and the Exchequer had to help with a loan. Convinced of the need for both a better fleet and more money, the government decided to authorize a second issue of writs, this time directed to inland areas as well. There was some opposition, as in Devonshire, a coastal county, and Oxfordshire, an inland county. Ship money was not in origin a device to raise revenue to maintain the regime but gradually the potentialities of this tax excited greater atten-tion, and organization was introduced. For a year, from March 1635 to March 1636, the Treasury had been in commission, Laud being the dominant figure. Then Juxon became Lord Treasurer, and Nicholas was given responsibility over ship money. There was a third issue of writs and then a fourth. Writs were again issued in 1638 and 1639. The money was used for ships – indeed London was only asked for money rather than ships in 1639 – but as the total spending on the navy declined it meant in practice that revenues could be diverted, and thus the financial position of the government was being supported. A popular success might still have been of great advantage, but in the end the value of both the King's diplomacy and navy was contemptuously dragged in the dust by the Dutch squadron which destroyed Spanish shipping off Dover.[3]

At the end of 1635, an opinion was obtained from the judges which apparently attempted to take into account local reluctance to bear costs when it was suspected that only the ports, or some of them, benefited. It was declared that in respect of threats such as piracy, money might be levied on the ports and 'maritime parts', but that when the safety of the kingdom was concerned the whole realm should bear the cost (Doc. 28 [4]). This opinion was not signed by Hutton, and Croke did not wholly assent. The second point was again put to the judges for confirmation and clarification in February 1637. This time they expanded their explanation of the sovereign's responsibility to act in the defence of the realm and to determine whether a threat existed (Doc. 28 [5]). Some important judges – Croke, Hutton, and apparently Bramston – did not agree, but they signed the collective opinion for the sake of conformity. It was later said that Finch had used bribes and threats. The theory was that the King, having power to act in emergencies for the safety of the

[3] *Ship Money Papers*, pp. x–xi. Dietz, pp. 266–7, 274–5, 278–81. M. D. Gordon, 'The Collection of Ship Money in the Reign of Charles I', *TRHS* 1910, 3rd. ser. iv. 143–4.

country, must act in anticipation of emergencies. He could determine the existence of danger, apprehended or immediate. It was a duty as much as a power.[4]

This opinion discouraged Hampden's lawyers from relying upon a direct challenge to the legality of ship money. So while it was a basic argument that society was governed by fundamental rules, it suited the defence to concentrate upon a few issues, for example the validity of the particular writ and whether the immediate circumstances justified the procedure adopted by the Crown. Bramston and Davenport would find against the writ because it did not appear by the record to whom the money was due, and because the writ was wrong in law: the King had power to command the service but not to receive the money. Hampden's counsel, St John and Holborne, tied the points together: the writ was for a ship, or part of a ship, and not for money; it made no mention of immediate war or even depradations, and it allowed a generous seven months – surely time in which to call a Parliament. Holborne, unlike St John, apparently wanted to undermine the theory that the King could decide whether an apprehended danger existed, but a frontal assault was futile. So although their arguments are quite different, both counsel concentrated upon the point which was hardest for the Crown to rebut in the context of legal proceedings: it was that public knowledge, and the very procedure adopted and admitted by the Crown, revealed that there was not an apprehended danger. Therefore, as St John said, the King without Parliament had no power to take emergency action which touched the property of the subject. Thus the levy became a tax, and even if an extraordinary justification could be shewn, there was time enough for this to be handled in the proper forum for extraordinary taxes, namely Parliament. This line of attack, based upon political facts, was difficult for the judges to get their teeth into without also discussing Parliament. If, in retrospect, some resulting remarks were ill-considered, it must be remembered that the topic had been introduced by Hampden's counsel, and it was not irrelevant to argue that on the evidence of the 1620s Parliament was pretty useless as a means of raising money within a reasonable time. Littleton, for the Crown, was probably most effective in arguing that Parliament had nothing to do with it since the question was one of defence.[5]

[4] Gardiner, viii. 94–5. It was claimed that Bramston had secured a modification of the opinion by forcing the insertion of a phrase which made it clear that it only applied in times of necessity. Bramston, pp. 68, 78–9, 80. B. Whitelock, *Memorials*, i. 72.

[5] For *Hampden's Case*, see *State Trials*, iii. 825–1316. Extracts are in Gardiner, *Docs.*, pp. 109–24, and Kenyon, pp. 109–16. Gough, pp. 69–75. Gardiner, viii. 272–80. Holdsworth, vi. 49–55. Bramston, p. 80. D. L. Keir, 'The Case of Ship-Money', *LQR* 1936, lii. 546–74. C. Russell, 'The Ship Money Judgments of Bramston and Davenport', *EHR* 1962, lxxvii. 312–18.

The case had initially come before the Exchequer but had been adjourned into the Exchequer Chamber on Hampden's demurrer. The arguments of counsel, two on either side, were spread over several days between November 6th and December 18th. After several tense months, seven judges had decided for the Crown and five for Hampden. With the exception of Croke and Hutton, the minority judges placed most emphasis on technical points. In fairness to those who voted for the Crown, it must be said that the arguments made for Hampden could be interpreted as confining the discretion of the King within limits which were too narrow for most contemporaries to digest.[6]

One of the men who decided against the Crown was the Chief Baron, Humphrey Davenport. None the less, as senior judge of the Exchequer, he would have to announce the judgment in his court. The dissenters included Bramston and John Denham, Baron of the Exchequer, who had been absent because of ill-health for part of the time and who wrote a brief judgment against the Crown. Hutton, Charles I's 'honest judge', was subsequently accused by Thomas Harrison, a parson, of being a traitor. For this contempt – the words had been uttered before the court of Common Pleas – Harrison was sued by the Crown in King's Bench and fined £5,000. Hutton also preferred his own bill in the King's Bench and was awarded £10,000 damages. The most celebrated judgment against the Crown was that given by Croke. There are some major differences of emphasis between his notes, his judgment, and his explanation to the King, but he evidently felt that he stood alone on fundamentals. The very practice of conformity meant that once judgment had been given in the Exchequer Chamber, his conscience and judgment, as well as those of other men, must be 'regulated' accordingly. The sum in dispute was insignificant – 20s – but 'it may be as well £20 hereafter, and no judge to mitigate or control it'. The precedents of the Exchequer Chamber bound all judges thereafter, and yet 'this charge without a Parliament is illegal'. Accepting that a majority opinion was binding, he understood the political implications surrounding this case. In effect, if one took his point of view, it meant that Exchequer Chamber could legislate for it could make a levy that was illegal into one that was legal (Doc. 20).[7] It is true that Parliament could reverse this, but then it could also reverse previous statutes. Too much concentration on *Hampden's Case* does not help in understanding all the animosities, complications and quarrels surrounding ship money, but it is vital to an understanding of the role in government now being played by the judges sitting in Exchequer Chamber. In 1638, the King's Bench

[6] Rushworth, ii. 598.
[7] In dealing with Croke, I have stressed the point most relevant to this study. For the points made by Croke and other judges with respect to the case before them, see Keir *op. cit.* and *State Trials*.

considered an action of trespass brought by Lord Say and Sele in respect of cattle seized in distress because he had not paid ship money. The court accepted the argument of the Attorney General that counsel were not permitted to argue against something that had been determined in Exchequer Chamber, the decisions of which stood until reversed by Parliament. Another to be frustrated, this time at the hands of Chief Justice Finch, was Sir Richard Strode.[8]

Hampden was one of those who suspected Charles's foreign policy and feared a papist movement at home. Although defeated at law, he had grounds for satisfaction. His case had attracted much attention, and it was reported from Chester that the statements of the minority judges had increased the difficulties of collection. However until 1638, the Crown obtained 90 per cent of the moneys assessed, a great success by Tudor–Stuart standards of collection. It would seem that most paid out of compliance. They did not accept the legality of the levy, whatever the judges might say. In 1637 some success against pirates had been achieved, and this may have helped, but in 1638 there was a falling off and by 1639 only a fraction was being collected. Further writs were issued, even after it had been decided to call a Parliament. Parliament failed, and General Leslie crossed the Tyne. A proclamation of August 20, 1640 – on the same day another proclamation resurrected feudal military obligations – required payment of all arrears of ship money. The King was ignoring a serious warning given in the Short Parliament that reprisals might be taken against the tax and against the judges. He was trapped in his Scottish crisis, but this was a military rather than a naval problem, although the importance of ships in this theatre and in respect of European diplomacy could still be appreciated. Unfortunately, Charles's competence and intentions were now thoroughly open to question.[9]

Society could not reject the legality of ship money without condemning the action of the judges. One of the first actions of the House of Lords in the Long Parliament was to declare the levy illegal, and the House of Commons followed suit. There were many themes. In 1639 cynics noted that whereas Doctors' Commons was assessed by the Lord Mayor for ship money, the Inns of Court, the two Inns of the serjeants, the Inns of Chancery, Herald's House, and City Halls escaped. So long as London was responsible for providing ships, it meant that the City, not the Crown, took responsibility for raising ship money and prosecuting defaulters in King's Bench.[10]

---

[8] Hutton, 131 (122 *English Reports*). B. Whitelock, *Memorials*, i. 72. Gardiner, viii. 278–9. Cro. Car., 524 (79 *English Reports*). Holdsworth, vi. 65–6.

[9] *CSP Dom.* 1637–8, p. 451. Steele, i. no. 1827.

[10] *Records and Documents Concerning Serjeant's Inn, Fleet Street*, collected by H. C. King, London 1922, p. 123. Pearl, p. 89.

One of the main points was that the whole affair came to be seen as a well-prepared policy executed in stages. Certainly, the space accorded to ship money in the Privy Council Registers is indicative of the importance attached to it by the govenment. In June 1635 Lord Keeper Coventrye, addressing the judges of assize, urged them to encourage people to pay and indicated the justifications for the tax. 'The wooden walls are the best walls of this kingdom' (Doc. 19). The approach was not novel, and judges on circuit were expected to exhort the people. Whitelocke considered going on circuit as a progress whereby the whole kingdom was called together (Doc. 7). In 1619, along with mayors, sheriffs, and other officials, they had been told to utilize every public occasion to stress the importance of contributing willingly for the repair of havens in Suffolk. But Coventrye was insistent on the subject of ship money (Doc. 19). Great men and judges might exhort, but the writing was on the wall. A grand jury at the Northamptonshire quarter sessions presented ship money as a grievance. The sheriff, who forwarded this to the Privy Council, was rebuked and warned about his defaults. The opinions of the judges given in 1635 and 1637, combined with the urgings of successive Lord Keepers to the justices of assize, created a picture in which the judges were seen as collaborating with the government's plot and pre-judging issues which might be raised in a challenge (Docs 28, 29). Indeed, the two opinions were more of a grievance than the decision in *Hampden's Case*. On the other hand opinions were of limited value, and Hampden had given the government an opportunity to enshrine its policy as a judgment of the Exchequer Chamber. The opinions had limited the grounds on which Hampden could fight, and then the judgment against him was used to bar future challengers. In other revenue matters, for example the financing of an army, it might be wondered whether there were any bounds to the King's power if he could utilize the same procedure. It seemed that ship money had become a regular tax, and that the power of legislation had been usurped from King and Parliament by the King and the judges.[11]

It was believed that Charles had tried to extend ship money into that kind of national tax which James I had failed to get in 1610. The government's denial of this intention to the Short Parliament was probably true, but ship money and other levies had been linked with the state of parliamentary authority before *Hampden's Case*. Along with other affairs, including the proposed Contract of 1610, ship money represented the constant struggle of the Crown not merely to survive financially but to escape from the unsatisfactory assessments and methods of collection associated with fifteenths, tenths, and subsidies. Up to 1638 success in collection, partly due to the collection of arrears after the great legal

---

[11] *State Trials*, iii. 837. Rushworth, ii. 294–8, 352–9; iii. 985–8, 991–2. *CSP Dom.* 1619–23, p. 17.

battles, was threatening to undermine one of Parliament's principal cards, if and when that assembly should be called again. Likewise, the final issue of writs was suspicious. In 1628 when writs had gone out to all the counties, it was made clear that the King would persevere with Parliament if the money was paid. This scheme was dropped, but no one could be certain in 1640 that some such device was not in the air, and in fact the King would offer to sell his rights (Doc. 31).[12]

From the accession of Elizabeth, and especially since 1588, the counties had been increasingly burdened although the peaceful years of James I's reign had entailed considerable relief in respect of military expenditure. Lord Treasurer Dorset had even suggested unavailingly that this might be recognized by a parliamentary increase of taxation to the Crown. The wars of the 1620s again changed the situation. In 1625, the trained bands of Essex were required to garrison Harwich and points on the coast. That county grumbled and demanded assistance or remuneration. It was intimated that the counties of Cambridge, Hertford, Huntingdon and Suffolk should assist with contributions, but spokesmen of these counties did not see it that way. Clearly the unity of England was on two levels. Communities were insistent on seeing a national justification for parliamentary taxes – and on this occasion there had been pointed reference to subsidies granted by Parliament – but there was little sense of common purpose when the question was that of paying the bill for defence. Perhaps this owed much to the confused strategies of the first two Stuarts, but the element had not been lacking in the last years of Elizabeth's wars. As already noted with respect to ship, money those directly involved saw that others should contribute; those not directly involved had difficulty in seeing this. The justifiable stress on parliamentary taxes is of tremendous importance in the history of that institution. At the same time it was not always an argument in favour of Parliament. It could be an excuse for not paying money. Parliament, especially in view of its poor record with regard to supply, might seem a cheap way out. When Hampden raised the question of Parliament he had a variety of honest reasons, but he was also appealing to some of the most stubborn elements of English provincialism.[13]

Financial burdens imposed since the middle of Elizabeth's reign were creating a cumulative reaction. The 1630s were notable for one major alleviation: the country was at peace after Buckingham's wars and thus the burden of military costs was lightened. The King was still interested in the creation of a 'perfect militia', but without the test of need he could be deluded that things were being done although pretence or even

[12] Gordon, p. 145. Dietz, pp. 244–5.
[13] L. Boynton, *The Elizabethan Militia, 1558–1638*, London, 1967, p. 211. *CSP Dom.* 1625–6, pp. 104, 106–7, 116, 119, 133.

degeneration in the military system was the order of the day. There had been long-standing disputes over the position and payment of muster masters. Since statutory authority had lapsed, it was ruled by Hutton in 1619 that the authority for these men and their remuneration was a matter of prerogative 'which . . . is of a higher transcendent nature than the best man of that bench ought to meddle with'. None the less in many counties, these professionals were slighted, ignored or unpaid. The Council, apparently in ignorance, took little notice of the deterioration and of the flouting if its orders, but the general muster order of April 1635 adopted a different tone, castigating the deputy lieutenants for their incompetence and neglect. But some could now believe that enforced payment of the muster master was in breach of the Petition of Right. At the end of 1638, there was growing Privy Council concern over musters. On December 5th it was ordered that all persons were to be charged according to the lands which they held in the county. On the 16th, it was specified that those with a certain income were liable to find a horse and a lance. Charles was trying to raise an army, and he was imposing military costs on counties far from the scene of action. Yet these areas were also being assessed for ship money. It was too much, and in any case the authorization of the charges was questioned. Although ship money had previously been paid substantially, nothing was collected in Buckinghamshire from the beginning of 1639, and a similar trend was evident everywhere. However, the judges were called upon and they provided the King with an opinion that his dual position did not erase the duty of inhabitants in the northern counties to defend the borders of England. In particular, their resolutions concerning tenant services were acted upon. Pym would link ship money with military impositions in his speech of grievances to the Short Parliament, and discussion of ship money drifted into debate over the burden of military charges. It would be pointed out that for Yorkshire, a county acutely conscious of military failure and defeat, military exactions had been vastly greater than ship money.[14]

Strafford and Laud

The policies of the 1630s left the government discredited behind a mantle of legality. The dwindling response to ship money, which paralleled conflict and failure in Scotland, indicated that the end had come. Against this background, Strafford and Laud are important less because they set their stamp upon a decade of 'thorough' than because of their reputation and the things for which they were feared. Strafford was seen – nearly all his enemies accorded him this credit – as the man

[14] Boynton, pp. 227, 244–97. Barnes, *Somerset*, pp. 244–80. *P.C. Registers*, IV. Aug.–Dec. 1638, pp. 589, 608–9. *Ship Money Papers*, p. 91. *CSP Dom.* 1639, p. 100; 1639–40, p. 50. Rushworth, iii. 1134. Gardiner, ix. 114–15.

capable of pulling things together for the King and providing him
with the means to carry out what was surmised to be his chosen policy.
Laud was conceived as the evil genius behind this surmised policy, a
rapprochement with Roman Catholicism, both internally and inter-
nationally.[15]

In the 1620s Wentworth, critical of so many aspects of government,
was never critical of the King. Always a candidate for office – he was
interested in obtaining the Presidency of the North in 1626 – he could
interpret the events of 1628–9 as outlining the futility and decay of
Commons activity while serving as a reminder that the King could
always exercise the whip-hand if he chose. The Crown was the source of
power, and Wentworth – imprisoned over forced loans in 1627 and a
leader in 1628 – offered the prospect of administrative reform. This was
also the King's mood, and for a time the commission into fees would
enjoy its most hopefully energetic period. Perhaps the importance of
this endeavour has been sadly underestimated. The fact is that Wentworth, Noy, and others had collaborated with Privy Councillors in
examining intimate details of administrative structure before they
accepted office. Wentworth, a member of James's commission, was
again appointed in 1630. He retired in 1634 but came back again in 1636.
They were pursuing a great grievance which had been raised in Parliament, and the theoretical acceptance of Spelman's proposals (Doc. 14)
must have seemed promising. Wentworth would also make some
attempt to reduce legal fees in the Council of the North. The transition
of men like Wentworth and Noy into government is less dramatic than
it might seem and has been described as consistent with the integrity of
their constitutional views. Yet even if the underlying hypothesis – that
Charles could appear in both personal endeavour and policy as a
genuine reformer – has any merit, it cannot be ignored that Wentworth's
inclusion in the ranks of government was marked by self interest. His
conversion, before the death of Buckingham, represented a deal
whereby he was willing to work in a system dominted by the Duke. He
was ready, in effect, to be a dependant. His barony and the Presidency
of the Council of the North stamped him as the 'great apostate'.
Furthermore, it was a mistake to elevate such a person in his own
backyard. As representative of the King, Wentworth was the last person
to pay heed to the subtle arrogances of northern life. His appointment,
immediate energy, and aloof mien were enough to damn him there for
ever. The affairs of Lord Fauconberg and his son, Henry Bellasis,
should have been a warning. Ten years later, Wentworth would have

[15] For Wentworth's career, see C. V. Wedgwood, *Thomas Wentworth, First
Earl of Strafford, 1593–1641*, London, 1964. H. Kearney, *Strafford in Ireland,
1633–41*, Manchester, 1959. For Laud, see H. Trevor-Roper, *Archbishop
Laud, 1573–1645*, London, 2nd. rev. ed. 1962.

even fewer friends in the north. On the other hand, he was never a favourite and, hardly liked by Charles, he was positively disliked by the Queen and her circle. There was little compensation for this cool reception, since Ireland removed him from the logical prize, the centre of power.[16]

In Ireland, Wentworth managed to build up powerful elements of opposition without creating sufficient support or confidence. When he became Lord Deputy in 1632 – he was made Lord Lieutenant in 1640 – confidence sadly needed to be restored. After James's policy of trying to combine colonization with pacification, Charles had struck a bargain with Irish peers and Catholic leaders, but nothing was done and Charles stood before the Irish Catholics as one who had broken his promise. Wentworth, faced with this situation, staffed the administration with Englishmen of his choice, but his efforts to enhance revenue – including commissions for defective titles – were an affront to the Anglo-Irish and to the companies. Nor was he easy on the Catholics: in 1632–3 he raised £20,000 for not enforcing the recusancy laws, but in 1634 he imposed the thirty-nine articles and the oath of supremacy. When he called Parliament, the Anglican bishops more than counter-balanced the Catholic nobles. By the end of the decade, he could report that he had established and endowed the official church, turned a debt into a surplus, and raised an army to keep the peace. This force seemed impressive by some European standards, and the Irish Parliament voted four subsidies, nearly £200,000. It was only a façade. He had rooted out exaction, feathered his own nest, and alienated most sections of Irish society. He had not created positive support. The position crumbled when he left: fighting in Ireland and news of Protestants being massacred would have a dramatic effect upon English politics in November 1641. But in 1640, Englishmen could think that Charles had an Irish government, without debt, assured of supply, and backed by a sizeable army, the skill and savagery of which was exaggerated. It looked very impressive, and it was assumed that Strafford would seize any opportunity to do a repeat performance in England. The Scots, after his recent speeches in Ireland, could assume the same. The Short Parliament confirmed this impression. This meeting was brief enough to reveal, indeed to create, unanimity among the opposition, without being long enough to expose discord. Coventrye, who had died before this Parliament met, had advised Charles to let it sit 'without an unkind dissolution', and Strafford was probably opposed to the manner of the King's dismissal although he acceded to the decision. The unavoidable obstacle was the Scottish army, hence the occasional enthusiasm in the south as General Leslie strengthened his hold on the north in the summer

[16] Gardiner, vi. 128. Wedgwood, p. 105. Judson, p. 12.

of 1640. The Scots were never liked, and their insurgence was a spur rather than a deterrent to some M.P.s. There was fearful anger, and it seemed that if Strafford won he would enable the King to dominate as he chose.[17]

Strafford's own religious position has been likened to that of Pym, but in Ireland he was suspected by Protestants of leaning towards the Catholics, and his enforcement of current Church rules strengthened this impression. This was also the quagmire in which Laud sank. At the beginning of the century, the Catholic minority – despite wild plots and some theories of assassination – were not a serious threat. James saw this, though it did not mean that he would hesitate to tighten up execution of the recusancy laws for financial or immediate political reasons. He also knew that his hopes of establishing an alliance with a great Catholic power pointed in another direction. As for radical Protestants who went so far as to reject the authority of bishops they were another minority, but they were a definite threat to established things and to the state. The era of high church policy associated with Laud had its own *raison d'être*, but it also represented an attempt to restrain dissidents. Archbishop Abbot (1611–33) was lax but he declined, and Laud was beginning to dictate the mood long before he acquired the Archbishopric of Canterbury. Yet, if he and his friends could capture the hierarchy, they lacked grass roots. Conformists under Abbot became disenchanted as Laud, leader of an intellectual minority, increasingly found support only in the King, himself the leader of a dwindling political minority. The two held hands and fell together, but it cannot be said that they were overwhelmed by some radical Protestant movement.

Laud was an irritant, and perhaps it was symbolic that some young men of Lincoln's Inn drank a health to his confusion in May 1640. His ceremonial demands on the Church and his moral 'puritanism' towards society might have infuriated, without causing too much damage, had he maintained credibility. Whether it was a matter of punishing gentry for enclosing or wenching, the suspicion grew that the principal motive was to collect fines and thus raise revenue.[18] Indeed Pierrepont would couple the workings of Laud's hierarchy with the wrongful authority supposedly claimed by the judges (Doc. 29). Laud was a minister in the fullest sense – his role as leader of the Treasury commission, 1635–6, was probably vital – and the increasing role of bishops in Privy Council and commission of the peace associated them

[17] Foss, vi. 283. Wedgwood, pp. 283–4, 309 n. 50.
[18] Rushworth, iii. 1180. It was later said that: 'ship money was taken away, the Star Chamber was taken away, and the High Commission was taken away, for a man could not meddle with a wench but he must be questioned'. Cited P. Tyler, introd. to Usher, p. xxxiv.

with unpopular administrative and political devices. There had been a warning of the possible dangers in 1621, when the Commons had been worried at the prospect of clergy becoming J.P.'s. It was this involvement which Bagshaw challenged. Their regular attendance in the House of Lords in the 1620s and support of the official line was not forgotten. All these themes account for the coming assault upon the bishops. On May 10, 1641, the House of Commons voted in favour of the proposition that bishops should not have a vote in Parliament, exercise judicial authority in Star Chamber – the abolition of which was evidently not anticipated – or bear any authority in temporal matters. It was further stipulated that clergymen should not be members of the commission of the peace.[19]

The bishops were believed to be associated with some kind of Catholic plot which could be discerned in Charles's inept foreign policy, in Laud's theology, in the attempt to bring the Scottish church to heel, and in Strafford's Irish administration. Everything – notably the courts and financial sinews which maintained the government – became *ipso facto* supports for the developing plot, belief in which began to spread from 1638 and coincided with the Scottish conflict and the collapse in ship-money collection. Although it must be taken with a pinch of salt, for other divisions had by then occurred, an outstanding description of this supposed plot, and the way in which it explained and even oc- casioned all other aspects of Charles's government, is provided by the Grand Remonstrance of November 1641. In fact, nothing could have been less true of Charles and his ministers, from Laud and even Windebank to the most clearly anti-papist of all, Strafford. However they entrapped themselves in the snares of this reputation, partly because their actions were tortuous, and partly because their sense of public relations was so bad as to make a Tudor weep. More than one, 'continuing a Roman Catholic', obtained a letter from the King attesting to his loyalty and requiring the judges 'not to cause or suffer him to be prosecuted'. It was stated that William Petre had 'particular employ- ment in our service, which he cannot so well discharge if he be troubled for his religion'. In 1640 the *'etcetera'* oath, designed against Catholics, was so poorly handled in its inception that it served to heighten the flames of rumour. Even those who did not believe all the rumours were disgusted. D'Ewes wrote that he could honour 'a virtuous papist' but that he abhorred self-professed Protestants who inveighed against popery while working to destroy the truth. It was noted that England was at peace while European Protestants suffered and presumed mari- time opportunities were squandered. The government could not fight because it lacked money, and it could not get money because it would not compromise with Parliament. Instead it financed its feeble survival

[19] *Commons Debate, 1621*, iii. 111. *Commons Journals*, ii. 101–2.

by sapping the wealth of the country. There was little positive evidence for most of this, but much was feared.[20]

There were many serious grievances, but the different strands of accusation might not have come together had not religion provided the bond. It was not 'puritan' beliefs but a deep fear of popery which crippled Charles, just as it had driven Prynne, a conservative, into national politics. In the 1630s, Prynne and others built up an attack against those bishops who they felt could be accused of excess and abuse. It was not an attack against the office of a bishop. Prynne and most of the critics believed in episcopacy. The mood explains the drama of Bagshaw's Reading. Bagshaw subsequently affirmed that England was founded upon a state of episcopacy, that he had only spoken against abuses, and that Pym was of like mind. His Reading had taken up the question as to whether clergymen could be J.P.s, denied that heretics could be convicted by the ordinary alone, and argued that certain types of punishment for a cleric – deprivation, excommunication, fine, imprisonment – could be void in law. Above all he had questioned the position of the bishops in the House of Lords, pointing out that Elizabeth's Act of Supremacy had been passed with their presence but without their votes in support. He had translated vague popular objection into legal terms. That was all, but others would feel compelled to go further. Prynne – who did not become an M.P. until 1648 – became convinced in 1641 that the country could not be saved without the destruction of episcopacy. Faith in Charles, hitherto seen as a victim of clerical intrigue, dwindled and Prynne developed the notion that monarchy and episcopacy could not coexist. A popish design involved subordination to Rome, but this was contrary to the imperial nature of the English Crown. It was still possible to be a monarchist, for the aim was to preserve monarchy, and the device of treating Charles as a real King after the outbreak of hostilities was not merely an exercise in delusion.[21]

In inception, it was the anti-Catholic rather than the Puritan revolution, and even Laud blundered around with evidence of a Catholic plot. It is true, of course, that his rigour had given the radicals cohesion and purpose, and that the destruction of the High Commission and of censorship would enable them to flourish. But as with those other radicals who emerged for a time in the army, before their weakness was exposed, it cannot be suggested that they controlled the early Long Parliament and its activities or represented the dominant mood of that assembly.[22]

---

[20] *CSP Dom.* 1638–9, pp. 223, 607. D'Ewes, *Autobiography*, cited G. P. Gooch, *English Democratic Ideas in the Seventeenth Century*, New York, 1959, pp. 82–3.
[21] Bagshaw, *Vindication*. W. Lamont, *Marginal Prynne*, London, 1963, pp. 69, 96, 109, 116.
[22] Rushworth, iii. 1310–34.

The Judges Trapped

Ministerial futility and popular fears combined to produce the idea that the bench was inextricably allied with government policies in opposition to the majority feeling of the parliamentary classes. Clarendon accused the House of Commons of 'exorbitancy' and 'contempt of the laws', and he suggested that the concurrence of the Lords stemmed from 'the irreverance and scorn' with which the judges had come to be regarded, 'who had been always before looked upon there as the oracles of the law'. The judges, he told the Long Parliament, were the delinquents, and he said that their judgment against Rolle had in effect given tunnage and poundage to the Crown.[23]

By 1637, the reputation of the judges was wilting. Hyde reported that the worst news was 'that the plague is in town, and no judges die'. Despite the professed unanimity of the judges, society thought that ship money was illegal just as it had reached a similar conclusion over practices supposedly condemned by the Petition of Right. The morality and competence of judges who took another view was open to question. None the less, as can only be expected, their decisions had often upset the Crown, and their actions on circuit had by no means been conformist. In 1632, Chief Justice Richardson was accused by Laud of encroaching upon ecclesiastical jurisdiction. Reproved by the Privy Council he was subsequently forced to withdraw an ordinance issued when on the western circuit. Denham, while on the previous circuit, had dismissed the validity of instructions issued to the Council in the North. He had required J.P.s to ignore compositions and to enforce the statutes against recusants. He was, in consequence, removed from the circuit at Wentworth's request. These were clear cases of Council interference, but those travelling the circuits were expected to support official policy. In these instances they were clearly doing the contrary. However, one's impression must be that the judges became more careful and obedient as the 1630s progressed. Posterity would give due emphasis to some sturdy examples of their judicial independence while not fully digesting the subsequent attempts at impeachment.[24]

It was difficult to think of attacking the judges because the men who sat in Parliament had a deep respect for the law and for the responsibility of those who served it. It was hard to reconcile this genuine emotion with the conviction that certain judgments were wrong. Many M.P.s, as J.P.s, exercised in their little way a similar responsibility, and one of the features of 1621 had been the strength of feeling in this respect. Licences which side-stepped their authority had been resented – 'no government in the country if the ministers of justice should be thus

[23] Clarendon, i. 88–9. Rushworth, iii. 1360–1. *State Trials*, iii. 293.
[24] B. Whitelock, *Memorials*, i. 73. Campbell, *Chief Justices*, i. 396. Reid, pp. 425–6. Rushworth, ii. 191–3.

contemned' – and Coke had stressed the insult offered to J.P.s. But by 1640 the J.P.s were not merely protesting. They were in revolt.[25]

It needed the extraordinary circumstances which surrounded the meeting of the Long Parliament to provide a platform for so unusual a step as a frontal attack on the judges. Yet most of the grievances against them existed when the Short Parliament met, and they were outlined by Pym who made much of the former imprisonment of M.P.s. 'That the judges presume to question the proceedings of the House. It is against nature and order that inferior courts should undertake to regulate superior. The court of Parliament is a court of the highest jurisdiction, and cannot be censured by any other law or sentence but by its own.' He went on to condemn 'extra-judicial judgments and impositions of the judges without any cause before them, whereby they have anticipated the judgment which is legal and public and circumvented one of the parties of just remedies, in that no writ of error lies, but only upon the judicial proceedings'. With particular reference to monopolies and Star Chamber, he claimed that 'the great courts do countenance the oppressions'. Among the points listed by the Commons on April 28, 1640, for conference with the Lords were 'the complaints which have been made concerning the denial of justice in the courts of Westminster to the subject's prejudice in point of the property of his goods'.[26]

The Short Parliament was dissolved, and the King and his Council failed to take note of the ominous threat. The very offer to sell ship money for twelve subsidies suggests political incompetence, and it made the judges appear in an even worse light than before (Doc. 31). The persecution and imprisonment of men who failed to aid, or who refused, ship money struck an increasingly discordant note.[27] The activity of Convocation added another. Perhaps most important of all is that old conclusion which sees the Short Parliament as revealing to its members the common nature of their grievances. At first sight this Parliament was quite conventional, certainly a contrast to the early days of the Parliament which would meet in November. The House of Lords reminded the Commons about the need for supply, and the Commons spent much time on consideration of a fast, in which pursuit Secretary Windebank scuttled around in busy fashion. There is hardly a hint of future events. When the next Parliament met, Windebank was regarded as one of the evil men, and the House of Lords was clearly hostile to the government. Perhaps this Parliament was indeed too short.

[25] *Commons Debates, 1621*, ii. 118; vi. 252.

[26] Kenyon, pp. 197–203. Rushworth, iii. 1148.

[27] When seven aldermen were summoned before the King's Bench because of their refusal to contribute to a loan, Thomas Soames told the bench that *his* honesty would not be affected by becoming an alderman. Pearl, p. 100.

The most important charge against the judges, not one which could easily be expressed in legal terms, was that they had shared in the plans of a treacherous set of Councillors. The two most important points were the practice of giving extra-judicial opinions prior to litigation, especially when they were unanimous, and the decision in *Hampden's Case*. Such other points were collected as would aid the accusation. It does not follow that the incidents dragged up had created much of a stir at the time. Yet once included in the articles of impeachment they attracted attention, and authors such as Rushworth included them in the appropriate place in their narrative. These were not great constitutional cases, but they were fair examples of what had been going wrong. The cases of Danvers, Pargiter, and Jenings centred on their imprisonment for various matters, including denial of military demands, and the refusal of the judges to discharge them until certificates were produced that they had paid ship money (Doc. 28 [10]). Bramston would claim that he was honestly convinced that these men were not bailable at law. Then there was that point about corn. Berkeley had accepted Noy's argument that corn was covered by statute. It was therefore possible for the King to open up another line of revenue 'by licenses and dispensations for selling corn at other prices' (Doc. 28 [2]). Berkeley had also ruled, on a reference to him, that the plea, demurrer, and answer of John Overman and other soap makers should be expunged saving four words and ten lines (Doc. 28 [3]). A number of malpractices were alleged with respect to his conduct in ecclesiastical cases (Doc. 28 [9, 11]).[28]

The sweeping nature of the Long Parliament's attack upon the judges is partly obscured by deaths and new appointments. A true picture can be gained by looking at the bench as it existed at the beginning of 1639 and not forgetting the deaths of Dudley Digges, Master of the Rolls, in that year and of Lord Keeper Conventrye who passed away, as it was said, in a seasonable time, January 1640. Those directly accused were Finch, translated from Chief Justice to Lord Keeper, Chief Justice Bramston, Chief Baron Davenport, Justices Berkeley and Crawley, and Barons Trevor and Weston. Denham and Hutton had died in 1639. Jones and Vernon, both of whom would certainly have been impeached, died on 9 and 16 December 1640 respectively. This left only the aged Croke, who had been allowed to retire when eighty years old, while retaining his allowances, salary and title. He was to be excluded by the House of Commons in their vote against those judges who had delayed justice to Rolle and others. Croke apart, every judge who had been involved in the ship-money decision was either dead or under attack.[29]

Finch was the obvious target, although Pym appears unsuccessfully to have urged restraint. If Strafford was the representative of lay

[28] Rushworth, ii. 149, 165–6, 414–16. Bramston, p. 79.
[29] B. Whitelock, *Memorials*, i. 94. Foss, vi. 295.

advisers and Laud of ecclesiastical, then Finch had been the obvious choice among the judges. The King, said Falkland, was surrounded by unjust judges, pernicious councillors, and disconscientious divines. Finch had been Speaker in 1629, and in 1640 – when he presided over the House of Lords – his earlier conduct was condemned by the Commons and declared a breach of privilege. He had often spoken as though he were the voice of officialdom. Appointed Chief Justice after the removal of Heath, he had expressed his intention of relying upon the wisdom of fellow judges on the Common Pleas bench: 'I shall think it no disparagement to see with their eyes, to hear with their ears, and to speak with their tongues.' Shades of a famous future utterance by a Speaker of the House of Commons, but Finch had gone on to speak warmly of the King's favour, not merely for this elevation but also for promoting his career in the past. He repeated the point in his defence, but stressed that he was only an adviser to the King (Doc. 24). Charged, like Strafford, with conspiracy to produce arbitrary and tyrannical government, he was alleged to have practised unlawfully to increase the forest boundaries in Essex and to have procured undue returns of jurors whom he had threatened and awed into producing verdicts. As Chief Justice and also as assistant to the justices in eyre, he had directed the refusal of a traverse offered by the county. In this context, it is worth noting that early in 1641 the House of Lords ordered that no one was to be judge in both a superior and an inferior court for the same case. Ship money provided the major accusation, and note was taken of his argument that Parliament could not take this right away from the Crown. 'No act of Parliament can bar a King of his regality', he had said, presumably meaning that the prerogative was so inseparable that a statute purporting to take it away was void. As Chief Justice, he was also accused of improper practices in so far as it was alleged that he had sat in his chamber releasing persons arrested on outlawries and otherwise overruling his fellow Justices. Finally, it was charged that as Lord Keeper he had influenced the King against Parliaments, and had both advised and framed the dissolution of the Short Parliament. Finch was allowed to address the Commons on December 21, 1640, but Rigby immediately called for impeachment (Doc. 25). He fled and was sequestered from Parliament. It was ordered that he was to be taken into custody if found. [30]

Shortly after the opening of the Long Parliament, Hyde and others spoke against the judges. They stressed ship money, and when Hampden spoke on this subject he was most critical of Bramston and the other King's Bench judges. On November 24th, it was argued that the judges

[30] Roberts, p. 78 n. 2. Rushworth, ii. 255–7, 1331. *Lords Journals*, iv. 115, 156. *State Trials*, iii. 1235. *Lord Somer's Tracts*, ed. W. Scott, London, 1810, iv. 129–33.

were not competent to handle a matter which concerned the whole kingdom. Two days later, the House of Lords set up a committee to examine abuses in courts of justice and in the practice of imprisonment. This had direct relevance to the tactics used to enforce ship-money payments, and particular attention was paid to the case of Francis Freeman, a constable, who had been committed for fifteen weeks without cause shewn (Doc. 23). On December 7th, Falkland made a notable speech against the judges. They were, he said, 'the authors of all our oppressions in giving wrong judgments contrary to their oaths'. The remedy was simple: 'take away the judgments and the judges together'. It could never be too often repeated that although kings could do no wrong, bad judges could advise them that evil actions were just. On this same day Sir John Wray exclaimed, 'let the common law destroy them that would have destroyed it'.[31]

The day after Finch's flight, the House of Lords bound over the six other alleged culprits in £10,000 each to be present and to answer charges being prepared by the House of Commons. It was soon obvious that the attack would now be concentrated on Berkeley who in the eyes of critics had a particularly long and unfavourable record and who, quite apart from the constitutional issues, was also suspected of other ill-doings in the exercise of his functions. At the end of December and the beginning of January, the other judges were bailed: they were to appear when required. A House of Commons committee was formed, and on the 19th Hyde urged Members to provide particulars which would aid in the formulation of charges. On the following day a unanimous resolution of the House of Lords – later to be incorporated in a formal order – vacated all records of ship money: 'the extra-judicial opinions enrolled in the Exchequer Chamber, and in other courts, concerning shipping money, and all the proceedings thereupon, are illegal, in part and in whole, and contrary to the laws and statutes of this realm, contrary to the rights and properties of the subjects of this realm, and contrary to former judgments in Parliament, and contrary to the Petition of Right.' Thus the guilt of the judges was almost presupposed, and on February 12th the articles of accusation against Berkeley were formally presented (Doc. 28). Impeached for high treason, he was arrested on the bench of his court and placed in the Tower. This was said to have 'struck a great terror in the rest of his brethren then sitting in Westminster Hall and in all his profession'.[32]

[31] Rushworth, iii. 1339–41. *The Journal of Sir Simonds D'Ewes from the Beginning of the Long Parliament to the Opening of the Trial of the Earl of Strafford*, ed. W. Notestein, New Haven, 1923, pp. 3–4, 63 n. 12, 117, 118. *Lords Journals*, iv. 98.

[32] *D'Ewes* (Notestein), pp. 178, 180, 253–4, 263, 352–3. *Lords Journals*, iv. 114–15, 116, 119, 122, 136, 161, 173. B. Whitelock, *Memorials*, i. 117.

The accused judges could not be replaced, and there was anxiety over their continued exercise of judicial duties. It was argued in the Commons that they were not fit to go on circuit, but the Speaker intervened to say that it had already been decided that they should not go. Yet Bramston was one of the judges considered fit to advise the House of Lords that Strafford deserved to undergo 'the pains and forfeitures of high treason by law'. The situation was difficult and embarrassing, Parliament was involved with other things, and some must have began to realize the difficulties of translating accusations into proof even if full use was made of the theory of treason employed in Strafford's trial. On July 6th, the House of Commons asked the Lords to set a date for the impeachment of Berkeley, and in the afternoon the charges of crimes and misdemeanours against the other judges were transmitted to the upper House. Hyde spoke on the matter, there was a bitter contribution from Holles (Doc. 30), and William Pierrepoint spoke harshly against Berkeley (Doc. 29).[33]

After the summer recess the Commons, hardly prepared to present a case, were drifting into that conflict of ideas which would produce the divisive vote on the Grand Remonstrance. On October 23rd, the House of Lords announced that they intended to proceed, and on the 26th Berkeley was called to the bar. The accusations were read, and he said that he was not guilty. The Commons, next day, agreed somewhat feebly that they must consider how to make good the impeachment, and on the 28th there was discussion and production of proofs. Pym requested further time: 'it having been long since any traitors were tried'. Strafford, it will be remembered, had been eliminated through attainder. The difficulty of presenting a credible case was again apparent. On October 29th the postponement of Berkeley's impeachment was moved after the House had failed to produce any ideas. 'The Speaker put the House in mind that they had appointed to consider of the manner of Justice Berkeley's trial, but all men remained silent.' In May 1642, when an actual trial was supposed to be imminent, lawyer M.P.s, not satisfied that it was a matter of treason, were unco-operative and eventually asked to be excused from participation. This was regretted by those who believed, in the words of a contemporary, that 'the judgment of ship money transcended all that Strafford ever did'.[34]

By October 1642 every King's Bench judge was either with the King or in prison. Berkeley was therefore allowed to keep essoins for the

[33] D'Ewes (Notestein), p. 367. Somers, Tracts, iv. 300–4. C. Russell, 'The Theory of Treason in the Trial of Strafford', EHR 1965, lxxx. 30–50.

[34] The Journal of Sir Simonds D'Ewes from the First Recess of the Long Parliament to the Withdrawal of King Charles from London, ed. W. H. Coates, New Haven, 1942, pp. 33, 41, 42, 48, 49, 51. Lords Journals, iv. 402, 403, 405. HMC Cowper, ii. 315.

Michaelmas term. In September 1643, the remnant of the House of Lords found him guilty, not of treason but of high crimes and misdemeanours. He was fined £20,000 – he paid half – and forever disabled. Bramston had thrown in his lot with the parliamentary cause, and was sacked by Charles in October 1642. His reputation thus restored, he would be Parliament's candidate for his old job as Chief Justice of England at the time of the Uxbridge proposals. As his son and apologist remarked: 'they thought him not criminous when they made this proposal'. He withdrew, however, from public service. Trevor, heavily fined in 1642, was imprisoned but released after payment. Vernon was also fined. Crawley joined the King at Oxford, and in 1645 Weston was disabled from being a judge 'as though he was dead'.[35]

Other judges of more recent appointment were victims of the civil war. John Banks, who as Attorney General led the prosecution in *Hampden's Case*, had been made Chief Justice of the Common Pleas in January 1641. He was impeached after the outbreak of hostilities as was Justice Foster who sided with the King. Littleton and Heath also cast in their lot with Charles. Littleton, counsel for Rolle, had become Recorder of London and then Solicitor General. As such he played a leading part with Banks in the prosecutions of Hampden and others. In January 1640, he was appointed Chief Justice of the Common Pleas over the head of, but probably with the agreement of, Banks. He was made Lord Keeper at the beginning of 1641 in place of the departed Finch. Heath had made quite a recovery in royal esteem. Despite petitioning the King to reconsider, he had been dismissed in 1634 amid rumours of bribery and of his opposition to ship money. He had resumed practice, becoming a King's serjeant in October 1636. His many interests included an association with Vermuyden. Their title and lease of lead mines in Derbyshire were challenged but upheld in 1638. He was made a Justice of the King's Bench in January 1642 and Chief Justice in the following year. Thomas Malet, made Justice of the King's Bench in July 1641, was imprisoned briefly in the spring of 1642 for his clear opposition to parliamentary policies, notably the Militia Ordinance. When war began, he was seized by a troop of horse and spent two years in the Tower. Indeed Parliament had few legitimate judges to shew. There were forgiven men, such as Vernon, and Edmund Reeve, appointed Justice of the Common Pleas in 1639. Reeve ignored the King's proclamation to adjourn to Oxford, and in 1643 he sat alone in his court.[36]

---

[35] Rushworth, ii. 166. Bramston, p. 88. *Lords Journals*, vi. 211. Clarendon, iii. 209–10.

[36] *CSP Dom.* 1634–5, p. 209. Campbell, *Chief Justices*, i. 415. PRO, D.L.5/32, ff. 452–6.

The Long Parliament

In midsummer 1641 the Long Parliament passed, and the King accepted, a variety of legislation. Hitherto there had been little statutory activity save for the attainder which condemned Strafford, the Triennial Act of February 1641, and the act of May 10th which declared that the present Parliament could not be dissolved without its own consent. There was little theory behind these measures which, in a rather desperate and scrambling fashion, endeavoured to solve the real or imagined problems of the moment, notably the paying off of the Scottish army which occupied the northern counties of England. After midsummer 1641, the King gave his assent to only one important piece of legislation: the bill to remove bishops from the House of Lords which passed early in 1642. The Militia Ordinance of 1642 ignored the requirement of regal participation and, thus introducing the question of the legitimate rights of sovereignty, paved the way to civil war.

The principal legislation[37] of the Long Parliament passed in a period of about nine weeks. Some acts concerned supply. That of June 22nd gave Charles tunnage and poundage for only two months – expressive of distrust, it was renewed regularly until the outbreak of war – and legalized past impositions. New impositions were prohibited, and monopolies were declared to be illegal. In August, ship money was abolished by a statute which reversed the decision in *Hampden's Case*. Other statutes defined and limited the forest laws, the boundaries of Stannary jurisdiction, and prevented further attempts along the lines of distraint of knighthood. In actuality these grievances had already ceased to exist, but Parliament was securing control over taxation and it had placed its hand strategically on the fiscal jugular of royal government.

A second group of statutes, those which can be described as structural, concerned the legal life of England. In July the commissioners of ecclesiastical causes, commonly known as the High Commission, were abolished by the sincere, if inaccurate, device of repealing the relevant clause in Elizabeth's 1559 Act of Supremacy. Other legislation, repealed in 1661, deprived the ecclesiastical courts of the right to administer lay punishments and the long debated *ex officio* oath. The decision in the *Five Knights' Case* was reversed, and an amended procedure established whereby those in prison might secure a hearing under *habeas corpus* proceedings. It was stipulated that the judges were to decide upon the application within three days if the prisoners had been committed by the Privy Council. The Star Chamber was abolished, as were 'the like' jurisdictions of the two provincial Councils, the County Palatine of Chester, and other tribunals, not all of which were specified. These other courts were not abolished. They were merely deprived of one aspect of jurisdiction.

[37] For extracts from these statutes, see Gardiner, *Docs.*, pp. 144 ff.

The statutory achievements of the Long Parliament were limited because the men who gathered in November 1640 wanted to cut out sores in the body politic which immediately offended them. Eighteen of the M.P.s had been imprisoned in 1627 for their refusal to pay the loan, and a further eighteen were relatives of those who had refused. Over twenty, some different from the above, had been imprisoned for other political reasons. Hampden had not been alone in refusing ship money. At least seventeen other M.P.s had followed the same course, and thirty-three had opposed or hampered collection. Of the forty-six M.P.s who had been sheriffs in the years, 1635–40, it is known that fourteen had been reprimanded by the Privy Council for procrastination, and nine others had been reminded of their responsibility to collect arrears. Holles caught the emotions of these men when he spoke of those who had betrayed the subject, making the law speak another sense, and exposing the subject to oppression (Doc. 30). Wicked men and poisoned institutions were assailed, but political events prevented further achievement. Many grievances were so commonly understood – the structure of office and fees, the fiscal feudal system – that nothing was done even though they were raised. It must be presumed that they might have been tackled had the expected rapprochement with Charles occurred and government continued normally from, let us say, August 1641. Our knowledge of the course of events should not blind us to the suggestion that there were many themes – the structure of administration, the Westminster courts, the status of the provincial courts, the disordered arrangements of ecclesiastical jurisdiction – which would have caused concern without the particular political upheavals of Charles's reign. So many aspects of law and of legal procedures were open to question. The defeat of Bacon's procedure of bills of conformity in 1621 had left a void, but now a bill for the general relief of creditors and for the relief of those debtors who were unable to satisfy was rejected on August 30, 1641. This Parliament lashed out, but it had neither time nor opportunity to give consideration to the long-term grievances of society.[38]

It is probable that most statutes passed by this Parliament concerned matters on which the King had indicated that he would compromise. Thus on March 6, 1641, some months prior to the actual legislation, he had agreed to a limitation of forest boundaries. Although only their Star Chamber jurisdictions were abolished – these after all represented the immediate political grievance – there was much opposition to the two provincial Councils, and Hyde chaired a committee which considered them (Doc. 27). The House of Commons declared generally against the Council of the North, but the House of Lords was reluctant to go beyond reproof. Even so, the conciliar jurisdiction at York was

[38] Keeler, pp. 14–15. *Commons Journals*, ii. 277.

K

finished. Charles admitted this when he said that the Council was shattered but not legally abolished. In the west, the members of the Council of the Marches took note of a vote in the House of Commons that their jurisdiction over the four shires was illegal. It was an old dispute which aroused great passion but which had nothing particular to do with the policies of Charles I (Doc. 27). They decided not to deal further with these counties and to proceed cautiously with other suits.[39]

Hyde achieved an outstanding success when the court of Chivalry, or Earl Marshal's court, was constrained. This tribunal was concerned with questions of arms, Heralds' fees, and wrongs done to gentlemen. It had passed through a weak stage during the reign of James when, among other things, it was argued by some of the Heralds that the Earl Marshal could not hold court without the Constable. James held 'his own honour engaged to defend the power and reputation of that court which is of so high a nature, so ancient, and so immediately derived from his Majesty, who is the fountain of all honour'. From around 1622 the court revived, and business seems to have increased in the 1630s following the advice of Sir Henry Marten and other civilians that it had power to award damages for scandalous words. Actually, although not to the same degree, it had previously entertained complaints about insulting acts and words, and the most common type of case was the allegation of 'scandalous words provocative of a duel'. Objection centred upon the court's power to award damages, and what might have been a normal complaint was exaggerated by the relationship which could be drawn between the odd case and the government's fiscal policies. In 1639, the court considered a complaint brought by Sir Popham Southcote, a soap patentee, whose position in the West country had been supported by proclamation. He claimed that faced with obstruction his appeal to the mayor of Exeter had been refused, which was admitted, with offensive words derogatory to knighthood, which was denied. In the Short Parliament, after Pym's speech on grievances, Hyde rose to object that the Earl Marshal's court had not been mentioned. In the Long Parliament, as one of the most powerful of committee chairmen, he pressed his assault. In February 1641, it was reported that the court had no power to hold plea of words, that the Earl Marshal could not sit without the Constable, and that the court was a grievance. Sittings were suspended, and the court ceased to operate for the time being. This would be applauded in the Grand Remonstrance. It was a sweeping victory for Hyde and one that had not entailed legislation. The Earl Marshal apparently tried to appear sweetly reasonable – Hyde later penned a sardonic description of his behaviour (Doc. 27) – and the affair is an instructive example of political tactics. Statute was not involved, and therefore the King was not involved. However, the Earl

[39] *Lords Journals*, iv. 177. Brooks, p. 30. Skeel, pp. 159, 161–2.

Marshal's court represented a limited grievance which could be grasped. A far greater grievance was the whole structure of administration and fees. This, despite perversions associated with the 1630s, had little to do with immediate fears, and the men of the Long Parliament were as futile as Charles's commissioners. Concentration upon immediate issues meant that the reform movement was unbalanced. Despite the energy of some Commonwealth reformers, hated practices survived to flourish under the Restoration, some institutions were destroyed with nothing put in their place, and the structure of English administrative and legal institutions was left unbalanced for generations to come.[40]

Even in destruction, the members of the Long Parliament could not achieve all that they desired. The Restoration was largely a restoration of Charles I's system as amended by the legislation of 1641. The position of the judges was not altered, they would still be regarded as men of the administration, and some like Jeffreys and Scroggs would be celebrated. Yet although it rather fizzled out, the attack upon the judges in 1640-1 was sustained by an intensity of conviction which makes it a central episode of the period. The idea had been sown that they ought to stand apart from administration and politics.

Charles I's judges were neither dishonest nor particularly subservient, but they were the King's servants and important officials heading major institutions. They had not questioned the implications of their position, and many of them, as a matter of normality, were ambitious men with careers in the state to make. When Coke opposed the procedure of consultation in *Peacham's Case*, Houghton had doubts, but Bacon noted that 'he is a soft man and seemeth desirous to confer, alleging that the other three judges had all served the Crown before they were judges, but that he had not been much acquainted with business of this nature'.[41] Subsequently, as Hyde put it, the judges gave tunnage and poundage to the Crown, and George Croke's position in *Hampden's Case* amounted to a statement that they could make legal that which in his opinion had previously been illegal (Doc. 20). Charles was too successful in signalling his belief in their authority and virtue, and he should have been warned by events in the 1620s which indicated that the judges and the Houses of Parliament might be on a collision course. Lord Keeper Coventrye had said that 'justice and sovereignty in his Majesty do kiss each other' (Doc. 19), and the government of the 1630s had indeed been a government of lawyers who placed all possible faith in the legal justification of the past. Convinced, usually with reason, of the King's rights, they relied upon the marriage of law and politics. But

---

[40] *CSP Dom.* 1619–23, pp. 318, 321. *APC* 1621–23, pp. 364–6. Q. C. Squibb, *The High Court of Chivalry*, Oxford, 1959, pp. 37, 56, 57, 59–60, 62–7. Steele, i. no. 1788. Gardiner, *Docs.*, p. 213.

[41] *Life and Letters of Bacon*, ed. Spedding, v. 101.

politics has to be a matter of immediate action whereas law is often more a reflection of past action. Lawyers can envisage and attempt to circumvent future problems, but they cannot know what problems will arise. Politics is often concerned with situations which have not been anticipated or which are the subject of dispute and misunderstanding. A statement of legal right may produce the claim that the law should be changed, and this is certainly an element in the early Stuart period. Far more important, however, was the growing belief that judges were slavish and self-interested. Hence the claim was that the law was mis-stated and that it was the judges who should be changed. After the judgment in *Hampden's Case* some gentry and townsmen would still conform, but this dwindling success did not promise survival. There was nothing unusual about the introduction of new principles as though they were part of a pre-existing law, but once men are politically aroused they will not accept this and they will accuse the regime of wrongful innovation. Charles's ministers and judges were to be accused of legislating without Parliament. As Hobbes wrote, 'no man's error becomes his own law, nor obliges him to persist in it' (Doc. 32).

DOCUMENTS

1. The judges and the House of Lords, 1614

FROM H.M.C. Hastings, iv. 255–7, 262–3.

[Monday, May 23, 1614]

Lord Chancellor [Ellesmere]

My Lords: the lower House do not desire to meet with your Lordships but to confer with you about the point of impositions.

Upon these arguments on both sides it was put to the question whether we should hear the judges before we met with the lower House, and it being put to the question, the Lords of the Privy Council and all the bishops being of opinion that it was fit to hear the judges before we should determine whether or no to meet with the lower House, the Lords of the Council and bishops carried it by mene [sic.? nine] voices.

The judges present [Coke, Hobart, Tanfield, Warburton, Croke, Altham] . . . went into my Lord Chancellor's lodging and stayed there some half an hour, and then the Lord Chief Justice of the King's Bench made a speech, the effect whereof here followeth.

Lord Coke

May it please your Lordships: I take it to be the thing in charge given us by your Lordships to deliver unto you our opinions about the point of impositions, the which, my Lords, is a matter so great in consequence that none of us having thought of it heretofore we must beseech your Lordships to spare and pardon us herein at this time, for I vow unto your Lordships, for myself, and I think I may say for my brethren, that we never turned over book, saw record, or any other thing that might give us light in this matter. My Lords: the things we should speak to are to the point of impositions, the which what can we say to give answer to this general proposition? For impositions are of several kinds and rating, some of exported commodities, some imported, some domestic. My Lord: this is a matter great in itself, and great in consequence, and therefore we humbly thank those Lords that were of opinion we should not be heard, but seeing it is your pleasures we must speak. For my part, I will not look above me nor about either the one way or the other, but as we are sworn to deliver our opinions in matters judicial coming before us, betwixt party and party, so are we in matters betwixt the King and the subject. But, my Lords, in this matter as yet we can deliver no opinion, for I protest unto your Lordships I am not yet myself satisfied in the point, for it is not *magna* but *maxima questio juris*, and again I must thank from my heart those noble Lords that would not have heard us, for this is a great matter in point of profit to the King, and it seems the subjects do think it a great grievance to them. Therefore, I am loath to speak *in hoc individuo*. The King, I say, takes it not only to be a flower but a sovereign prerogative of the Crown. If it be a prerogative it is warranted by law, for the King hath no prerogative to impose that the law giveth him not power to do. I have read out of the book of Leviticus that we should first hear, understand, and then judge, but till we have heard and understood we cannot tell your Lordships our opinions; and, my Lords, I think it should be good to hear somewhat from the lower House, and that answered by the King's counsel, and then us to judge of it. For my part I will not argue the case, it being against our oath so to do. We are called by our writ to advise the King when it is his pleasure to have us speak and to advise and assist your Lordships when you please to have us speak, but not to dispute. Therefore the King is much prejudiced that he hath no counsel here, as the Attorney and Solicitor, whose place and duty it is that the[y] should attend this House, and not to be of the lower House; for so I must call it, having the presidence so to do of former times, and not to term it as nowadays it is the Commons House, for I know no Commons House but the lower House of Parliament. Your Lordships cannot but remember how my predecessor, my Lord Flemyng, and Baron Clarke were thought of in the case of currants which was argued in the Exchequer Chamber. He was a great scholar, and no doubt I ought so to think of him, gave his judgment according to his conscience. Yet the same case remaineth like a scole that is put as it were *super domum pestilentem* which every man flyeth from as they do the plague. If that your Lordships will undertake to dispute the matter, we will upon the hearing of it argued on both sides, if it be your pleasures, to deliver our opinions.

For my part I will deliver my conscience, for I fear not the face of any man, but because as yet we are no way provided to speak of it *in statu judiciali*. I must again thank the Lords that would not have us heard. My conclusion of this short and undigested speech is this: that whosoever should incline to take away a sovereign prerogative should shew too much popularity, and on the other side should speak that a King should keep those things if they be against law, in us that are judges it should be perjury, and in others too great baseness and flattery.

*   *   *

[Tuesday, May 24th]

Lord Chancellor

My Lords: if I should speak much I should lose much by the way, being an old man and my memory weak. My Lords: I must tell you that *in conceptis verbis* the lower House desire a conference and your Lordships are disputing whether you should give them a meeting. What will that do but, as a Lord said, to gaze, for to confer is to dispute the matter and lay record against record and book against book. For the one you have not the King's counsel here to do it, and for the other, you hear my Lords, the judges, say they have not in the least manner at any time considered of this case. And on the other side they go both high and low and look of all things that concern their purpose, and we can say nothing having not seen records. They perhaps will tell us of the law of nature and nations, being learned and able gentlemen who have studied this case long. If any man in this House think himself able to dispute with them, let him do it; for my part I must desire to be excused. I think both the King's necessity on the one side and the people's good on the other must be regarded, but who can love the Kingdom so well, can the lower House, as the King that is *pater patriae*? The King hath no prerogative but that that is warranted by law and the law hath given him, and therefore if they find themselves aggrieved, let a writ of error be brought and then the appeal must be brought, not unto the lower House but unto your Lordships, and then if so be you find error then to determine it upon the hearing of the King's counsel, otherwise being found no error in the pleading by your Lordships the matter is to go down again unto the King's Bench and there the Chief Justice is to give sentence in the cause.

*   *   *

Lord Danvers

My Lords: if the want of counsel be the matter, we cannot confer with the lower House; if we made known so much unto them, no doubt they would spare the King's counsel in that House, and then there were no impediments and hindrances why we might not argue and dispute the matter.

2. *Ignoramus, 1615*

FROM G. Ruggle, *Ignoramus*, trans. R. Coddrington, London, 1662,
Act 2, Scene 6.

Musaeus: What is that which liveth by right and by wrong; which
  hath both a great heart and no heart; which is both an ambidexter
  and a bifront; which speaketh much and speaketh nothing; which is
  jest in earnest and earnest in jest; which speaketh English, Dutch,
  French and Latin, yet speaketh neither English, nor Dutch, nor
  French, nor Latin; which writeth laws that they may be misprisions,
  and which writeth misprisions that they may be laws; which maketh
  a finite infinite, truth no truth, and no truth, truth?

Trico: Which maketh truth no truth, who should this be but *Belzebub
  Cydonius*?

Musaeus: It is he, and it is not he.

Trico: Who loves to speak in an unknown tongue? It is a popish priest.

Musaeus: It is something like him, but not the same.

Trico: What a blockhead I am, now I have it.

Musaeus: What, or who is it?

Trico: It is your master, Ignoramus.

Musaeus: You are an Oedipus.

Trico: Who was father to this monster?

Musaeus: *Francus Soloicophanes*, his mother's name was *Barbara
  Latina*.

Trico: Where was he born?

Musaeus: In great *Puritania*.

Trico: In what city?

Musaeus: Either *Aurelia* or *Argentina*.

Trico: What doth he feed upon?

Musaeus: The common law.

3. James I instructs the House of Lords about its judicial responsibilities, March 10, 1621

FROM 'The Hastings Journal of the Parliament of 1621', ed. Lady Elizabeth de Villiers, *Camden Miscellany xx*, 1953, pp. 27–9.

The lower House have shewed great modesty in their proceedings and in their places have proceeded as far as they can in the information, for they are no court of record neither can give oath; it is you that have the power of judicature. As for the things objected against the Chancellor and the Treasurer, I leave them to answer for themselves and to stand and fall as they acquit themselves, for if they cannot justify themselves they are not worthy to hold and enjoy those places they have under me.

All this while I have been telling you of my desire to have my people righted, but now I desire you to do your King justice. For though Sir Edward Coke be very busy and be called the father of the law and the Commons House have divers young lawyers in it, yet all is not law that they say, and I could wish, nay I have told Sir Edward Coke, that he would bring precedents of good Kings' times . . . or precedents of my time, and not either of Henry the 6th, a poor weak prince governed by his Council, or of Richard the 2nd, who was murdered, and such like princes and times when one house was up today and another tomorrow, and the Crown tossed up and down like a tennis ball. I hope in his vouching precedents to compare my actions to usurpers' or tyrants' times you will punish him, for the Star Chamber which is an inferior court to this will punish *pro falso clamore*.

* * *

Now my Lords, I have somewhat to say to you: you need not search precedents whether you may deal in this business [the examination of patents] without the lower House for there is no question yours is a House and a court of record. You need not stick upon it, for the lower House they are but a House of customs and orders and their House hath come from yours; for though heretofore a long time since you were but all one House, yet upon the division all the power of judicature went with your House.

Now to speak as a judge these things are necessary for you to observe: first the party accused; secondly the accusers; thirdly the matter of the accusation; fourthly witnesses and proofs. That is (1) Sir Giles Mompesson (2) the lower House (3) patents (4) matters of record and the parties that are to be sworn. In your judgment learn not of accusers how to judge but judge as you see cause, for things must be judged by real proofs, and in questions of law judges are to speak if it concern any particular party much more to hear them when the matter is upon a question of law and that it concerns me. Laws are not to look backward and forward; for the prevention of abuses of things to come make as severe laws as you will find, for those things that are prejudicial for the present shall be taken away. I will join with you, as I say, leaving me that latitude that is fitting for you to leave to your King. I honour Parliament but more verity. In former times Kings sat not in the Parliament by representation but person, as I do now, both Houses making then but one. I know not the mysteries of the omnipotency of a Parliament. I think him an enemy to monarchy and a traitor to me that mentions my actions with such Kings as I have told you.

I am accountable to none but to God and my people for my government. If I had known these abuses I would have seen a reformation, but they come to my knowledge now in Parliament as though nothing could be done but in Parliament. I hope both my lords the bishops, you, my Lords that are made by me and other that are of the ancient nobility, will do me right against these tongues that wrong me both for the love you bear to me and your own honours; for Buckingham, since he came to me, being so near to me, hath been more troubled than ever any that served me, that I may say his time hath been a purgatory to him and that he hath had more ease this Parliament than he hath had of a long time before, for now he is not pestered and troubled at his chamber with projects or projectors. . . . So now everybody would be glad to be rid of their patents and envy and speak much against patents and courtiers, but after the Parliament is ended . . . they will come again and be glad to regard those near about me and then Buckingham shall be troubled again, some coming to beg something of me.

*　　*　　*

For the judges they are men of great understanding and gravity, but for common lawyers they are wind instruments, their tongue being their pipe. A bagpipe is a greater noise than a viol, although a viol hath better music and heavier. This is now a time of bringing all things to proof, nay a day of judgment. I fear not to appear before sun and moon when I come to trial, such hath been all my actions in my time. . . .

4. The judges discuss the nature of a Parliament, 1623

FROM Hutton's *Reports*, 61–2 (122 *English Reports*).

Memorandum. That on Monday the seventeenth of February, at Serjeant's Inn, upon the assembly of all the Justices to take consideration upon the statute of 35 Elizabeth c.1, for the abjuration of sectaries; the Attorney General and Serjeant Crewe[1] being there, after the perusal of the statute, and the continuances thereof, it was first upon debate considered whether this statute was in force, or discontinued, and upon the perusal of the proviso in the statute of subsidy,[2] and upon reasoning the matter, these points were resolved.

1. If a Parliament be assembled, and divers orders made, and a writ of error brought, and the record delivered to the higher House, and divers bills agreed, but no bills signed, that this is but a convention, and no Parliament, or session, as it was *anno* 12 James[3] in which (as it was affirmed by them which had seen the roll) it is entered that it is not any session or Parliament, because that no bill was signed. . . .

2. It was agreed, that if divers statutes be continued until the next Parliament, or next session, and there is a Parliament or a session, and nothing done therein as to continuance, all the said statutes are discontinued and gone. Then it was moved, whether this statute was discontinued, *et seriatim* Jones, Chamberlain, Hutton, Denham, Houghton, Doddridge, Winch and Bromley declared their opinions, that this statute is discontinued; and that the statute of subsidy is a Parliament, and that every Parliament is a session, but not *è converso*, for one Parliament may have divers sessions. . . . And that this proviso is not to any other purpose, but to continue their proceedings in the same estate, as if this Act had not been made; and if this proviso had not been, than this statute had been discontinued by this Act of Subsidy, but when this ends and is determined, then is the session ended, then it is a session, *scilicet* a Parliament; which ought to be pleaded, at the Parliament holden, etc. and all the commissions of subsidy are accordingly; and the proviso call it a session. Then this being done, the Lord Chief Baron did not deliver any opinion, for he said, that he had not considered the statute; and afterward it was desired that the Lords would deliver their opinions, and thereupon the Lord Hobart declared his opinion

---

[1] Ranulph Crewe, Chief Justice of the King's Bench, 1625–6.
[2] 1621.
[3] 1614.

accordingly: that it seemed to him that it was a session, and that it was not safe to meddle with such law, and that he would never refuse to declare his opinion with his brethren. After, the Lord Chief Justice Ley made a long discourse, concerning the purpose and intent of Parliament, *scilicet*, that it was not their purpose to destroy so good laws, and therefore it was not any such session as was within the intent of the preceding Parliament, which was, that these should determine when it is a Parliament or session, in which good laws are made.

And Doddridge said that it was fit to see the commission, and that that which hath been said was not to bind anyone, but everyone spoke what then he was advised of and peradventure might change upon better consideration. And afterwards upon Tuesday on an assembly of the two Chief Justices, the Chief Baron, Justice Houghton, Baron Denham, Hutton, Chamberlain, and Jones, the Attorney General brought the commission *de* 12 Elizabeth June 1 . . . and the commission to dissolve this Parliament, 28 February *anno* 19 James, had the same words, saving that he recite that he had given his royal assent to an Act of Subsidy, by which it was intended that it should not be a session. And upon view of the commission, the Lord Chief Justice moved that the King was mistaken in this, that he had given power to dissolve this Parliament, which had not any session, and if it be a session, then he had no power to dissolve it, and then it is as it were, a recess; and a Parliament cannot be discontinued or dissolved but by matter of record, and that by the King alone; and if the Parliament yet continue, then this statute also continue during the Parliament by the proviso. But that would not serve, for first, it is against the intent of the King and against his proclamation; and also the case is truly put in the commission, as to the matter in fact, and he is not misinformed, but mistaken in the law, and then the commission for the dissolving is good. . . . But because that all the judges were not at this conference, therefore it was deferred until the next term; and in the interim, the grand Secretary and the Attorney General were to inform the King that the statute is obscure, and had not been put in *jure*, and that we could not agree.

5. Sir Edward Coke comments on the nature of a Parliament

FROM Sir Edward Coke, *The Fourth Part of the Institutes of the Lawes of England*, 1669, pp. 27–8.

The passing of any bill or bills by giving the royal assent thereunto, or the giving any judgment in Parliament, doth not make a session, but the session doth continue until that session be prorogued or dissolved; and this is evident by many precedents in Parliament ancient and late.

★   ★   ★

The diversity between a prorogation and an adjournment, or continuance of the Parliament, is that by the prorogation in open court there is a session, and then such bills as passed in either House, or by both Houses, and had no royal assent to them, must at the next assembly begin again, etc., for every several session of Parliament is in law a several Parliament; but if it be but adjourned or continued, then is there no session, and consequently all things continue still in the same state they were in before the adjournment or continuance.

★   ★   ★

We have been the longer and more curious for the clearing of this point for two reasons. 1. For that the adjournment or continuance ... is much more beneficial for the Commonwealth for expediting of causes than a prorogation. 2. In respect of a clause in the Act of Subsidy in the Parliament holden in *Anno 18 Jacobus Regis*, which is but declaratory of the former law ...

★   ★   ★

When a Parliament is called and doth sit, and is dissolved without any act of Parliament passed, or judgment given, it is no session of Parliament, but a convention.

6. Part of the debate in the House of Lords as to whether Cranfield should be deprived of all his offices, 1624

FROM *Notes of the Debates in the House of Lords, Officially taken by Henry Elsing, Clerk of the Parliament, A.D. 1624 and 1626*, ed. S. R. Gardiner, Camden New Ser. 1879, xxiv. 88.

Pr[ince]
This offence, simply of itself, not so great, but considering how he came in upon reformation and proved a shark for himself, etc., to lose them.

South[amp]ton
The Tr[easur]er's faults far greater than the Lord St Albans's. For unfaithful to the K[ing]: extortion and tyranny, and a wolf to all the kingdom. St Albans but a few.

L[ord] Keeper
The Lord St Albans's fault as great as any. For bribery; yea, by contract, which destroyed the formality of his place. No such proved against the Treasurer for his judicature. Faulty for extortion, whereby he destroyed also the formality of his place. No fault can be greater than a judge to be corrupt.

7. Justice Whitelocke complains about the behaviour of Lord Treasurer Marlborough, 1627

FROM *Liber Famelicus of Sir James Whitelocke*, ed. J. Bruce, Camden Soc. Old Ser. 1858, lxx. 108–9.

Memorandum, that our wages, which for the memory of man had always been paid the last day of Easter term and Michaelmas term, or the day after at the farthest, was unpaid the end of this Michaelmas term, 1627, whereupon four of the judges were sent from all the rest to the Lord

Treasurer, to desire his care of it—Jones, Whitelocke, Harvey, Croke. To whom the Earl of Marlborough [Ley], Treasurer, gave sleeveless and cunning answers, but craftily and deceitfully, underhand, did abuse the judges with delays, for he promised he would take present order with Sir Robert Pye, clerk of the warrants, that they should be first paid, which he did by word of mouth, but by his writing gave order for others. . . . But this old dissembler, that had been one of our own company, used us worse than any man before him. He was wont to be called 'Volpone', and I think he as well deserveth it now as ever. Being himself indebted to some of the judges, for moneys he had borrowed of them when he was Chief Justice of the King's Bench, he gave a private warrant for the payment of them underhand, but Sir Robert Pye very honestly refused to execute it, and returned answer that it was a general duty for the whole order, and that it should be done for all at once, and that none ought to be preferred or singled from their fellows. . . .

★   ★   ★

Memorandum, that the Treasurer dallied out all the vacation, and all Hilary term, without payment of our wages, whereupon myself and Doddridge and Jones caused writs of *liberate* upon the statute of 18 Henry VI[4] to be drawn, thereby to charge the clerk of the Petty Bag, but the Lord Keeper [Coventrye] told us to stay, and he would interpose. . . .

★   ★   ★

Another wonder fell out this term, for whereas the judges, ever sithence their compounding for the charge of the circuit, were paid their circuit money the last day of the term preceding the circuit, now at this time one penny was not paid so they were put to this straight, either to deceive the whole kingdom, whom by their summons they had called together, or spend their own money in the King's service. These monstrous enormities in the state happened by the crooked dealing of the Treasurer.

[4] 18 H.VI. c. 1.

L

8. An order in the Court of Requests, January 26, 1629

FROM PRO, Entry Books of the Court of Requests, Requests 1/58.[5]

Whereas the last term upon the exhibiting of a bill of complaint to the King's most excellent majesty by James Harrington, one of the fellows of Wadham College in Oxford, against William Smith, Warden of the said College, defendant, a commission under his Majesty's Privy Seal was awarded forth of this court unto John Prydeaux, John Warner, Richard Corbett, doctors of divinity, [   ][6] Lapworth, doctor of physic, and Francis Smith, esq., authorizing them, or any four, three, or two of them to call the parties before them and to examine witnesses upon the contents of the said bill and thereupon to determine the differences between them if they could, or else to certify their proceedings into this court on the morrow after the Purification of the blessed Virgin Mary next coming. Now forasmuch as this Court was this day informed by Mr Dayrell, counsellor at law, that the matters of the said bill being between the Warden and a fellow of that college concerning[7] his fellowship there appertain to the proper determination of the right reverend father in God, the Lord Bishop of Bath and Wells, visitor thereof, before whom the cause at the granting of the said commission depended, and doth yet depend, whereof this court was not heretofore informed, never meaning to impugn the privileges and statutes of the said house nor jurisdiction of the said Lord Bishop. It is therefore ordered that the said commissioners nor any of them shall no further proceed in the execution of the said commission, and whatsoever they have already done therein is and shall be suppressed and made void.

[5] This volume is not foliated, but entries can be found by date.
[6] Blank.
[7] The words, 'the orders and statutes', are deleted.

9. Richard Chambers opposes the seizure of his goods, 1629

FROM PRO Exchequer. K.R. Entry Books, Public Record Office, E. 125/6. ff. 210, 320.

[January 30, 1629]. Whereas by an order made the seven and twentieth day of November the last Michaelmas term (amongst other things) it was ordered by the court that an injunction should be awarded under the seal of this court to stay all further proceedings upon several writs of replevin then sued forth by divers merchants for the delivery of certain goods detained in his Majesty's possession for certain duties alleged to be due to his Majesty. And that the sheriffs of the city of London should thereby take notice neither to proceed in execution of the said writs of replevin then sued forth nor of any other such writs to be sued forth for the delivery of any other goods being in the King's storehouses, as by the said order more at large appeareth. Now, upon the motion of Sir Robert Heath, knight, his Majesty's Attorney General, and upon reading of the said order, informing this court that one Richard Chambers of London, merchant, did on the nine and twentieth day of this present month of January come into the Custom House of London in the forenoon and there demanded of Abraham Dawes and Richard Carmarthen, esquires, his Majesty's officers there, certain goods and merchandise now remaining in the King's storehouse upon Customhouse Quay, and it so appeareth by affidavit made in this court. And for that they told the said Mr Chambers that they had no power to deliver the said goods unto him, thereupon the said Chambers shewed the said Mr Dawes and Mr Carmarthen a written paper which he called a replevin, and brought one Phillips, an officer to the sheriffs of London, for to execute the same, as appeareth likewise by the said affidavit. It was therefore humbly desired by his Majesty's Attorney General on his Majesty's behalf that the said order of the twenty-seventh day of November should be explained as well for the stay of proceedings upon all plaints as writs of replevin to be brought by any person whatsoever. Whereupon, it is this day ordered and declared by the court that the sheriff's officers of London shall not execute any kind of replevin brought . . . for such goods contrary to the said order of the seven and twentieth day of November as aforesaid, but that the said parties are to take such course for the same, if they be unduly detained, as the law doth allow.

*   *   *

[May 18, 1629]

Whereas Richard Chambers of London, merchant, hath lately exhibited an English bill into this court against Abraham Dawes, esq., Richard Carmarthen, esq., John Holloway, esq., and Bryan Rogers, gent., defendants, touching certain goods of great value which were seized by them or some of them as officers and farmers of his Majesty's customs, and still detained in his Majesty's storehouse of London for some duties pretended to be due to his Majesty. And whereas also by the said bill the said Richard Chambers hath humbly prayed that this court would be pleased to give order that his Majesty's Attorney General might likewise answer to the said bill as by the said bill amongst many other things therein contained more fully and largely may appear. Now, upon the motion of Mr Noy, on the behalf of the said Richard Chambers, in the presence of his Majesty's Attorney General, informing this court that the said bill came in almost three weeks sithence and that after divers rules given here in court, according to the course of this court, the said Abraham Dawes, Richard Carmarthen, John Holloway, and Bryan Rogers did on Tuesday last put in their answer to the said bill, but that his Majesty's Attorney General hath not as yet put in any answer to the same; and therefore and for other reasons by him, the said Mr Noy, alleged in court, it was now by him humbly desired that the said goods so seized and detained as aforesaid might be redelivered to him, the said Richard Chambers. It is thereupon this present day ordered by this court, by and with the consent of the said Mr Attorney General, that the said Mr Attorney shall this day put in his answer to the said bill and then upon the motion of the said Mr Noy again tomorrow the court will give such further order in the said cause as shall be fitting.

10. Charles I consults the judges with respect to the Petition of Right and parliamentary privilege, 1628 and 1629

FROM *The Autobiography of Sir John Bramston*, ed. Lord Braybrooke, Camden Old Ser. 1845, xxxii. 48–54.

. . . (As I find reported by Sir Nicholas Hyde, then Lord Chief Justice of the King's Bench, under his own hand, which I with my hand transcribed, and have by me), the 16 of May [1628], the King sent for him, and Richardson, Chief Justice of the Common Pleas, to attend him at Whitehall, where the King delivered them a case, and required them to assemble all the judges, and to give their answer thereunto under all their hands. The case was, 1. whether in no case whatsoever the King may not commit a subject without shewing cause? Whereto the same day they made answer. We are of opinion, by the general rule of law, the cause of commitment by his Majesty ought to be shewn; yet some case may require such secrecy, that the King may commit a subject without shewing cause for a convenient time. Which being delivered to his Majesty, subscribed by them all, the King gave them (the two Chief Justices) another case, and required their answer as before. The case was, 2. whether a *habeas corpus* be brought, and a warrant from the King, without any general or special cause returned, the judges ought to deliver him before they understand the cause from the King? They answer that, upon an *habeas corpus* brought by one committed by the King, if the cause be not generally or specially returned, so that the court may take knowledge thereof, the party ought, by the general rule of law, to be delivered; but if the case be such as requireth secrecy, and may not presently be disclosed, the court in discretion may forbear to deliver the prisoner for a convenient time, to the end the court may be advertised of the truth thereof. This was also subscribed and delivered as the former, when his Majesty gave a third case: 3. whether, if the King grant the Commons' Petition, he doth not thereby conclude himself from committing or restraining a subject for any time or cause whatsoever without shewing cause? [It was answered that] every law after it is made hath its exposition, and so this Petition and answer must have an exposition, as the case in the nature of it shall require, to stand with justice, which is to be left to the court of justice to determine, which cannot particularly be discerned until such case shall happen. And, although the petition be granted, there is no fear of conclusion, as in the question is intimated. . . .

I also find reported by [the] said Sir Nicholas Hyde, Chief Justice, that upon the 2nd day of March, 1629, the King directed an adjournment of the Commons House until the 10th day of the same month, which received some opposition, and some Members behaved themselves so as gave offence to his Majesty, whereupon the next day (3 March) the two Chief Justices and Chief Baron were sent for to the Council, where also was his Majesty, and a declaration was read of the speeches used and the behaviour of divers of the Members of the Commons House the day before. Which being done, the King commanded the said three judges to meet and answer such questions as should be proposed to them by his Attorney, and for their assistance they should call such of his learned counsel as were in town. Whereupon they, the Attorney and Solicitor, Serjeant Crec [sic][7a] and Serjeant Davenport met, and these questions were proposed, and the answers made by uniform consent, as followeth. Whether a Parliament man offending the King criminally or contemptuously in the Parliament House, and not there punished, may be punished out of Parliament? We conceive that if a Parliament man, exceeding the privilege of Parliament, do criminally or contemptuously offend his Majesty in the Parliament House, and not then punished, may be punished out of Parliament.

Whether the King, as he hath power of calling or dissolving of a Parliament, hath not also an absolute power to cause it to be adjourned at his pleasure? Whether, if the King do command an adjournment to be made, he hath not also power to command all further proceedings in Parliament to cease at that time? We conceive the King hath power of commanding adjournments of Parliament, as well as of calling, proroguing, and dissolving. But for the manner there, and for the more particular answer to these two questions, we refer ourselves to the precedents of both Houses.

Whether it be not an high contempt in a Member of the House, contrary to the King's express command, tumultuously to oppose the adjournment? The King's express commandment being signified for adjournment, if any after that shall oppose it tumultuously, farther or otherwise than the privilege of the House will warrant, this we conceive is a great contempt. Upon delivery of this answer, his Majesty sent this further question: can any privilege of the House warrant a tumultuous proceeding? To which they answer: we humbly conceive that an earnest, though disorderly and confused, proceeding in such a multitude may be called tumultuous, and yet the privilege of the House may warrant it.

If a few Parliament men do conspire together to stir up ill affections in the people against the King, and to leave the Parliament with such a loose [sic], and by words or writing put in execution, and this not punished in Parliament, be an offence punishable out of Parliament? We conceive this punishable out of Parliament.

Whether if some Parliament men shall conspire together to publish papers containing false and scandalous news against the lords of the King's Council, or any one or more of them, not to the end to question them in a legal or parliamentary way, but to bring them into hatred of the people, and the government into contempt, and to make discord between the Lords and Commons, if this be an offence punishable out of Parliament? We conceive this punishable out of Parliament.

If two or three, or more, of the Parliament shall conspire to defame the King's government, and to deter his subjects from obeying or assisting the King, of what nature is this offence? The nature of this offence will be greater or less, as the circumstances shall fall out upon

[7a] Possibly Thomas Crew.

the truth of the fact. This answer not satisfying, his Majesty sent this addition, written with his own hand. It is true the circumstances of the fact will aggravate or diminish when particular men come to be tried, but I must know what the nature of the offence is being proved? We, in all humbleness, are willing to satisfy your Majesty's commands, but until the particular of the fact do appear we can give no directer answer than before.

I find further reported by the same Sir Nicholas Hyde, at the beginning of this term, [Easter 1629], all the judges and Barons of the Exchequer were assembled at Serjeant's Inn, in Fleet Street, by the King's commandment, and Mr Attorney General, on his Majesty's behalf, proposed these questions, which were answered as followeth.

Whether the statute 4 Henry VIII, intitled an Act for Richard Strode,[8] were a general law, concerning all Parliament men, or only the said Richard Strode, and seven others, particular men who joined with him in preferring bills in Parliament? They answer, it is a particular act for them, no general law.

Whether if any subject have received probable information against another subject of treason or of traitorous attempts or intentions against the King or state, that subject ought not to make known to the King, or to the King's commissioners, when he shall be thereunto required, what informations he hath received, and the grounds thereof, to the end the King, being informed truly may, prevent the danger? And if such subject in such case shall refuse to be examined, or answer the question which shall be so demanded of him, for the enquiries and discoveries of the truth, whether it be an high contempt in him, punishable in the Star Chamber, as an offence against the general justice and government of the kingdom? They answer, this not concerning not [sic] himself, but another, nor to draw him into danger of treason or contempt by his answer, his refusal to answer is a contempt, punishable in the Star Chamber.

Whether it be a good answer for any one that is thus interrogated, and shall refuse to answer, to say he was a Parliament man when he received these informations, that he spake thereof in the Parliament House, and therefore the Parliament being now ended he refuseth to answer to any question concerning the same but in Parliament House, and no other place? They answer, if he had refused to answer absolutely, and peremptorily, it were punishable; if he make an excuse which is no good plea, or excuse but an error in judgment, it is no offence punishable.

Whether a Parliament man offending the King criminally or contemptuously in the Parliament House, and not there punished may not be punished out of Parliament? They answer, if this be not done in a parliamentary way, he may be punished out of Parliament. If one

[8] 4 H.VIII. c. 8.

Parliament man resolve, or two or more conspire together, to raise false and scandalous rumours against the Lords of the Privy Council and the judges, not to the end to question them in a legal course or parliamentary way, but to blast them, and to bring them into hatred with the people and the government into contempt, whether this be not an offence punishable out of Parliament? They answer, it is an offence punishable out of Parliament.

If a Parliament man in the Commons House shall by way of digression say thus falsely, though [sic.? that] King's counsel at law and all, though the judges and the Privy Council have conspired together to trample the liberties of the subjects and privileges of Parliament under foot, is this an offence punishable out of Parliament, the words being spoken a month before the Parliament dissolved, the speaker of them never punished, not suffered for them by the House, nor after the speaking of them any legal proceedings had against any of them against whom the words were spoken? They answer, we desire to be spared to answer this question, it concerning ourselves, and being included in the former question. If a Parliament man being called *ore tenus*, being charged that he submitted not to an examination for such things as did concern the King and government of the state, and were affirmed to be done by a third person, and not by himself, if he confess his hand to that refusal, and make his excuse and plea because of the privilege of Parliament, whether he ought to be overruled to answer? The answer: we are of opinion that the justest way for the King and party is not to proceed *ore tenus*, because it being a point in law it is fit to hear counsel before it be overruled; and, in case of an *ore tenus* by the rules in the Star Chamber, counsel is not admitted.

Mr Attorney General read out of a paper the effect of a speech made in Parliament by Sir John Eliot, wherein amongst other things were contained: that the King was led by ill counsel; that the Lord Treasurer was the head of the papists, and that he was a chief maintainer of priests and Jesuits, and the Bishop of Winchester was hinderer of religion, and he would have all proclaimed as enemies to the state that should exact or demand for his Majesty tunnage and poundage, and they accessory that should pay the same, and that he never knew any blasted in Parliament but a curse followed. His question hereupon was – that if the substance of this be proved, whether he were to be censured or not? They answer, they desire to be spared to give any answer to a particular case which might peradventure come before them judicially. But they all disliked many parts of the speech, and did conceive it to be not according to a parliamentary proceeding.

11. Charles I, in his 'Declaration Shewing the Causes of the late Dissolution', denounces attempts by the House of Commons to interfere with councillors and judges, March 10, 1629

FROM S. R. Gardiner, *Constitutional Documents of the Puritan Revolution, 1625–60*, Oxford, 1962, pp. 93–5.

We are not ignorant how much that House [of Commons] hath of late years endeavoured to extend their privileges, by setting up general committees for religion, for courts of justice, for trade, and the like; a course never heard of until of late: so as, where in former times the knights and burgesses were wont to communicate to the House such business as they brought from their countries; now there are so many chairs erected, to make enquiry upon all sorts of men, where complaints of all sorts are entertained, to the unsufferable disturbance and scandal of justice and government, which, having been tolerated awhile by our father and ourself, hath daily grown to more and more height; insomuch that young lawyers sitting there take upon them to decry the opinions of the judges; and some have not doubted to maintain that the resolutions of that House must bind the judges, a thing never heard of in ages past: but in this last assembly of Parliament they have taken on them much more than ever before.

They sent messengers to examine our Attorney General (who is an officer of trust and secrecy) touching the execution of some commandments of ours, of which, without our leave first obtained, he was not to give account to any but ourself. They sent a captious and directory message to the Lord Treasurer, Chancellor, and Barons of the Exchequer, touching some judicial proceedings of theirs in our court of Exchequer.

They sent messengers to examine upon sundry questions our two Chief Justices and three other of our judges, touching their judicial proceedings at the gaol delivery at Newgate, of which they are not accountable to the House of Commons.

And whereas suits were commenced in our court of Star Chamber against Richard Chambers, John Fowkes, Bartholomew Gilman, and Richard Phillips, by our Attorney General, for great misdemeanours; they resolved that they were to have privilege of Parliament against us for their persons, for no other cause but because they had petitions depending in that House; and (which is more strange) they resolved that a signification should be made from that House, by a letter to issue under the hand of their Speaker unto the Lord Keeper of our Great Seal, that no attachments should be granted out against the said Chambers, Fowkes, Gilman, or Phillips, during their said privilege of Parliament. Whereas it is far above the power of that House to give direction to any of our courts at Westminster to stop attachments against any man, though never so strongly privileged; the breach of privilege being not in the court that grants, but in the party or minister that puts in execution such attachments. And therefore, if any such letter had come to the Lord Keeper, as it did not, he should have highly offended us if he had obeyed it. Nay, they went so far as they spared not the honour of our Council Board, but examined their proceedings in the case of our customers, interrogating what this or that man of our Council said in direction of them in the business committed to their charge. And when one of the members of that House, speaking of our counsellors [sic] said we had wicked counsel; and another said that the Council and judges sought to trample under feet the liberty of the subject; and a third traduced our court of Star Chamber for the sentence given against Savage, they passed without check or censure by the House. By which may appear, how far the members of that House have of late swollen beyond the rules of moderation and the modesty of former times; and this under pretence of privilege and freedom of speech, whereby they take liberty to declare against all authority of Council and courts at their pleasure.

They sent for our sheriff of London to examine him in a cause whereof they had no jurisdiction; their true and ancient jurisdiction extending only to their own Members, and to the conservation of their privileges, and not to the censure of foreign persons and causes, which have no relation to their privileges, the same being but a late innovation. And yet upon an enforced strain of a contempt, for not answering to their satisfaction, they commit him to the Tower of London, using that outward pretext for a cause of committing him, the true and inward cause being, for that he had shewed himself dutiful to us and our commandments in the matter concerning our customs.

In these innovations (which we will never permit again) they pretended indeed our service, but their drift was to break, by this means, through all respects and ligaments of government, and to erect an universal over-swaying power to themselves, which belongs only to us, and not to them.

12. The plea and demurrer exhibited by Sir John Eliot in the court of Star Chamber, May 22, 1629

FROM PRO, State Papers Domestic, Charles I, S.P. 16/143, no. 5.

The plea and demurrer of Sir John Eliot, knight, to the information of Sir Robert Heath, knight, his Majesty's Attorney General.

This defendant believeth that the King's Majesty at the time in the information mentioned did summon a Parliament to be holden as in the information is set forth and that the same continued by prorogation as in the said information is also expressed. And that this defendant was during the said Parliament a Member of the House of Commons. But this defendant conceiveth he is not bound by the laws and customs of this kingdom to make answer to the matters by the said information laid to this defendant's charge for the reasons following.

First: for that the matters and things by the said information laid to this defendant's charge are set forth to be done, committed or said in the Commons House of Parliament in the time of Parliament, this defendant being then a Member thereof. And this defendant is informed by his counsel that by the laws of this kingdom no person or persons whatsoever ought to inform our Sovereign Lord the King of any matter proposed, spoken, debated, agreed or otherwise consulted of by any Member of the same House until the same were shewn to the King by the advice and consent of all the Commons assembled in Parliament; and that if any such information should be made no credence ought to be given thereunto. And this defendant sayeth it doth not appear by the said information that any the matters in the said information contained were shewn to his Majesty by the advice and consent of the House of Commons, and therefore no credence ought to be given to the matters contained in the information, neither ought this defendant to be charged with the same.

Secondly: for that as this defendant believeth the liberties, franchises, privileges and jurisdictions of Parliament are the ancient and undoubted birthright and inheritance of the subjects of this kingdom of England; and the urgent affairs concerning the King, state and defence of the realm and of the Church of England and redress of mischiefs and grievances which happen within this realm are proper subjects and matters of counsel and debate in Parliament; and in the handling and proceeding of these businesses every member of the House of Parliament hath and of right ought to have freedom of speech to propound, treat, reason and bring to conclusion the same, and the Commons in Parliament have and ought to have liberty and freedom to treat of such matters in such order as in their judgment shall seem meet; and every member of the said House hath and ought to have freedom from all impeachment, imprisonment and molestation (other than by censure of the House itself) for or concerning any speaking, reasoning, doing or declaring of any matter or matters touching the Parliament or parliament business. And all such accusations, condemnations, executions, fines, amercements, punishments, corrections, charges and impositions put or had unto or upon any member of the House of Parliament, unless by the House itself, for any bill, speaking, reasoning or declaring of any matter or matters concerning the Parliament communed or treated of are and ought to be utterly void and of none effect. And it appears by the said information, as this defendant conceiveth, that the matters laid to this defendant's charge are by the said information supposed to be committed in the Commons House of Parliament in time of Parliament and are concerning affairs of Parliament, and therefore this defendant conceiveth by the laws and customs of this realm the same are only examinable and determinable by the House of Commons or by a parliamentary course of proceeding and not otherwise.

Thirdly: for that the whole Parliament is the great Council of the Kingdom and therefore this defendant by the laws and customs of this realm ought not to disclose or reveal what was done, spoken or debated in the Commons House unless by consent of the Commons House of Parliament.

Fourthly: for that it appears by the said information that at the time when the matters laid to this defendant's charge are supposed to be done or spoken, the House of Commons was neither dissolved, prorogued nor adjourned. And this defendant sayeth that as he is informed by his counsel in the Parliament holden at Westminster in the sixth year of the reign of the late King Henry the Eighth, it was enacted that no knight, citizen, burgess or baron of Parliament which then after should be elected to come or be in any Parliament should depart from the same Parliament nor absent himself from the same till the said Parliament should be fully finished, ended or prorogued except he or they should have licence of the Speaker and Commons in such Parliament assembled.[9]

Lastly: for that it doth not appear by the said information but that the said Parliament as yet continueth, it being not therein set forth that the same is dissolved, prorogued or adjourned.

The which matters this defendant is ready to aver and prove as this

[9] 6 H.VIII. c. 16.

honourable court shall award, for which causes and for divers other imperfections in the said information contained this defendant demandeth the judgment of this honourable court whether he shall be enforced to make any other or further answer to the said information. And humbly prayeth to be from hence dismissed.

Bramston. William Holte. Robert Mason.

13. Privy Council orders with respect to peers accused of contempt, 1629

FROM *APC*, May 1629–May 1630, pp. 7, 102.

[May 6, 1629]
Whereas in the last session of Parliament upon a question raised in the higher House whether the peers of this realm were to be attached upon process of contempt out of the court of Chancery, an order was conceived for the privileging of peers in that behalf, yet with caution to reform the same if cause should upon precedents or better reason be shewed in that or any other Parliament or to the like effect. And whereas it was intended by the Lords of Parliament to take into further consideration the matter aforesaid, and upon view of precedents, and such other motives as might be of importance, to settle such a course as no failure of justice should be in cases concerning any of the peers of this realm for want of due correction, but before any course [was] settled therein the Parliament was dissolved. Forasmuch as the matter aforesaid is of great consequence, touching on the one side the common justice of the kingdom, especially in the courts of Star Chamber, Chancery, and other courts of equity, and on the other side the privilege of the nobility, of both which his Majesty is and ever will be most sensible and careful. Therefore his Majesty being now present in Council did declare his royal pleasure to have this question settled with the most mature deliberation and advice, and hath therefore required that their Lordships give order to all the judges to take this business into a serious consideration, and upon conference among themselves and upon view of precedents resolve what just coercive process from any of the courts aforesaid ought to be awarded against a peer of this realm for

breach of any decree or other contempt, and to certify their opinions therein to the Board, where the same is also to be taken into consideration so that his Majesty may be speedily informed of the advice as well of his Privy Council as of his judges, and may thereupon settle such a course as no failure of justice may be hereafter. This having been ordered in his Majesty's presence, the Board do pray and require the aforesaid judges to take notice hereof and with all convenient expedition to proceed accordingly.

*   *   *

[July 29, 1629]

Since which said fourteenth year of Queen Elizabeth we [the judges] find it hath been an usual practice in the said court [of Chancery] (and the precedents are very frequent) to serve such process in the like case upon peers of the realm for contempts. And upon further advisement thereof among ourselves we find that there is no other coercive course to be taken against a peer of the realm in such cases save only the process afore mentioned. And it is agreeable to the course of the common law, for by the common law a *capias* doth lie against peers of the realm for contempts by them committed. All which we humbly certify and leave to your lordships further consideration.

Upon due consideration whereof, and of an order of the higher House of Parliament dated the tenth of February last, and of a former order of the higher House made in the fourteenth year of the late Queen Elizabeth, whereby the Lord Cromwell was discharged of an attachment awarded out of the Chancery, it appeared . . . that in both orders there was a proviso that if at any time during those Parliaments or then after in any other Parliament there should be shewed sufficient matter that by the prerogative of the Crown or by the common law or custom of this realm or by any statute, law, or sufficient precedents, the persons of any of the Lords of Parliament in such case were to be attached or attachable, then and from thenceforth, that to take place which should be so ordered or warranted. And that the said judges have grounded their opinions as well upon the rule and reason of the common law as upon precedents of the court of Chancery before the fourteenth year of Queen Elizabeth, there being no other coercive means in many cases of contempt to do justice for relief of such as shall have cause to complain. Therefore his Majesty, having deliberately advised thereof and having heard the opinions of all the Lords now present, who having severally delivered their votes, did all unanimously concur with the aforesaid report of the judges, was thereupon pleased to approve the advice given as well by the said Lords as by all the judges of the realm. And accordingly doth ordain that the peers of the realm upon process of contempt out of any of the courts aforesaid are and ought to be attached and attachable. And willeth that this course be duly kept and observed by all the courts aforesaid until his Majesty shall find cause to make some other determination in Parliament concerning the same.

14. 'Considerations offered by Sir Henry Spelman, knight, touching the suppression of unjust fees': at the inner Star Chamber on Monday, May 3, 1630

FROM PRO, Commission into Fees, E. 215/2/134.

The considerations following being offered by Sir Henry Spelman, knight, to the consideration of their Lordships and the rest of his Majesty's said commissioners were now read by the right honourable the Lord Viscount Wentworth, and especially well approved of by their Lordships and the said other commissioners.

Considerations touching the suppression of unjust fees
1. That every officer be stinted to a certain number of clerks, and that he shall not take for their admission, and such as have been trained up in those offices.
2. And if necessity require him to have more he take them by allowance of the Justices there.
3. That he shall allow his clerk that doth the business a third, fourth, fifth, or such part as shall be agreed of, of the fee himself hath for the same doing nothing, if he be not his menial servant.
4. That he shall not abridge his clerk of his wages or allowance in any one thing under pretence of having a surplusage in another.
5. That he shall suffer no clerk or servant to receive any overplus or gratuity for his writing or business.
6. That upon notice of any such offence he shall discharge his clerk or servant from serving any more in that place for one whole year.
7. That the officer or master himself shall deliver whatsoever is written by the clerk or servant to the client or suitor, and shall receive his whole fee himself, and not by the demand or hand of his clerk or servant.
8. That whosoever receiveth divers fees shall deliver a particular note of them to the client (if he require it) showing for what every of them are.

9. That the fees agreed of and made certain be hanged up in a table in every court and office respectively.

10. That in the same table mentioned be made under a particular title of the suppressed fees, that they may presently be known to have been suppressed if at any time hereafter they creep up again.

11. That the reformed fees may also have some note upon them to shew they have been reformed and abated.

12. That a pattern or scantling be likewise assigned for the manner of writing, the largeness of the paper and parchment roll, and for the number, length and content of the lines. And that the same pattern be hanged up also in every office that the suitor may see whether it be observed and himself well dealt with.

13. That both the officers and masters and the clerks and servants be sworn to the premises, and not to use sleight or deceipt to lengthen their writing or to raise the charge of the client or suitor, or to protract or delay him unnecessarily.

14. That the fees being generally settled a book may be printed of them and a proclamation made commanding all men upon pain of his Majesty's high indignation carefully to observe them. And that no man give or offer, take or receive, either directly or indirectly any thing to the contrary.

15. That in the mean time as any unjust fees shall be discovered, his Majesty will be pleased by his writ of Privy Seal into that court or office or to the persons delinquent directed to command them to forbear henceforth, and not to take them any more.

16. That after all this there be standing and perpetual commissioners (as were sometimes for supportation of Magna Carta) to take cognizance once in seven or ten years of abuses touching fees, officers, and innovation of offices, and to remedy the same or certify his Majesty.

Nec sic extinguitur Hydra

17. When King John had made a reformation by his charter of some fees touching the Great Seal (which were then excessively enhanced) he caused the Archbiship of Canterbury, and other inferior bishops present at his coronation to denounce a sentence of excommunication against all that should do contrary.

15. Privy Council order, with assent of the judges, clarifying the privileges and limits of the Stannaries, February 18, 1632

FROM G. R. Lewis, *The Stannaries*, Cambridge, Mass., 1908, Appendix I. pp. 249–51.

This day (his Majesty being present in Council) certain articles and propositions produced by his Majesty's Attorney General concerning the jurisdiction of the Stannaries were read and approved of by the Board. Only some few particulars thought fit to be added were by his Majesty recommended to his said Attorney General; who is likewise required to cause a fair transcript thereof to be signed by the judges, before they go their circuit and to return the same to this Board, to the end it may be kept in the Council chest.

The rules following to be observed in his Majesty's courts at Westminster and his court of the Stannaries were agreed of before the Board, his Majesty being present in Council, and afterwards subsigned by the Lord Warden of the Stannaries and all the judges of his Majesty's said courts at Westminster and his Attorney General. And the transcript thereof ordered to be entered into the register of Council causes and the original to remain in the Council chest.

The workers about the tin, whether in mine or stream, the carrier, washer, and blower of tin, and the necessary attendants about the works have privilege that they ought not to be sued out of the Stannary (except it be in causes concerning life, member, or freehold) for any cause arising within the Stannary. And if they be sued elsewhere, the Warden may demand *conusans* or the party may plead his privilege.

Besides these there are other tinners that do no handwork as are the owners of the soil, owners of the bounds, owners of the blowing houses, and their partners, buyers and sellers of black tin, or white tin before the deliverance, these may sue one another, or working tinners, or any other man, for any matter concerning tin, or tin works, in the Stannary court.

Both these tinners and the workers may sue one another in the Stannary for all causes personal not concerning freehold, life, or member, arising within the Stannary or elsewhere arising.

One tinner may sue a foreigner in all like causes personal, arising within the Stannary, but a tinner may not sue a foreigner in the Stannary for matters personal rising out of the Stannary.

M

Of those later sort of tinners, such only are intended as within some convenient time make profit or endeavour to make profit to the coinage.

For the manner of trying whether one be a tinner or not, the use in Cornwall is by plea, and if issue be joined, and found for the plaintiff it is not peremptory but a *respondes*.

In Devon it is by oath of the party.

For the Extent of the Stannaries

We cannot yet discern but that the Stannaries do extend over the whole county of Cornwall.

In Devon there hath been long question concerning the extent of the Stannary, as appeareth in sundry petitions in Parliament.

This is a question of fact and not of law.

But for repose and quietness hereafter, whether it be convenient to award a commission to some able persons who may enquire by oath of lawful and indifferent men of the bounds of each Stannary for information only, or whether it be more fit to leave it without further enquiry and as it hath been heretofore we humbly leave it to your Majesty's wisdom, with this: that until the matter of fact be further known, this question concerning the bounds of the Stannary in the county of Devon may remain without prejudice, by occasion of any former opinion delivered concerning this question of fact. But:

The exemption of tinners from toll is over the whole county.

The power to dig and search for tin is over the whole county saving under houses, orchards, gardens, etc.

The tin wrought in any part of the county must be brought to the coinage.

The privilege of emption or preemption is of tin gotten over the whole county.

Judgments had in the Stannary court are leviable in all parts of the county.

Fines and amercements set in the Stannary court may be levied over the whole county by process of the Stannary.

For trespasses in tin works, process may be executed in the whole county.

Water courses for the tin works or tin mills may be made in any place of the county.

Signed:

Pembroke and Montgomery.   Thomas Richardson
                            Robert Heath
                            Humphrey Davenport
                            John Denham
                            Richard Hutton

William Jones
George Croke
Thomas Trevor
George Vernon
James Weston
Robert Berkeley
Francis Crawley

William Noy

16. An example of conditions in the Fleet, November 29, 1632

FROM PRO, Commission into Fees, Waste Book, E. 215/1/22, f. 155.[10]

David Waterhouse, esq., prisoner in execution in the Fleet, examined, saith that he hath been a prisoner there near about twenty years, and upon his first commitment he paid five marks to the then Warden, Mr Wilkenson, for that he was a parlour commoner (the hall commoners paying but half, as he hath been informed). And touching the lodgings in the Fleet he saith that there was a rate in anno 3 Eliz. what should be paid for lodgings in chambers whereto he refers himself, but he saith that since that time there have been many new buildings made in the Fleet, and he conceiveth that the orders of 3 Eliz. do not extend to the chambers built sithence.

*   *   *

That for the return of a day writ he hath within two years last past usually paid 2s 6d. . . . That he hath also during the said times usually paid 12d the forenoon and 12d the afternoon to the keeper that hath attended on him abroad. And that he conceiveth a knight or person of greater quality do in their bounty give sometimes 4s and sometimes 5s.

And he further saith that in the time of Mr Harris, the Warden, some prisoners were thrust into the common gaol upon differences between the Warden and them . . . but whether for matter of fees or lodgings he knoweth not.

And that there are divers committed to the same place by the now

[10] This is f.155 in a file which begins at f.138.

Warden, as Mr Browne for stabbing of Sir William Essex as he conceiveth.

That if the prisoners require to have of the best beer by the can they
pay a penny a can, if by the jug but a penny a quart as he conceiveth.
Which can is not a quart. But how much the tapster payeth for leave to
sell beer in the Fleet he knoweth not.

That in the first fee of 5 marks the fee to be freed from irons is
included.

That in his own particular he knoweth not of any exaction of grievance committed by the Warden or his ministers, but hath heard divers
complain whose names he doth not now remember.

And more he knoweth not.

David Waterhouse

17. A complaint about practices in the courts of law, *circa* 1632

FROM PRO, State Papers Domestic, Charles I, S.P. 16/230, no. 18.

Grievances worthy [of] reformation in the practices of the courts of
equity, *videlicet* the court of Chancery, the court of Requests, the
court of Wards, the Duchy court, and the Exchequer Chamber.

In the court of Chancery by the statute made in the 15th of King Henry
VI, cap. 4, it is enacted that no writ of *subpoena* be granted from
thenceforth until surety be found to satisfy the party so grieved and
vexed for his damages and expenses, if so be that the matter cannot be
made good that is contained in the bill. Which damages and costs are
so small at this day that it is little or no satisfaction to the party grieved,
neither is there any security given to satisfy the party so grieved his
costs and expenses according to the words of the statute. But at this
day every man that will takes out a *subpoena* before any security given as
aforesaid or bill exhibited. Which begets many long and tedious suits to
the great impoverishing and vexation of the people which are the
defendants, and is a great means for divers contentious persons to
revenge themselves of their adversaries and to wrack their malice upon
them, the plaintiff being *amicus curiae* and commonly paying little or
small costs to the party grieved.

The like proceeding being by English bill and information in the court of Wards and court of Requests, which are courts grown up and established since the making of the said statute and proceed by way of bill, answer, and decree as the court of Chancery doth. Likewise the Duchy court and Exchequer Chamber which have the like proceeding and are an equal grievance to the people and of the same nature and condition with the other, the fees and allowances in these courts imitating the court of Chancery.

Grievances worthy [of] reformation in the practices of the courts of common law.

It is a great grievance to the people the outlawring of divers of the King's people upon indictments of trespass, battery, and personal actions, and divers others not being felony, and for small finds to the King. Whereby the parties so outlawed are in danger to lose all their goods, and personal estates, and leases, except error can be found in the outlawry or it be reversed, the charge of reversing one of which outlawries is commonly £7 or £8 and sometimes cannot be reversed but in Parliament if it be in the King's Bench. But the party outlawed is secretly outlawed, the county courts being obscurely holden, and proclamation only there made in a confused manner, many names being proclaimed together, whereas by the statute made in 31 Elizabeth[11] the party ought to be proclaimed first in the open county court, next in the general quarter sessions, and last at the parish church door where he doth or did lately inhabit. Whereas now by combination between the under-sheriff and the clerks of several courts which make out the process of outlaws rather desiring the party should never appear than otherwise.

The like grievance is by outlawing a man in a foreign county, where he doth not nor never did dwell, for debt, which to vex the party sued and by the false returns of the sheriffs is effected.

The last, which is not the least grievance to the people, is that every man that will, learned or unlearned, is a common solicitor of causes, whereby many tradesmen and such others stir up many suits amongst the people and get great sums of money to follow and solicit causes, whereas by law none but the King, lords, and great persons ought to have solicitors, but their causes ought to be pleaded and followed by their counsel and attorneys, which are allowed by public authority. These solicitors sue out process, draw bills and sometimes pleas, and follow the cause and make proofs, which offence in the solicitors is maintenance by the law. And often the solicitors share with the party if any thing be obtained by the suit which he stirs him up to. That this innovation being but new may be quite suppressed.

[11] 31 Eliz. c. 3.

18. Opinion of the judges to the effect that 'liberty may not be given to prisoners by force of a *habeas corpus*', 1636

FROM Hutton, 129–30 (122 *English Reports*).

Memorandum. Upon petition exhibited to the King by the prisoners of quality, which were in execution in the Fleet, King's Bench, and Marshalsea, to have liberty in the time of infection, and for preservation of their lives to have liberty by writs of *habeas corpus* to go into the country, upon security given to the Warden and Marshal for their return. The King (out of the great care of their safety) referred their petition to the Lord Keeper Coventrye, and that he, with the advice of the judges, should consider by what way it might be done. And the eighteenth day of June, we attended the Lord Keeper at Durham House; and there upon conference and consideration of a former resolution which was at Reading in Michaelmas term last, before the said Lord Keeper (where were present all the judges, besides my self). That these abusive *habeas corpus* were not lawful, and that the Warden and Marshal were then called and warned, that they should not suffer their prisoners to go into the country, as they had used to do, by colour of such writs. This which follows was subscribed:

We are of opinion, that the writ of *habeas corpus* is both ancient and legal; but as the writ doth not, so no rule can authorize the keeper of the prison to give liberty to his prisoner, by colour of such writ, but the same is an abuse against law, and an escape in the keeper, if he let the prisoner go by such writ.

We find that neither in the twenty-fourth year of Elizabeth, when the term was adjourned to Hertford, nor in the thirty-fourth of Elizabeth, in which year it was adjourned to Hertford, nor in the thirty-fifth of Elizabeth in which year it was adjourned to St. Albans, nor in 1 James in which year the term was adjourned to Winchester, nor in the first of King Charles, in which year it was adjourned to Reading, (in all which years there were great and dangerous infections of the plague) there was no such course to set prisoners out of prison by *habeas corpus*, but we find it a novelty begun of late years.

But we think, that if the danger of infection shall grow so great, as it shall be found necessary to provide for the safety of the prisoners (who may at all times provide for themselves by paying their debts, and yielding obedience to justice) then a course may be taken that some certain house may be assigned for the Warden of the Fleet, in some good town, remote from the infection, and the like for the Marshal of the King's Bench, in some other town, where they may remove such prisoners as have been petitioners to his Majesty, and there keep them as prisoners, *sub arcta et salva custodia*, as they should be kept in their proper prisons, and not to be as house keepers in their own houses; and by this means they will have the like to avoid the infection, as other subjects have, and not make the infection a cause to abuse their creditors, or delude the course of justice.

John Bramston	1.	Humphrey Davenport	6.
Richard Hutton	2.	William Jones	7.
George Croke	3.	Thomas Trevor	8.
George Vernon	4.	Robert Berkeley	9.
Francis Crawley	5.	Richard Weston	10.

To Sir John Bramston, knight, Lord Chief Justice of England

My very good Lord, – I have acquainted his Majesty with your resolution, and your brethren, about writs of *habeas corpus*. His Majesty doth exceedingly approve the same, and hath commanded me to let you know that his Majesty would not recede from that which you have certified, and prays you and the rest of my Lords, the judges, to observe it constantly, according to that resolution under your hands: – Your Lordship's assured,

Thomas Coventrye, C.S.

Hampton Court, 19 June, 1636

19. Lord Keeper Coventrye instructs the judges to encourage ship money payments, 1635 and 1637

FROM *State Trials*, iii. 825–30, 837–8, 841–2, 845–6.

[June 17, 1635]

My Lords the Judges: the term being done and ended, the assizes are at hand. You are to divide yourselves for your several circuits. Circuits are for the service of the King and the good of the people; they are the execution of the King's laws, and administration of justice. In the term, the people follow and seek after justice; but in the circuit, justice followeth and seeketh after the people. So gracious is the frame and constitution of the King's government, that twice a year, at the least, justice followeth the subjects home to their own doors; which, as it is a great ease to the trouble, charge, and travail of the country, so it giveth the people a better knowledge of justice; and the end of it, that they may bless God and the King for the same.

* * *

Of the trial of capital offenders, I shall say ... little; that part of justice moveth in a frame, and if all officers under you did their parts, you should walk in so straight a path, that you would find it very hard to tread awry; therefore you had need to heed them narrowly, lest they pervert justice. Look to the corruptions of the sheriffs and their deputies; the partiality of jurors; the bearing and siding with men of countenance and power in their country. When you meet with any such, your proceedings ought to be severe and exemplary against them, otherwise justice shall be overborne, howsoever in your own persons you bear yourselves with never so much uprightness.

* * *

I have but one thing more to give you in charge, and it is a thing of great weight and importance; it concerneth the honour of his Majesty and the kingdom, and the safety of both. Christendom is full of war, and there is nothing but rumours of war. What hath been done of late years abroad by fire and sword, it were a pity and grief to think of; yet we have by the goodness of God, and his Majesty's provident care, all this while enjoyed a most happy peace and plenty. .... It hath ever been accounted the greatest widsom for a nation to arm, that they may not be enforced to fight; which is better than not to arm, and to be sure to fight. Therefore his Majesty in these doubtful times hath not only commanded that all the land-forces of the kingdom should be set in order and readiness, but to set to sea a royal fleet at his Majesty's great charge, but with the assistance of the maritime places of this kingdom.

* * *

The dominion of the Sea, as it is an ancient and undoubted right of the crown of England, so it is the best security of the land; for it is impregnable so long as the sea is well guarded. Therefore, out of all question, it is a thing of absolute necessity, that the guarding of the sea be exactly looked unto; and those subjects whose minds are most fixed upon the honour of their King and country, will with no patience endure to think of it, that this dominion of the sea, which is so great an honour, should be either lost or diminished. Besides, for safety sake, the dominion of the sea is to be kept and the seas guarded. The wooden walls are the best walls of this kingdom; and if the riches and wealth of the kingdom be respected for that cause, the dominion of the sea ought to be respected; for else, what would become of our wool, lead, and the like, the prices whereof would fall to nothing if others should be masters of the seas? . . . Therefore, upon advice with his Council, he hath resolved that he will forthwith send forth new writs for the preparation of a greater fleet the next year, and that not only to the maritime towns, but to all the kingdom besides. For since that all the kingdom is interested both in the honour, safety and profit, it is just and reasonable that they should all put to their helping hands.

Now that which his Majesty requireth from you, and doth command, is, that in your charges at the assizes, and in all places else, where opportunity is offered, you take an occasion to let the people know how careful and zealous his Majesty is to preserve his honour, and the honour of this kingdom, and the dominion of the sea.

*　　*　　*

[February 14, 1637]
My Lords: I have but one particular more, and that is of great importance; whereof by special direction and command from his Majesty, I am to speak unto you at this time. . . . His Majesty hath now the third time sent forth writs to require the aid of his subjects for the guarding of the dominion of the sea, and safety of the kingdom. This his Majesty did upon great deliberation and advice, and upon important and weighty reasons. In the first year, when the writs were directed to the ports and maritime places, they received little or no opposition; but in the second year, when they went generally throughout the kingdom, though by some well obeyed have been refused by some, not only in some inland counties, but in some of the maritime places; and actions have been brought against some that have been employed in the execution of these writs.

*　　*　　*

I may say, for the most part, the subjects have shewed themselves most dutiful and obedient in this service of his Majesty. And this year the sum imposed upon the county of York being £12,000 is brought in already by the sheriff, and so is most part of Lancashire, and other shires. But when his Majesty heard of some refusals, though he had cause to be sensible of it, yet he was far from being transported with passion, but thought good to resort to the advice of you his judges, who are sworn to give him faithful and true counsel in that which pertaineth to the law; and this his Majesty, as well for the direction of his own course, as for the satisfaction of his subjects, required you to deliver your opinions herein, to which you returned an answer under your hands.

*   *   *

The command from his Majesty is that I should publish this your opinion in this place, and give order that it should be entered in this court, in the high court of Chancery, and in the courts of King's Bench, Common Pleas, and Exchequer; for this is a thing not fit to be kept in a corner. And his further command is that you the judges do declare and publish this general resolution of all the judges of England, through all parts of the kingdom, that all men may take notice thereof, and that those his subjects which have been in an error, may inform themselves, or be reformed. You have great cause to declare it with joy, and you can hardly do it with honour enough to the King, that in so high a point of his sovereignty, he hath been pleased to descend, and to communicate with you his judges; which sheweth, that justice and sovereignty, in his Majesty, do kiss each other. His further pleasure is, that you let all know it is not his purpose by this resolution to stop, or check, the actions or suits which any have brought, or shall bring, concerning this; for it is his Majesty's command, that all such as proceed in any action about the same have equal and meet justice, and that they be suffered to proceed in course of law, so as you call the King's learned counsel unto their proceedings, that they may not be surprised.

Now, my Lords, I have little more to say, but this I am sure of, that if any contrary opinion shall yet remain amongst men, it must proceed from those that are sons of the law ... and you the judges of the realm have been accounted the fathers of the law; then, in good faith, it will ill become the son to dispute against the father. Having thus delivered unto you what I received in command from his Majesty, as his Majesty doth, so do I, leave it to your judgments.

20. George Croke on *Hampden's Case*, 1638

FROM 'Notes of the Judgment Delivered by Sir George Croke in the Case of Ship-Money', ed. S. R. Gardiner, *Camden Miscellany vii*, 1875, pp. 1–3.

This is a case of as great consequence as ever came judicially into any court, therefore it behoveth us to be as careful in delivering judgment in it. I have deliberately scanned what hath been said of both sides at the bar by the counsel. I have considered maturely of what hath been delivered by my brothers; upon hearing of their grave judgments I endeavoured as much as in me lay to conform my own opinion to theirs, much suspecting that my own judgment was not guided aright when I heard them all judicially upon their oaths give their judgment against my single opinion. Yet because every one hath a private conscience to satisfy and give account of to God, I cannot be swayed by anything that hath been yet said to give my judgment with the multitude; but in my opinion judgment ought to be given *for* the *defendant*.[12] However, when judgment shall be given in this court one way or other, mine and all other men's judgments and consciences must be regulated accordingly; but to shew that judgment ought not to be given against Mr Hampden, I shall deliver my reasons, *which shall stand upon these po[sitions]*.

1. That the writ of 4th August directed to the sheriff of Bucks to provide a ship, with munition, etc., *at the charge of the inhabitants of the county* and to rate *them*, etc., is against the common law, *for that is not by assent in Parliament*.

2. That it is against divers statutes.

3. That no pretence of *prerogative, royal power*, necessity, *or danger, doth or* can make it good.

4. That it is not warranted by any precedents vouched, especially not by *any* one record judicial; *but rather in my understanding express records against the legality of these writs. To examine the parts of this writ.* To examine the part of this work.

5. That the motives of the writ are not sufficient to lay *this* charge *upon the county, and are not warranted by former precedents*.

6. If they were, yet the command of the writ is against the law.

7. If the *writ* were legal, yet the manner of assessment by the sheriff *as it is certified is* not warranted *by the writ*.

8. That the *certiorari and sci[re] facias* issued not *out* legally, *and so consequently no judgment can be given against the defendant thereupon*. The *mittimus* is that *the Barons shall proceed secundum legem et consuetudines Regni Anglie; so* we are not to judge here according to conveniency or state policy, but according to the common law *and custom of England we are to judge*. We find in our books, records, or statutes; if we cannot find it to be law by these we cannot judge it to be law. Therefore Mr Littleton . . . says that we shall never intend that to be law which never was put in *iure*, and upon which no action hath been brought. This reason applied to our case induces me to conceive that this writ is not *agreeable to the* common law, because before this time there was never any such writ to charge a county.

The common law of England sets a freedom in the subjects in respect

[12] Croke scratched out the words, 'against the King'.

of their persons, and gives them a true property in their goods and estates; so that without their consent (that is to say their private actual consent or implicity in Parliament) it cannot be taken from them. And as to this purpose the law distinguishes between bondmen, whose estates are at their lords' will and disposition, and freemen, whose property none may invade; for in our case here is a charge laid upon the free subject without his consent, and therefore not warranted by the law.

21. Extension of the limits of the honor of Peveril, May 31, 1639

FROM extract printed in *Deputy Keeper's Reports*, xvi. appendix 3, p. 42.

... The jurisdiction of the honor of Peveril shall for the future extend itself as well in and through all those places which of old were within the jurisdiction of the said honor, as in and through the whole wapentakes or hundreds of Broxton and Thurgarton, by Leigh, in the county of Nottingham (to wit) in all parts of those wapentakes which previously were not within the jurisdiction of the said honor, and that all the towns, townships, hamlets, and places within the wapentakes aforesaid which before were not within such jurisdiction shall henceforth be called the additional limits of the honor Peveril.

22. A Star Chamber fine, 1640

FROM PRO, Enrolment book of writs and letters of privy seal, E. 403/ 2568, f. 136v.

Charles by the grace of God, King of England, Scotland, France, and Ireland, defender of the faith, etc. To the Treasurer and under treasurer

of our Exchequer, now and for the time being, greeting. Whereas
Henry Lort, esq., was fined to our use in our court of Star Chamber the
sum of two thousand five hundred pounds for depopulations, upon the
prosecution of George Ellis, the relator in that cause, two thousand
pounds whereof being already paid and five hundred pounds residue
thereof remaineth unpaid. And whereas the said George Ellis hath
disbursed in following the said suit on our behalf for the execution of
commissions, riding charges and otherwise the sum of four hundred and
fifty and five pounds as appears by certificate from our Attorney
General, and was ordered to be paid unto him by the Lords of our
Council, and hath also been very careful in the prosecution of this cause
for our service, we therefore graciously please the said sum shall be
paid unto him. And do hereby will and require you out of the residue
of the said fine of two thousand five hundred pounds which remaineth
due to us and unpaid by the said Henry Lort as aforesaid to pay or
cause to be paid to the said George Ellis or his assigns the said sum of
four hundred [and][13] fifty and five pounds in satisfaction of the charges
by him expended and his pains taken in prosecuting the said cause. And
these our letters shall be your sufficient warrant and discharge in this
behalf. Given under our Privy Seal at our Palace of Westminster the
sixteenth day of November in the sixteenth year of our reign.

23. The case of Francis Freeman, December 1, 1640

FROM *Lords' Journals*, iv. 101.

The Earl of Dover reported to the House [of Lords] the petition of
Francis Freeman of Wilby, in the county of Northampton, that the said
Freeman, for that he being a constable had not been forward to levy
ship money, was sent for up by a messenger, one Davenport, by the
Lords of the Council; but, upon Freeman's refusing to obey unless the
said messenger would show his warrant, the messenger drew his sword
against the said Freeman, and coming up to London made complaint of
Freeman and divers other inhabitants in Wilby; whereupon Serjeant
Francis, serjeant at arms, apprehended the said Freeman and divers

13 Crossed out.

others upon a general warrant expressing no particular cause and demanded fifty pounds of him and compounded for ten pounds. Freeman being committed to prison, and lay fifteen weeks as prisoner, all the judges of the King's Bench (Justice Croke only excepted) denied him bail and liberty, though they had granted him his *habeas corpus* and no particular cause was given for his imprisonment. He further signified to the House that the Lords committees had sent for the Lord Chief Justice, Justice Croke, and Mr Justice Berkeley, to know why Freeman and the rest were not released. They answered that the return, as it appeared before them, stood in generals, and so did not know to the contrary but that it might have been for treason. It was further alleged that Mr Attorney General had an information depending against the said Freeman and others in that court. Hereupon the opinion of the Lords committees being made known to the House, that it was unanimously resolved of by all the Lords committees that both the warrants from the Lords of the Council and also the proceedings of the Judges were directly against the Petition of Right; thereupon it was ORDERED for the present that Serjeant Francis, the serjeant at arms, shall repay to Freeman and others the ten pounds in money which he received of them; and also that Mr Attorney General shall enter in the King's Bench a *non vult prosequi* to the information against Freeman and the rest.

24. Lord Keeper Finch speaks to the House of Commons, December 21, 1640

FROM *State Trials*, iv. 1–8.

Mr Speaker: I do first present my most humble thanks to this honourable assembly for this favour vouchsafed me, in granting me admittance to their presence, and do humbly beseech them to believe it is no desire to preserve my self or my fortune but to deserve the good opinion of those that have drawn me hither. I do profess in the presence of Him that knoweth all hearts that I had rather go from door to door and crave *da obolum Belizario, etc.*, with the good opinion of this assembly, than live and enjoy all the honours and fortunes I am capable of. I do not come hither with an intention to justify my words, my actions, or my opinions, but to make a plain and clear narration for myself, and then humbly to submit to the wisdom and justice of this House myself, and all that concerns me.

* * *

I have now, Mr Speaker, been fifteen years of the King's counsel. From the first hour to this minute, no man is able to say that ever I was author, adviser, or consenter to any project. It pleased the King, my gracious master, after I had served him divers years, to prefer me to two places: to be Chief Justice of the Common Pleas and then Keeper of his Great Seal. I say it in the presence of God, I was so far from the thought of the one, and from the ambition of the other, that if my master's grace and goodness had not been, I had never enjoyed these honours.

* * *

Mr Speaker: I had once the honour to sit in the place that you do. From the first time I came thither to this unfortunate time, I do appeal to all that were here then, if I served you not with candour. Ill office I never did to any of the House, good offices I have witnesses enough I did many. I was so happy, that upon an occasion which once happened, I received an expression and testimony of the good affection of this House towards me. For the last unhappy day, I had great share in the unhappiness and sorrow of it. I hope there are enough do remember, no man within the walls of this House did express more symptoms of sorrow, grief, and distraction, than I did.

After an adjournment for two or three days, it pleased his Majesty to send for me, to let me know that he could not so resolve of things as he desired, and therefore was desirous that there might be an adjournment for some few days more. I protest I did not then discern in his Majesty, and I believe it was not in his thoughts, to think of the dissolving of this assembly; but was pleased, in the first place, to give me a command to deliver his pleasure to the House for an adjournment for some few days, till the Monday following, as I remember, and commanded me withal to deliver his pleasure, that there should be no further speeches, but forthwith upon the delivery of the message come and wait upon him. He likewise commanded me, if questions were offered to be put, upon my allegiance I should not dare to do it. How much I did then in all humbleness reason with his Majesty, is not for me here to speak. Only thus much let me say, I was no author of any counsel in it. I was only a person in receiving commission. I speak not this, as any thing I now produce or do invent, or take up for my own excuse, but that which is known to divers and some honourable persons in this House to be most true. All that I will say for that is humbly to beseech you all to consider that if it had been any man's case, as it was mine, between the displeasure of a gracious King, and the ill opinion of an honourable assembly. I beseech you lay all together, lay my first actions and behaviour with the last. I shall submit to your honourable and favourable constructions.

For the shipping business, my opinion of that cause hath lain heavy upon me. I shall clearly and truly present unto you what everything is, with this protestation, that if in reckoning up my own opinion what I was of, or what I delivered, any thing of it be displeasing, or contrary to the opinion of this House, that I am far from justifying of it, but submit that and all other my actions to your wisdom and goodness. Mr Speaker: the first writs that were sent out about the shipping business, I had no more knowledge of, and was as ignorant as any one Member of this House, or any man in the kingdom. I was never the author nor adviser of it, and will boldly say, from the first to this hour, I did never advise nor counsel the setting forth of any ship writs in my life.

Mr Speaker: it is true that I was made Chief Justice of the Common Pleas some four days before the ship writs went out to the ports and maritime places; as I do remember, the 20th of October 1634, they do bear *teste*, and I was sworn Justice the 16th of October. So as they went out in that time, but without my knowledge or privity, the God of Heaven knows this to be true.

Mr Speaker: afterwards his Majesty was pleased to command my Lord Chief Justice of the King's Bench, that than was, Sir Thomas Richardson, and Chief Baron of the Exchequer that now is, and myself, then Chief Justice of the Common Pleas, to take into consideration the precedents then brought unto us. Which we did, and after returned to his Majesty what we had found out of those precedents. It is true that afterwards his Majesty did take into consideration that if the whole kingdom were concerned that it was not reason to lay the whole burthen upon the Cinque Ports and maritime towns. Thereupon, upon what grounds his Majesty took that into his consideration, I do confess I do know nothing of it. His Majesty did command my Lord Chief Justice that now is, my Lord Chief Baron, and myself, to return our opinions. Whether, when the whole kingdom is in danger, and the kingdom in general is concerned, it be not according to law and reason that the whole kingdom and his Majesty and all interested therein should join in defending and preserving thereof? This was, in time, about 1634. In Michaelmas term following, his Majesty commanded me to go to all the judges and require their opinions in particular. He commanded me to do it to every one, and to charge them upon their duty and allegiance to keep it secret.

Mr Speaker: it was never intended by his Majesty (so professed by him) at that time, and so declared to all the judges, that it was not required by him, to be such a binding opinion to the subject, as to hinder him from calling it in question, nor be binding to themselves, but that upon better reason and advice they may alter it; but desire their opinions, for his own private reason. I know very well that extra-judicial opinions of judges ought not to be binding. But I did think, and speak my heart and conscience freely, myself and the rest of the judges being sworn, and by our oaths tied to counsel the King, when he should require advice of us, that we were bound by our oaths and duties to return our opinions. I did obey his Majesty's command, and do here before the God of Heaven avow it. I did never use the least promise of preferment, or reward to any, nor did use the least menace. I did leave it freely to their own consciences and liberty, for I was left the liberty of my own by his Majesty, and had reason to leave them the liberty of their own consciences. And I beseech you be pleased to have some belief that I would not say this but that I know the God of Heaven will make it appear, and I beseech you that extravagant speeches may not move against that which is a positive and clear truth.

Mr Speaker: in the discourse of this (as is between judges) some small discourses sometimes arose, yet never was any cause wherein any judges conferred, that were so little conference between me and them. Mr Speaker: against a negative, I can say nothing. But I shall affirm nothing unto you, but by the grace of God, as I affirm it to be true, so I make no doubt of making it appear to be so. This opinion was sub-scribed without solicitation. There was not any man of us did make any doubt of subscribing our opinion, but two: Mr Justice Hutton and Mr Justice Croke. Mr Justice Croke made not a scruple of the thing, but of the introduction. For it was thus: 'That whereas the ports and the maritime towns were concerned, there according to the precedents in former times, the charge lay on them. So when the kingdom was in danger, of which his Majesty was the sole judge, whether it was not agreeable to law and reason, the whole kingdom to bear the charge?' I left this case with Judge Croke.

The next term I spake with him. He could give me no resolution, because he had not seen the writs in former times. But did give his opinion that when the whole kingdom was in danger the charge of the defence ought to be borne by all. So of that opinion of his, there was no need of a solicitation.

I speak no more here than I did openly in my argument in the Exchequer Chamber. This is the naked truth. For Mr Justice Hutton, he did never subscribe at all. I will only say this, that I was so far from pressing him to give his opinion, because he did ask time to consider of it, that I will boldly say, and make it good, that when his Majesty would have had him sometimes sent for, to give his opinion, I beseeched his Majesty to leave him to himself and his conscience. And that was the ill office I did.

The judges did subscribe in November or December 1635. I had no conference nor, truly I think, by accident any discourse with any of the judges touching their opinions. For till February 1637 there was no speech of it, for when they had delivered their opinions I did return according to my duty to my master, the King, and delivered them to him, in whose custody they be.

In February 1637, upon a command that came from his Majesty, by one of the then Secretaries of State, the judges all assembled in Gray's Inn. We did then fall into a debate of the case then sent unto us, and we did then return our opinion unto his Majesty. There was then much discourse and great debate about it. Mine opinion and conscience at that time was agreeable to that opinion I then delivered. I did use the best arguments I could for the maintenance of my opinion. And that was all I did.

It is true that then, at that time, Mr Justice Hutton and Mr Justice Croke did not differ in the main point, which was this: 'when the kingdom was in danger, the charge ought to be borne by the whole kingdom.' But in this point, 'whether the King was the sole judge of the danger', they differed. So as there was between the first subscription, and this debate and consultation, some fifteen months difference.

It is true that all of them did then subscribe, both Justice Hutton and Justice Croke, which was returned to his Majesty, and after published by my Lord Keeper, my predecessor, in the Star Chamber. For the manner of publishing it I will say nothing, but leave it to those whose memories will call to mind what was then done. The reason of the sub-scription of Justice Hutton and Justice Croke, though they differed in opinion, grew from this, that was told them from the rest of the judges: 'that where the greater number did agree in their vote, the rest were involved and included'.

And now I have faithfully delivered what I did in that business till I came, which was afterwards, to my argument in the Exchequer Chamber. For the question was a *scire facias* issued out of the Exchequer in that case of Mr Hampden's, of which I can say nothing; for it was there begun, and afterwards rejourned, to have advice of all the judges.

Mr Speaker: amongst the rest, according to my duty, I argued the case. I shall not trouble you, to tell you what my argument was. I presume there are copies enough of it. Only I will tell you there are four things, very briefly, that I then declared. First, concerning the matter of danger and necessity of the whole kingdom. I profess that there was never a judge in the kingdom did deliver an opinion, but that it must be in a case of apparent danger. When we came to an argument of the case, it was not upon a matter of issue, but it was upon a demurrer. Whether the danger was sufficiently admitted in pleading, and therefore was not the thing that was in dispute, that was the first degree and step that led unto it. I did deliver myself as free and as clear as any man did, that the King ought to govern by the positive laws of the kingdom: that he could not alter nor change nor innovate in matters of law, but by common consent in Parliament. I did further deliver that if this were used to make a further revenue or benefit to the King, or in any other way but in case of necessity, and for the preservation of the kingdom, the judgment did warrant no such thing. My opinion in this business, I did in my conclusion of my argument submit to the judgment of this House. I never delivered my opinion, that money ought to be raised, but ships provided for the defence of this kingdom, and in that the writ was performed. And that the charge ought not to be in any case, but where the whole kingdom was in danger. And Mr Justice Hutton and Mr Justice Croke were of the same opinion with me.

I do humbly submit, having related unto you my whole carriage in this business, humbly submitting myself to your grave and favourable censures, beseeching you not to think that I delivered these things with the least intention to subvert or subject the common law of the kingdom, or to bring in, or to introduce any new way of government. It hath been far from my thoughts, as any thing under the heavens.

Mr Speaker: I have heard too that there hath been some ill opinion conceived of me about Forest business, which was a thing far out of the way of my study, as anything I know toward the law. But it pleased this Majesty, in the sickness of Mr Noy, to give some short warning to prepare myself for that employment. When I came there, I did both the King and commonwealth acceptable service. For I did and dare be bold to say, with extreme danger to myself and fortune, (some do understand my meaning herein) run through that business, and left the Forest as much as was there. A thing, in my judgment, considerable for the advantage of the commonwealth, as could be undertaken.

When I went down about that employment, I satisfied myself about the matter of perambulation. There were great difficulties of opinions, what perambulation was. I did arm myself as well as I could, before I did anything in it. I did acquaint those that were then judges, in the presence of the noble lords, with such objections as I thought it my duty to offer unto them. If they thought they were not objections of such weight as were fit to stir them, I would not do the King that disservice. They thought the objections had such answers as might well induce the like upon a conference with the whole country. Admitting me to come and confer with them, the country did unanimously subscribe.

It fell out afterwards, that the King commanded me, and all this before I was Chief Justice, to go into Essex, and did then tell me he had been informed, that the bounds of the Forest were narrower than in truth they ought to be, and I did according to his command. I will here profess that which is known to many. I had no thought or intention of enlarging the bounds of the Forest, further than H. and that part about it, for which there was a perambulation about 26 Edward IV. I desired the country to confer with me about it, if they were pleased to do it. And then according to my duty, I did produce those records which I thought fit for his Majesty's service, leaving them to discharge themselves as by law and justice they might do. I did never, in the least kind, go about to overthrow the Charter of the Forest. And did publish and maintain *Charta de Foresta*, as a sacred thing, and no man to violate it, and and ought to be preserved for the King and commonwealth. I do in this humbly submit, and what I have done, to the goodness and justice of this House.

25. Mr Rigby speaks against Finch, December 21, 1640

FROM *State Trials*, iv. 8–9.

Mr Speaker: Though my judgment prompts me to sit still and be silent, yet the duty I owe to my King, my country and my conscience, move me to stand up and speak. Mr Speaker, had not this siren so sweet a tongue, surely he could never have effected so much mischief to this kingdom. You know, sir, '*optimorum putrefactio pessima*', the best things putrefied become the worst. And as it is in the natural, so in the body politic; and what is to be done then, Mr Speaker? We all know '*ense recidendum est*', the sword, justice must strike, '*ne pars sincera trahatur*'.

. . . Now, Mr Speaker, hath not this kingdom seen, (seen, say I?) nay felt and smarted under the cruelty of this man's justice? So malicious as to record it in every court of Westminster; as if he had not been contented with enslaving of us all, unless he entailed it to all posterity. Why shall I believe words now. . . . Oh no, there be some birds in the summer of Parliament will sing sweetly, who in the winter of persecution will for their prey ravenously fly at all, upon our goods, nay seize upon our persons; and hath it not been with this man so, with some in this assembly?

Mr Speaker, it hath been objected unto us, that in judgment you should think of mercy, and 'be ye merciful as your heavenly Father is merciful'; now God Almighty grant that we may be so, and that our hearts and judgments may be truly rectified to know truly what is mercy. I say to know what is mercy. For there is the point, Mr Speaker. I have heard of foolish pity, foolish pity; do we not all know the effects of it? ... We see by the set and solemn appointment of our courts of justice, what provision the wisdom of our ancestors hath made for the preservation, honour, and esteem of justice; witness our frequent terms, sessions, and assizes, and in what pomp and state the judges, in their circuits, by the sheriffs, knights and justices, and all the country, are attended oft-times for the hanging of a poor thief for the stealing of a hog or a sheep, nay in some cases for the stealing of a penny, and justice too, *in terrorem*. And now shall not some of them be hanged that have robbed us of all our propriety, and sheered at once all our sheep and all we have away, and would have made us indeed poor Belizarius to have begged for half pennies, when they would not have left us one penny that we could have called our own?

Let us therefore now, Mr Speaker, not be so pitiful as that we become remiss; not so pitiful in judgment, as to have no judgment; but set the deplorable estate of Great Britain now before our eyes, and consider how our gracious sovereign hath been abused, and both his Majesty and all his subjects injured by these wicked instruments; for which my humble motion is, that with these particulars we become not so merciful as to the generality, the whole kingdom, to grow merciless, *Fiat Justitia*.

26. The House of Lords confirms the rights of peers, December 31, 1640

FROM G. W. Sanders, *Orders of the High Court of Chancery*, London, 1845, I. i. 207–8.

Ordo parliamenti

Ordered upon the question (*nemine contradicente*) that the nobility of this kingdom and Lords of the upper House of Parliament are of ancient right to answer in all courts as defendants upon protestation of honour only and not upon the common oath. And that the said order and this explanation doth extend to all answers and examinations upon interrogatories in all causes as well criminal as civil and in all courts and commissions whatsoever. And also to the persons of the widows and dowagers of the temporal peers of the land. And that the Lord Keeper of the Great Seal of England for the time being or the Speaker of the Lords House for the time being do forthwith give notice of it together with the explanation to all the courts of justice and the judges, clerks, and registers of them by causing our former order with this explanation to be recorded in all courts. And that all orders, constitutions, or customs entered or practiced to the contrary wheresoever may be abolished and declared void. And the Lord Keeper of the Great Seal for the time being or commissioners of the Great Seal out of Parliament-time shall see all practice to the contrary hereafter to be punished with exemplary severity to deter others from the like attempts.

27. The activities of Mr Hyde during the early months of the Long Parliament, 1640-1

FROM Edward Hyde, Earl of Clarendon, *The Life of Edward, Earl of Clarendon*, Oxford, 1857, i. 70-1, 72-3.

Within few days after their meeting, he renewed the motion he had made in the last [Short] Parliament against the Marshal's court . . . and told them what extravagant proceedings there had been in that court since the dissolution of the last Parliament; and that more damages had been given there, by the sole judgment of the Lord Marshal, for contumelious and reproachful words, of which the law took no notice, in two days, than had been given by all the juries, in all the courts in Westminster Hall, in the whole term, and the days for trial after it was ended. Upon which he got a committee to be named, of which himself sat in the chair; and found that the first precedent they had in all their records for that form of proceeding which they had used, and for giving of damages for words, was but in the year 1633; and the very entrance upon this inquisition put an end to that upstart court, which never presumed to sit afterwards. . . . The Earl Marshal seeing Mr Hyde . . . thanked him for having treated his person so civilly, when upon so just reason he had found fault with some of his actions: said, he believed he had been in the wrong; but that he had been misled by the advice of Sir Harry Marten and other civilians, who were held men of great learning, and who assured him that those proceedings were just and lawful. He said they had gained well by it, but should mislead him no more; and concluded with great professions of kindness and esteem, and offered him all offices in his power; when, in his heart, he did him the honour to detest and hate him perfectly; as he professed to all whom he trusted.

*   *   *

He was in the chair in that committee which considered of the illegality of the court of York; and the other, that examined the miscarriages of the judges, in the case of ship money, and in other cases of judicatory, in their several courts, and prepared charges thereupon against them. He was in the chair against the Marshal's court; in that committee which was against the court of York, which was prosecuted with great passion, and took up many weeks debate; in that which concerned the jurisdiction of the Lord President and Council of the Marches of Wales, which likewise held a long time, and was prosecuted with great bitterness and animosity; in which the inhabitants of the four neighbour counties of Salop, Worcester, Hereford, and Gloucester, and consequently the knights and burgesses which served for the same, were passionately concerned to absolve themselves from the burden of that jurisdiction. And all the officers of that court and Council, whereof some were very great men, and held offices of great value, laboured with equal passion and concernment to support and maintain what was in practice and possession, and their friends appeared accordingly.

28. The charges against Justice Berkeley, 1641[14]

The Articles of Impeachment of Sir Robert Berkeley, knight, one of the Justices of the Court of the King's Bench, by the Commons in this present Parliament assembled, in their own name and in the name of all the Commons of England, in maintenance of their accusation, whereby he standeth charged with high treason and other great misdemeanours, London, 1641.

1. *In primis*, that the said Sir Robert Berkeley, then being one of the Justices of the said court of King's Bench, hath traitorously and wickedly endeavoured to subvert the fundamental laws and established

[14] For the charges against Bramston and other judges, see *The Manuscripts of the House of Lords*, xi. 263–73.

government of the realm of England; and instead thereof, to introduce an arbitrary, and tyrannical government against law, which he hath declared by traitorous and wicked words, opinions, judgments, practices, and actions appearing in the several articles ensuing.

2. Whereas by the statute made in the five and twentieth year of the reign of the late King Henry the eighth,[15] prices of victuals are appointed to be rated in such manner, as in the said statute is declared; but it is manifest by the said statute, corn is none of the victuals thereby intended. Nevertheless some ill-affected persons, endeavouring to bring a charge upon the subjects contrary to law, did surmise that the prices of corn might be rated, and set according to the direction of that statute, and thereupon great gain might be raised to his Majesty, by licences and dispensations, for selling corn at other prices. And a command from his Majesty being procured to the Judges, and sent to them by William Noy, esquire, his Majesty's then Attorney General, to deliver their opinions touching the question, whether corn was such victuals as was intended to have the price rated within the said statute. In answer to which demand, the said Sir Robert Berkeley, then being one of his Majesty's Justices of the Court of King's Bench, in furtherance of the said unlawful charge, endeavoured to be imposed, as aforesaid, the 30th day of November, in the eighth year of his now Majesty's reign, did deliver his opinion that corn was such victual as was intended to have the price rated within the said Statute; which said opinion was contrary to law, and to the plain sense and meaning of the said Statute; and contrary to his own knowledge, and was given and delivered by him, with a purpose and intention that the said unlawful charge might be imposed upon the subject.

3. That an information being preferred in the court of Star Chamber by the said William Noy, his Majesty's then Attorney General, against John Overman and fifteen other soap-makers, defendants, charging them with several pretended offences, contrary to divers letters patents and proclamations, touching the making and uttering soap, and using the trade of soap-makers, and other offences in the said information mentioned, whereunto the defendants did plead, and demur as to part, and answer to other part of the said information. And the said plea and demurrer being overruled, for that the particulars therein insisted upon would appear more fully after answer and proof; therefore the defendants were ordered to answer without prejudice, and were to be admitted to such exceptions to the said information, and advantages of the matter of the plea and demurrer upon the hearing as shall be material; and accordingly the defendants did put in their answers, and set forth several

[15] 25 H.VIII. c. 2.

acts of Parliament, letters patents, charters, customs, and acts of Common Council of the City of London, and other matters materially conducing to their defence; and in conclusion pleaded not guilty. The said Sir Robert Berkeley, then being one of the Justices of the court of King's Bench, upon the 30th day of March in the eighth year of his Majesty's now reign, upon an order of reference to him and others by the said court of Star Chamber, to consider of the impertinency of the said answers, did certify the said court of Star Chamber, that the whole answers, excepting the four words and ten last lines, should be expunged, leaving thereby no more in substance of the said answers, than the plea of not guilty. And after upon a reference to him and others, by order of the said court, of the impertinency of the interrogatories and depositions of witnesses taken on the defendants' part. In the same case the said Sir Robert Berkeley, upon the second day of May, in the eighth year of his now Majesty's reign, certified that nine and thirty of the said interrogatories, and the depositions upon them taken, should be suppressed with answers (except as aforesaid) and depositions, although the same did contain the said defendants' most material defence. Yet were expunged and suppressed according to the said certificates; both which said certificates were contrary to law, and justice, and contrary to his the said Sir Robert Berkeley's own knowledge, and contrary to the said former order, whereby the advantages were saved to the defendants, as aforesaid. And by reason thereof, the said John Overman and the said other fifteen defendants were sentenced in the said court of Star Chamber, to be committed prisoners to the Fleet, and disabled from using their trade of soap-makers. And one of them fined in a thousand, five hundred pounds; two of them in a thousand pound apiece; four of them in a thousand mark apiece; the rest five hundred pounds apiece; which fines were estreated into the Exchequer without any mitigation. And the said defendants according to the said sentence were imprisoned, and deprived of their trade and livelihood, tending to the utter ruin of the said defendants, and to the overthrow of free trade, and contrary to the liberty of subjects.

4. That he the said Sir Robert Berkeley, then being one of the Justices of the court of King's Bench, and having taken an oath for the due administration of justice, according to the laws and statutes of this realm, to his Majesty's liege people; on or about the last of December subscribed an opinion in *haec verba*:

'I am of opinion, that as where the benefit doth more particularly redound to the good of the ports, or maritime parts, (as in case of piracy or depredations upon the Seas), there the charge hath been, and may be lawfully imposed upon them, according to precedents of former times; so where the good and safety of the kingdom in general is concerned, and the whole kingdom in danger, (of which his Majesty is the only judge), there the charge of the defence ought to be borne by all the realm in general; this I hold agreeable both to law and reason.'

5. That he the said Sir Robert Berkeley, then being one of the Justices of the court of King's Bench, and duly sworn as aforesaid, in February 1637 subscribed an extrajudicial opinion in answer to questions in a letter from his Majesty, in *haec verba*:

'*Charles Rex*, When the good and safety of the kingdom in general is concerned, and the whole kingdom in danger? Whether may not the King by writ under the Great Seal of England command all the subjects of this kingdom at their charge to provide and furnish such number of ships, with men, victuals and munition; and for such time, as he shall think fit, for the defence and safeguard of the kingdom, from such danger and peril; and by law compel the doing thereof in case of refusal, or refractoriness?; and whether in such case is not the King the sole judge, both of the danger, and when and how the same is to be prevented and avoided? *C.R.*'

'May it please your most excellent Majesty: we have according to your Majesty's command, severally every man by himself, and all of us together, taken into serious consideration the case and question signed by your Majesty, and enclosed in your royal letter. And we are of opinion that when the good and safety of the kingdom in general is concerned, and the whole kingdom in danger, your Majesty may by writ under the Great Seal of England command all your subjects of this your kingdom, at their charge to provide and furnish such number of ships, with men, victual and munition, and for such time as your Majesty shall think fit, for the defence and safeguard of the kingdom, from such danger and peril; and that by law your Majesty may compel the doing thereof in case of refusal, or refractoriness. And we are also of opinion that in such case your Majesty is the sole judge both of the danger, and when and how the same is to be prevented and avoided. *John Bramston, John Finch, Humphrey Davenport, John Denham, Richard Hutton, William Jones, George Croke, Thomas Trevor, George Vernon, Robert Berkeley, Francis Crawley, Richard Weston.*

6. That he the said Sir Robert Berkeley, then being one of the Justices of the court of King's Bench, and duly sworn as aforesaid, did on the [   ]16 deliver his opinion in the Exchequer Chamber against John Hampden, esquire, in the case of ship-money. That he the said John Hampden, upon the matter and substance of the case, was chargeable with the money then in question. A copy of which proceeding and judgment the Commons of this present Parliament have delivered to your Lordships.

16 Blank.

7. That he the said Sir Robert Berkeley, then being one of the Justices of the court of King's Bench and one of the justices of assize for the county of York, did at the assizes held at York [March 1637] . . . deliver in his charge to the grand jury that it was a lawful and inseparable flower of the Crown for the King to command not only the maritime counties but also those that were inland to find ships for the defence of the kingdom. And then likewise falsely and maliciously affirmed that it was not his single judgment, but the judgment of all his brethren, witness by their subscriptions. And then also said that there was a rumour that some of his brethren that had subscribed were of a contrary judgment; but it was a base and unworthy thing for any to give his hand contrary to his heart; and then wished for his own part that his hand might rot from his arm, that was guilty of any such crime, when as he knew that Mr Justice Hutton and Mr Justice Croke, who had subscribed, were of a contrary opinion, and was present when they were persuaded to subscribe; and did subscribe for conformity, only because the major number of the judges had subscribed. And he the said Sir Robert Berkeley then also said that in some cases the judges were above an act of Parliament; which said false and malicious words were uttered, as aforesaid, with intent and purpose to countenace and maintain the said unjust opinions, and to terrify his Majesty's subjects that should refuse to pay ship-money, or seek any remedy by law against the said unjust and illegal taxation.

8. That whereas Richard Chambers, merchant, having commenced a suit for trespass and false imprisonment against Sir Edward Bromfield, knight, for imprisoning him the said Chambers for refusing to pay ship-money, in the time that the said Sir Edward Bromfield was Lord Mayor of the City of London, in which suit the said Sir Edward Bromfield did make a special justification. The said Sir Robert Berkeley, then being one of the Justices of the court of King's Bench, in Trinity term last, then sitting on the Bench in the said court, upon debate of the said case, between the said Chambers and Sir Edward Bromfield, said openly in the said court that there was a rule of law and a rule of government, and that many things which might not be done by the rule of law might be done by the rule of government. And would not suffer the point of legality of ship money to be argued by the said Chambers, his counsel. All which opinions, declarations, words and speeches, contained in the third, fourth, fifth, sixth, seventh, and eighth articles, are destructive to the fundamental laws of this realm, the subject's right of property, and contrary to former resolutions in Parliament, and to the Petition of Right. Which resolutions in Parliament and Petition of Right were well known to him, and resolved, and enacted, when he was the King's serjeant at law, and attendant in the Lords House of Parliament.

9. That he the said Sir Robert Berkeley, then being one of the judges of the court of King's Bench, and being in commission of the peace, and duly sworn to execute the office of a justice of the peace in the county of Hertford, on or about the seventh of January 1639, at which time the general sessions of the peace for the said county were there holden. The said Sir Robert Berkeley, then and there sitting on the bench, did revile and threaten the grand jury returned to serve at the said sessions, for presenting the removal of the communion table in All Saints Church in Hertford aforesaid out of the place where it anciently and usually stood, and setting it altar-ways, against the laws of this realm in that case made and provided, as an innovation in matters concerning the Church; the said grand jury, having delivered to them in charge at the said sessions, by Master Serjeant Atkins, a justice of peace of the said county of Hertford, that by the oath they had taken they were bound to present all innovations concerning Church matters. And he the said Sir Robert Berkeley compelled the foreman of the jury to tell him who gave him any such information, and thereby knowing it to be one Henry Browne, one of the said grand jury, he asked the said Browne how he durst meddle with Church matters; who affirming that in the said charge from Master Serjeant Atkins, the said jury were charged so to do; he the said Sir Robert Berkeley told the said Browne he should therefore find sureties for the good behaviour, and that he the said Sir Robert Berkeley would set a great fine on his head, to make him an example to others; and thereupon the said Browne offered sufficient bail, but he the said Sir Robert Berkeley, being incensed against him, refused the said bail, and committed the said Browne to prison, where he lay in irons till the next morning, and used to the said Browne and the rest of the jurors many other reviling and terrifying speeches; and said he knew no law for the said presentment, and told the said Browne that he had sinned in the said presentment. And he compelled the said grand jurors to say they were sorry for what they had done in that presentment; and did bid them to trample the said presentment under their feet, and caused Browne to tear the said presentment in his sight. And he, the said Robert Berkeley, when as John Houland and Ralph Pemberton, late Mayor of St Albans, came to desire his opinion on several indictments against John Browne, parson of St Albans, and Anthony Smith, vicar of St Peters in St Albans, at the quarter sessions held for the said town of St Albans on the four and twentieth of June, 1639, for the removal of the communion table out of the usual place, and not administering the sacrament according to the law in that case provided. He the said Sir Robert Berkeley then told them that such an indictment was before him at Hertford, and that he quashed the same, and imprisoned the promoters; by which threatening and reviling

speeches, unjust actions and declarations, he so terrified the jurors in those parts, that they durst not present any innovations in Church matters, to their great grief and trouble of their consciences.

And whereas several indictments were preferred against John Brooke, parson of Yarmouth, by John Ingram and John Carter, for refusing several times to administer the sacrament of the Lord's supper to them without any lawful cause, at the assizes held in Norwich in [   ]¹⁷ 1633, he the said Sir Robert Berkeley, then being one of the judges of the assize, proceeded then to the trial on the said indictments. Where the matter in issue being that the said Brooke refused to administer the said sacrament, because the said Ingram and Carter would not receive tickets with their Sir-names before their Christian-names, which was a course never used amongst them but by the said Brooke. He the said Sir Robert Berkeley did then much discourage the said Ingram's counsel, and overruled the cause for matter of law, so as the jury never went from the bar, but there found for the said Brooke. And the said Sir Robert Berkeley bound the said Ingram to the good behaviour for prosecuting the said indictments; and ordered him to pay costs to the said Brooke for wrongfully indicting him. And whereas the said Carter, not expecting the trial at the same assizes he preferred his indictment, was then absent, whereupon the said Sir Robert Berkeley did cause to be entered on the said indictment a *vacat quia non sufficiens in lege*, and ordered an attachment against the said Carter, which said proceedings against the said Ingram and Carter, by the said Sir Robert Berkeley, were contrary to law and justice and to his own knowledge.

10. That the said Sir Robert Berkeley, being one of the Justices of the court of King's Bench, and duly sworn as aforesaid, Trinity term 1637 deferred to discharge or bail Alexander Jenings, prisoner in the Fleet, brought by *habeas corpus* to the bar of the said court, the return of his commitment being that he was committed by two several warrants from the Lords of the Council, dated the fifth of November, 1636. The first being only read in court expressing no cause, the other for not paying messengers fees; and until he should bring a certificate that he had paid his assessment for ship money in the county of Bucks, but remitted him. And in Michaelmas Term after, the said Jenings being brought by another *habeas corpus* before him, as aforesaid, and the same returned; yet he the said Sir Robert Berkeley, refused to discharge or bail him, but remitted him. And in Easter term, after several rules were given for his Majesty's Council to shew cause why the said Jenings should not be bailed, a fourth rule was made for the said Jenings, to let his Majesty's Attorney General have notice thereof, and notice was given accordingly;

¹⁷ Blank.

and the said Jenings by an other *habeas corpus*, brought to the bar in Trinity term after, and the same return with this addition of a new commitment of the fourth of May, suggesting he the said Jenings had used divers scandalous words in derogation and disparagement of his Majesty's government. He the said Jenings, after several rules in the end of the said Trinity term, was again remitted to prison. And he the said Sir Robert Berkeley did on the fifth of June last defer to grant his Majesty's writ of *habeas corpus*, for William Pargiter and Samuel Danvers, esquires, prisoners in the Gate-House and in the Fleet. And afterwards having granted the said writ of *habeas corpus*, the said Pargiter and Danvers were on the eighth of June last brought to the bar of the said court, where the returns of their commitments were several warrants from the Lords of the Council, not expressing any cause; yet he the said Sir Robert Berkeley, then sitting in the said court, deferred to bail the said Pargiter and Danvers, and the eighteenth of June last, made a rule for a new return to be received, which were returned the five and twentieth of June last, in *haec verba*:

'Whereas his Majesty finding that his subjects of Scotland, have in rebellious and hostile manner assembled themselves together, and intend not only to shake off their obedience unto his Majesty, but also as enemies to invade and infest this his kingdom of England, to the danger of his royal person, etc.

'For prevention whereof, his Majesty hath by the advice of his Council Board, given special commandment to all the Lord Lieutenants of all the counties of this realm, appointed for their rendezvous, in their several and respective counties, there to be conducted and drawn together into a body for this service. And whereas his Majesty, according to the laws and statutes of this realm, and the constant custom of his predecessors, Kings and Queens of this realm, hath power for the defence of this kingdom, and resisting the force of the enemies thereof, to grant forth commissions under his Great Seal to such fit persons as he shall make choice of, to array and arm the subjects of this kingdom, and to compel those who are of able body, and of able estates, to arm themselves; and such as should not be able of bodies, but of ability in estate, to assess them according to their estates, to contribute towards the charge of arraying and arming others being able of body, and not able in estate to arm themselves. And such persons as should be contrariant to commit to prison, there to remain until the King should take further order therein.

'And whereas the Earl of Exeter, by virtue of his Majesty's commission to him directed, for the arraying and arming of a certain number of persons in the county of Northampton, hath assessed William Pargiter being a man unfit of body for that service, but being of estate and ability fit to contribute amongst others, to pay the sum of five shillings towards the arraying and arming of others of able bodies, and wanting abilities to array and arm themselves.

'And whereas we have received information from the said Earl, that the said William Pargiter hath not only in a wilful and disobedient manner refused to pay the said money assessed upon him towards so important a service, to the disturbance and hindrance of the necessary defence of this kingdom; but also by his ill example hath misled many others, and, as we have just cause to believe, hath practised to seduce others from that ready obedience which they owe, and would otherwise have yielded to his Majesty's just command, for the public defence of his person and kingdom; which we purpose with all convenient speed to enquire further of and examine.

'These are therefore to will and require you, to take into your custody the persons of the said William Pargiter and Samuel Danvers; and them safely to keep prisoners till further order from this Board or until by due course of law they shall be delivered.'

Yet he the said Sir Robert Berkeley being desired to bail the said Pargiter and Danvers, remitted them, where they remained prisoners till the ninth of November last or thereabouts, although the said Jenings, Pargiter, and Danvers, on all and every the said returns, were clearly bailable by law; and the counsel of the said Jenings, Pargiter, and Danvers offered in court very sufficient bail. And he the said Sir Robert Berkeley, being one of the Justices of the court of King's Bench, denied to grant his Majesty's writs of *habeas corpus* to very many others his Majesty's subjects; and when he had granted the said writs of *habeas corpus* to very many others his Majesty's subjects, and on the return no cause appeared, or such only as was clearly bailable by law; yet he remanded them, where they remained prisoners very long; which said deferring to grant the said writs of *habeas corpus*, and refusals, and delays to discharge prisoners, or suffer them to be bailed, contained in this article, are destructive to the fundamental laws of this realm, and contrary to former resolutions in Parliament, and to the Petition of Right; which said resolutions and Petition of Right were well known to him the said Sir Robert Berkeley, and were resolved on and enacted, when he was the King's serjeant at law, and attendant in the Lords House in Parliament.

11. That whereas there was a cause depending in the court Christian at Norwich, between Samuel Booty, Clerk, and [   ][18] Collard for 2s in the £ for tithes for rents and houses in Norwich, and the said Collard moved by his counsel in the court of King's Bench for a prohibition to stay proceedings in the court Christian at Norwich, and delivered into the said court of King's Bench his suggestions, that the

[18] Blank.

said cause in the said court Christian was only for tithes for rents of houses in Norwich, which was determinable by the common law only. Yet he the said Sir Robert Berkeley, being one of the Justices of the said court of King's Bench, and sitting in the said court, deferring to grant a prohibition to the said court Christian in the said cause, although the counsel did move in the said court many several times, and several terms for a prohibition. And he the said Sir Robert Berkeley deferred to grant his Majesty's writ of prohibition to several other courts on the motions of divers others of his Majesty's subjects, where the same by the laws of this realm ought to have been granted, contrary to the laws of this realm, and his own knowledge.

All which words, opinions, and actions, were so spoken and done by him the said Sir Robert Berkeley traitorously and wickedly to alienate the hearts of his Majesty's liege people from his Majesty, and to set a division betwixt them, and to subvert the fundamental laws and established government of his Majesty's realm of England. For which they do impeach him the said Sir Robert Berkeley, one of the Justices of the court of King's Bench, of high treason against our Sovereign Lord the King, his Crown and dignity, and of the misdemeanours above mentioned.

And the said Commons by protestation, saving to themselves only the liberties of exhibiting at any time hereafter any other accusation or impeachment against the said Sir Robert Berkeley, and also of replying to the answer that he the said Sir Robert Berkeley shall make to the said articles, or any of them, or of offering proof of the premises, or any other impeachments or accusations that shall be exhibited by them, as the case shall according to the course of Parliaments require, do pray that the said Sir Robert Berkeley, one of the Justices of the court of King's Bench, may be put to answer to all and every the premises; and that such proceedings, examinations, trials, judgments, and executions, may be upon every of them had and used, as is agreeable to law and justice.

29. William Pierrepont speaks against Berkeley, July 6, 1641

FROM J. Rushworth, *Historical Collections of Private Passages of State*, London, 1659–1701, ii. 601–5.

The high treason is in the first article, in his endeavours to subvert the fundamental laws of this realm, and to introduce an arbitrary and tyrannical government, which hath been lately adjudged treason in the cause of the Earl of Strafford.

The other articles prove the first, by his opinions, certificates, judgments, by his denials of the benefit of our laws, which have been read by your Lordships. No fundamental law to the subject is left; our goods, our lands, our bodies, the peace of a good conscience, are by him given up to arbitrary tyrannical government.

Nothing hath been omitted to make a judge know the laws, to make him just, or fear him from being evil. We have Inns of Court peculiar to that study, judges from thence only chosen, seldom any but what have been twenty years there. Honours and revenues are given to judges, encouragement to do well. This judge had these. Judges are sworn according to law to serve the King and his people, according to law to counsel the King, and for not so doing to be at his will for body, lands, and goods. This judge took that oath. The laws the judges study impose the greatest punishment upon unjust judges, they shew that these punishments have been inflicted. More could not be done to persuade or fear a judge.

His offences shew in him great ambition, yet he was most timorous of displeasing the great in power. He did not only forbear doing what he was sworn to do, but was most active against our laws and in opposing and punishing any that did maintain them.

To have only received bribes, (though they blind the eyes, and though the desire to get money increaseth with age) that heinous crime in a judge had been, in comparison with his offences, a tolerable vice. For from such a judge, justice is also to be had for money. Ambition is violent, and ruins, whilst covetousness is making a bargain.

The words of his opinion and judgment are for the King's power. It is pleasing to the nature of man that others should obey his will; and well-framed dispositions of princes may easily be persuaded their power is unlimited when they are also put in mind that therefore they have more cause to do well, and for doing well are more renowned. For the most oppressive designs (which we have suffered under) the pretences of his

Majesty have ever been the good of his subjects. His is the sin that is to judge by the laws, and knows the laws are to the contrary, yet puts and confirms such thoughts in his Prince.

He that incites another to arbitrary government, when his self ends are thereby compassed, hates him for taking that power he persuaded him unto.

The writs, those monsters of necessity, to provide ships to avoid imminent danger that could not stay 40 days for the calling of a Parliament, were therefore to go out in September, to have ships ready in March. This hath been adjudged by your Lordships to be destructive to the fundamental laws of this realm, and to the subjects' right of property and liberty, etc., that I shall say but this concerning them: that this judge published them to be inseparable flowers of the Crown. And that we have lived to see for five years together imminent danger, and thus to be prevented.

This judge did advise to such a government, as future Kings here might exercise that highest tyranny, and the subjects want the benefit of restraints, known to the most slavish eastern nations where, if their Prince do unjustly, he hath hatred for it, and the dangers that follow that. This judge will have that hatred to go to our good laws: no such bondage as when the laws of freedom are misinterpreted by judges to make men slaves.

What can be considered of in a judge of law, to give his opinion and advice to his Prince, how the laws (the mutual covenants of Kings and subjects) are to be broken, but that his intentions are to have his Prince do ill, by making his evil servants to study and to be pleased with their wicked designs, because they see means to put them in execution, by making them to persuade their Prince, because in imminent danger his subject's goods are at his will, that there is such danger when there is not, and that they have only some by-ends of their own.

This judge will have the law to be what to him seems reason; the reason limited to him to judge of is what the common law saith is so, what a statute hath so enacted. For him to judge this or that is law, else a mischief shall follow, because the law in such a thing is imperfect, therefore he will make a law to supply it, or because that the law written in such particulars is against his reason, therefore his reason's to be the law; then must follow, as often as a judge's reason changes, or judges change, our laws change also. Our liberties are in our laws, where a subject may read or hear read, this is his, this he may do and be safe; and that thus the judge ought to give judgment, he is free. The excessive growths of courts of reason, conscience came from great and cunning persons; and though not the most sudden, yet the most dangerous and sure ways to eat out our laws, our liberties.

Unlimited power must be in some to make and repeal laws to fit the dispositions of times and persons. Nature placeth this in common consent only, and where all cannot conveniently meet, instructeth them to give their consents to some they know or believe so well of as to be bound to what they agree on. His Majesty, your Lordships, and the Commons are thus met in Parliament, and so long as we are often reduced to this main foundation our King and we shall prosper.

This judge will not allow us our knowledge or any reason; he will have our minds, our souls' slaves. A grand juryman gave his fellows true information; they present an innovation in the Church, are threatened and reviled for it. He that told this truth is charged (I shall use this judge's own words) to sin in that, and that he made others forswear themselves. This judge sent him to the common gaol, where he is laid in irons, and all this because he and they durst meddle with Church matters. He is forced to tear the presentment in pieces in open court. Our laws provide for the peace of our consciences, many acts of Parliament are for it, and the trust by those acts set to juries. This judge well knew all this. Your Lordships have heard what he did to the jury at Hertford. He would have us know no more divinity than to obey what the great of the clergy directed, no more law than what he said was so.

Judges in former times (but only such as were examples of punishment, as of injustice in cases of great and public concernment) forbare proceedings till the next Parliament. This necessitated the calling of Parliaments. This judge had as many such causes before him, as ever any had, yet he never desired the resolution of Parliament in any one, for the ways he went the necessity was never to have a Parliament. He would pull up that root of our safeties and liberties, which whilst we enjoy the malice or injustice of all other courts and persons can never ruin, and when near to ruin (as most near of late) this only sure remedy will help us; nothing can ruin a Parliament but itself.

The evils which we have suffered under, they were committed by the judges, or by them ought to have been and might have been prevented.

This judge assisted in causing the miseries we suffered in the Star Chamber and at the Council table. He denied the known rights which he ought to have granted us to stop our grievances in the ecclesiastical courts; he was the causer of our sufferings in other courts.

The best lovers of their laws and liberties, the most honest suffer most by an unjust judge, they most oppose his vices. Dishonest persons find such a judge to fit their purposes, the judge finds them for his, the bond of iniquity confederates them.

He that will do no wrong will suffer none which he can help. The man that knows himself born free will do his utmost to live so, and to leave freedom to his posterity. Were he in slavery, when by outward gesture thought to be most delighted, were his mind then known, there would be found vexation, and his busy thoughts employed to redeem himself and his posterity from thraldom. But to say: could this judge intend to make himself and his own posterity slaves? What he did was through error of judgment only. No, my Lords, what his aims and endeavours were is apparent. To consider man in the general, we shall find in every age he will be a slave to some few, that many may be slaves to him, he looks to himself only. This he would do, or forbear doing, to be great, to be rich, had he children or kindred, or had none. This highly unjust judge, by continuing sins, maintained his actions to preserve himself, he knows to be found guilty in one of his offences, the penalty of the law for it, therefore covers the offences committed with inventing and acting other.

For a judge to be unjust more hurts the public than any other. He is not suspected. What a judge doth is looked on as a thing that ought to be done. The most pernicious great man, that by cunning hath got to himself the heart and tongue of his Prince, his ill acts have died with him, if not taken up by others, and then they walk in darkness. No man will justify what he doth by saying such a favourite did it. But the unjust judgments of this judge were given in noon-day, were done in the face of the whole kingdom, in the hearing of such as might carry the news to all parts of the realm, and was therefore done; his unjust judgments were our records. We have seen wicked great men most craftily politic; they hated our laws, yet not meeting with active judges moulded to their purposes, they and their acts have died, the realm flourished. But of late, others less politic meeting with most unjust judges, every way as ill as they could wish them to be, then did the kingdom faint, under the load of its misery did long struggle. Now it's rising, I assure myself, your Lordships will assist to take off the burden.

If the designs of some would not have such a man to be at liberty, a warrant from some Lords of the Council would soon have laid him in prison, and given no cause. Had he moved this judge to be discharged or bailed, he could have obtained neither, if their ways would not have endured that man to live, a judge reviling the prisoner, and the counsel that moved for his discharge on bail, joined with the hate of some great man, might soon have moved a gaoler for unwholesome rooms and lodging, and ill diet for his prisoner, and they may soon take life away. Offenders in prisons are looked after to be safe only. Such as are brought in by power against law are abused.

Had a great man desired the estates of others, the breach of a proclamation might readily have been charged against them in Star Chamber. But they, it may be, could have answered and cleared themselves, and proved their answer by testimonies. Had they been referred to this judge he would have expunged the one, suppressed the other. Then followed fines to the value of their estates or more, then imprisonments of course till they paid such fines; your Lordships have heard what this judge did to the soap boilers.

The countryman followed the plough, and to his thinking he was assured of his right, property, and liberty, gave him ability to do it. He believed his neighbour, his landlord, his King could not take his goods from him without his consent. He knew the usual payments by law, and in extraordinary causes thought to have that care to choose such for the knights of his shire, or for his burgesses, as might be mindful of the cause of payment, and of his estate.

This countryman hath heard the opinions and judgment of this judge, hath seen his goods taken from him, without his, or his knights' of the shire, or burgesses' consent or advice. These have made him, his wife and children, to join in tears to wish they had never been born. They have made them think on many ways to keep safe that estate which was yet left them, have made them desire to sell all their goods, and hide the money. But then he remembers this judge, how that he shall be carried to prison, and remain there if he pay not what please others to assess him. Then they think idle persons (the drones and moths of the Commonwealth) to be a wise people, whilst the countrymen expect and can think of nothing but being beggars.

Where public and enormous offences have been committed, eminent and notorious punishments must be. Such will make your Lordships proceedings highly esteemed, else there will be so many offenders, and none without danger can be punished.

This judge, subverting our laws, took away the hearts of many. He subscribed for the King's power, but so as he put him on taking his subjects' goods, and of all other such ways be most dangerous. For we know his Majesty is not the last that suffers, and is not the King worth many thousands?

The place of this judge was to have given and preserved to the King the hearts of his subjects. The due execution of the laws had done this. And when such notice is taken of a Prince, none will conspire against him, who cannot feign to themselves safety before or after any fact committed, foreign enemies will not invade his kingdoms.

Thus hath his Majesty now got our hearts, and will for ever have them. This judge is to answer for what his Majesty and for what we have suffered.

I am commanded by the House of Commons to desire of your Lordships that the proceedings against Sir Robert Berkeley, knight, one of the Justices of his Majesty's court of King's Bench, may be put in as speedy a way of trial as the course of Parliament will allow.

30. Denzil Holles speaks against the judges, July 6, 1641

FROM *Lords' Journals*, iv. 303.

... That the gentlemen having represented unto your Lordships the sad object of justice perverted, liberty oppressed, of judgment turned into wormwood, the laws (which should be the bars of our gates, to protect and keep us, and all that is ours, in safety) made weak and impotent, to betray us into the hands of violence; instead of props to support us, become broken reeds to deceive us, and run into our sides when we lean upon them, even so many snares to entrap and entangle us. And all this by the perfidiousness of those who are entrusted with our laws, who call themselves the guardians and the interpreters of the law, but by their accursed glosses have expounded the text and made it speak another language and another sense than ever our ancestors the law makers intended. Our ancestors made laws to keep themselves, their posterity after them, in the possession of their estates; these judges could make the law itself rob us and despoil us of our estates. Were we invaded and prosecuted at any time for pretended crimes – or rather because we were free from crime?; and did we put ourselves upon a legal defence, and shelter ourselves under the buckler of the law, use those lawful weapons which justice and truth and the common right of the subject did put into our hands – would this avail us? No, these judges would make the law wrest our weapons from us, disarm us, take away all our defence, expunge our answers, even bind us hand and foot, and so expose us naked and bound to the mercifulness of our oppressions. Were our persons forced and imprisoned by an act of power, would the law relieve us when we appealed unto it? No, it would join hands with violence, and add bitterness to our sorrow. These judges would not hear us when we did cry; no importunity could get a *habeas corpus*; nay, our cries would displease them and they would beat us for crying; and overdo the unjust judge in the gospel, with whom yet importunity could prevail. . . . It is no wonder if the knights, citizens, and burgesses assembled in Parliament have sent up some of their Members to stand upon Mount Ebal, to curse these judges, to denounce a curse upon them who have removed our land marks, have taken away the bound stones of the propriety of the subject, have left no *meum* and *tuum*; but he that had most might had most right and the law was sure to be of his side.

31. Edmund Waller speaks against the judges, July 6, 1641

FROM Rushworth, iii. 1339.

My Lords: The articles against Judge Crawley you have read, and they have told you how these brothers of the coif are become *fratres in malo*, how these sons of the law have torn out the bowels of their mother.

This imposition of ship money springing from a pretended necessity, was it not enough that it was now grown annual, but they must entail it upon the state for ever, at once making necessity inherent to the Crown, and slavery to the subject? Necessity, which dissolving all law, is so much more prejudicial to his Majesty than to any of us, by how much the law has invested his royal state with a greater power and ampler fortune; for so undoubted a truth it hath ever been, that Kings as well as subjects are involved in the confusion which necessity produceth.

That this was a supposititious imposed necessity, and such as they could remove when they pleased; at the last convention in Parliament, a price was set upon it: for twelve subsidies you shall reverse this sentence. It may be said, so much money would have removed the present necessity. But here was a rate set upon future necessity: for twelve subsidies you shall never suffer necessity again, you shall for ever abolish that judgment. Here this mystery is revealed, this vizor of necessity is pulled off, and now it appears this Parliament of judges had very frankly and bountifully presented his Majesty with twelve subsidies to be levied on your Lordships and the Commons. Certainly there is no privilege which more properly belongs to a Parliament than to open the purse of the subject. And yet these judges, who are neither capable of sitting among us in the House of Commons, nor with your Lordships otherwise than as your assistants, have not only assumed to themselves this privilege of Parliament, but presumed at once to make a present to the Crown of all that either your Lordships or the Commons of England do or shall hereafter possess.

32. Extracts from *Leviathan*

FROM T. Hobbes, *Leviathan*, ed. 1651, pp. 125, 138, 139, 144, 146.

For judicature

They also to whom jurisdiction is given, are public ministers. For in their seats of justice they represent the person of the sovereign; and their sentence is his sentence.... There may arise a controversy between the party judged, and the judge; which because they be both subjects to the sovereign, ought in equity to be judged by men agreed on by consent of both; for no man can be judge in his own cause. But the sovereign is already agreed on for judge by them both, and is therefore either to hear the cause, and determine it himself, or appoint for judge such as they shall both agree on.

★   ★   ★

Use, a law not by virtue of time, but of the sovereign's consent

When long use obtaineth the authority of a law, it is not the length of time that maketh the authority, but the will of the sovereign signified by his silence (for silence is sometimes an argument of consent) and it is no longer law, then the sovereign shall be silent therein. And therefore if the sovereign shall have a question of right grounded, not upon his present will, but upon the laws formerly made, the length of time shall bring no prejudice to his right; but the question shall be judged by equity. For many unjust actions, and unjust sentences, go uncontrolled a longer time than any man can remember. And our lawyers account no customs law, but such as are reasonable, and that evil customs are to be abolished. But the judgment of what is reasonable, and of what is to be abolished, belongeth to him that maketh the law, which is the sovereign assembly, or monarch.

★   ★   ★

Provincial laws are not made by custom, but by the sovereign power

... The legislator is he, not by whose authority the laws were first made, but by whose authority they now continue to be laws. ...

★   ★   ★

Some foolish opinions of lawyers concerning the making of laws

Seeing then all laws, written and unwritten, have their authority, and force from the will of the Commonwealth; that is to say, from the will of the representative; which in a monarchy is the monarch, and in other commonwealths the sovereign assembly; a man may wonder from whence proceed such opinions, as are found in the books of lawyers of eminence in several commonwealths, directly, or by consequence making the legislative power depend on private men or subordinate judges. As for example, *that the common law, hath no controller but the Parliament*; which is true only where a Parliament has the sovereign power, and cannot be assembled, nor dissolved, but by their own discretion. . . .

★　　★　　★

The sentence of a judge does not bind him or another judge to give like sentence in like cases ever after

. . . No man's error becomes his own law, nor obliges him to persist in it. Neither (for the same reason) becomes it a law to other judges, though sworn to follow it. For though a wrong sentence given by authority of the sovereign, if he know and allow it, in such laws as are mutable, be a constitution of a new law, in cases, in which every little circumstance is the same; yet in laws immutable, such as are the laws of nature, they are no laws to the same, or other judges, in the like cases for ever after. Princes succeed one another; and one judge passeth, another cometh; nay, Heaven and Earth shall pass; but not one title of the law of nature shall pass; for it is the eternal law of God. Therefore all the sentences of precedent judges that have ever been cannot all together make a law contrary to natural equity. Nor any examples of former judges can warrant an unreasonable sentence, or discharge the present judge of the trouble of studying what is equity (in the case he is the judge) from the principles of his own natural reason. . . .

★　　★　　★

The abilities required in a judge

The abilities required in a good interpreter of the law, that is to say, in a good judge, are not the same with those of an advocate: namely the study of the laws. For a judge, as he ought to take notice of the fact,

P

from none but the witnesses; so also he ought to take notice of the law from nothing but the statutes and constitutions of the sovereign, alleged in the pleading, or declared to him by some that have authority from sovereign power to declare them. . . .

INDEX TO INTRODUCTION

INDEX TO INTRODUCTION

Abbot, George, Archbishop of Canterbury, 134
Admiral, Lord, 16, 17, 27, 120
Admiralty, court of, 17, 18, 94, 118, 124
Alford, Francis, 35
Andrews, Dr K. R., 17
Anne, Queen, 97
Antiquaries, Society of, 94
Apology of 1604, 48, 62
Armagh, Archbishop of, 45
Attorneys, 29, 32, 33, 35, 36, 40, 47
Attorney General, 29, 33, 37, 38, 40, 41, 43, 45, 47, 64, 67, 73, 76, 77, 79, 95, 104, 105, 109, 128. *And see* Bacon, Francis; Banks, Sir John; Coke, Sir Edward; Coventrye, Thomas; Egerton, Thomas; Heath, Sir Robert; Herbert, Sir Edward; Hobart, Sir Henry; Noy, William; Popham, Sir John; Yelverton, Sir Henry
Attorney general to the Queen, 41
Ayscough, Edward, 114

Bacon, Francis, Viscount St Albans, Attorney General, Lord Chancellor, 16, 27, 29, 34, 36, 37, 41, 42, 47, 50, 53, 59, 63, 64, 66, 86, 93, 108, 109, 111, 118, 145, 147
Bacon, Sir Nicholas, Lord Keeper, 48, 59
Bagshaw, Edward, 44, 48, 135, 136
Bail, 70, 71, 79
Banks, Sir John, Attorney General, Chief Justice of Common Pleas, 92, 95, 125, 128, 143
Barnes, Prof. T. G., 19, 104
Barristers, 32, 33, 35, 45, 47
Barton, rectory of, 34
Bastwick, John, 106
Bate, John, 54
Bate's Case, 41, 54–5, 56, 62

Beecher, Sir William, 60
Bell, H. E., 102
Bellasis, Henry, 80, 132
Berkeley, Sir Robert, Justice of King's Bench, 14, 20, 29, 52, 105, 123, 139, 141, 142–3
Bills of conformity, 64, 66, 114, 145
Bishops, 13, 21, 25, 44, 52, 68, 106, 134, 135, 136, 144
Blackstone, Sir William, 109
Bonham's Case, 15
Bourchier, Sir John, 66, 107
Bramston, Sir John, Chief Justice of King's Bench, 37, 41, 71, 125, 126, 127, 139, 140, 142, 143
Bristol, 124
Bromfield, Sir Edward, 123
Bromley, Sir Thomas, Lord Chancellor, 49 n. 29
Bromley, family of, 48
Brownker, Sir Henry, 57
Burford, court at, 96
Burlamachi, Philip, 85
Burroughs, Sir John, 97, 124
Burton, Henry, 106

Caesar, Sir Charles, 38
Calvin's Case, 49, 50, 62
Capel's Case, 49
Carew, Sir George, Master of the Wards, 100
Carleton, Dudley, Viscount Dorchester, Secretary of State, 48, 87
Cary, Lucius, Viscount Falkland, 20, 140, 141
Cavendish, Richard, 109
Cavendish, William, Earl of Devon, 72
Cavendish, William, Earl of Newcastle, 97
Cecil, Robert, Earl of Salisbury, Secretary of State, Master of the

Cecil, Robert—*Continued*
Wards, Lord Treasurer, 30, 34, 54, 55, 57, 100, 101
Cecil, William, Baron Burghley, Secretary of State, Master of the Wards, Lord Treasurer, 61, 100, 101
Chamberlain, John, 48
Chamberlain, Lord, 39
Chambers, Richard, 76, 77, 88, 123
Chancellor, Lord, 34, 37, 39, 40, 41, 44, 49, 50, 59, 60, 61, 64, 67, 72, 106, 129, 139, 143. *And see* Bacon, Francis; Bacon, Sir Nicholas; Bromley, Sir Thomas; Coventrye, Thomas; Egerton, Thomas; Finch, Heneage; Finch, Sir John; Hyde, Edward; Jeffreys, George; Littleton, Sir Edward; Puckering, Sir John; Williams, John
Chancery, court of, 18, 23, 28, 35, 49, 58, 59, 60, 64, 65, 66, 69, 81 n. 49, 98, 104, 108, 109, 110–11, 112, 113, 114, 115, 116, 118, 119, 120; Clerk of the Hanaper, of, 116; Cursitors of, 110; Examiners of, 35, 111; Masters of, 34, 35, 46, 66, 111; Six Clerks of, 110, 111, 116, 117
Channel Islands, 85, 90
Charles I, 13, 14, 19, 20, 22, 24, 25, 26, 27, 28, 31, 38, 39, 42, 44, 45, 46, 47, 48, 49, 51, 52, 53, 54, 60, 61, 64, 65, 67, 69, 70, 71, 72, 74, 76, 77, 78, 79, 84, 85, 86, 87, 88, 89, 90, 91, 92 n. 18, 93, 94, 98, 99, 103, 108, 113, 115, 116, 119, 120, 121, 123, 125, 127, 128, 129, 131, 133, 135, 136, 138, 140, 143, 144, 145, 146, 147, 148
Charles II, 22
Chester, county palatine of, 106, 128, 144
Chivalry, court of, 91, 146–7. *And see* Earl Marshal
Chudleigh's Case, 49
Cinque Ports, 18, 124
Clerks, 32, 33, 35
Coke, Sir Edward, Attorney General, Chief Justice of Common Pleas, Chief Justice of King's Bench, 16, 17, 22, 27, 32, 36, 37, 40, 41, 42, 43, 45, 50, 51, 52, 54 n. 3, 55, 62, 63, 64, 68, 69, 71, 73, 74, 78 n. 52, 82, 93, 96, 97, 99, 102, 104, 109, 113, 118, 121, 138, 147
Coke, Sir John, Secretary of State, 38, 76, 106
Common Pleas, court of, 18, 29, 43, 50, 69, 104, 109, 112, 113, 115, 116, 118, 119, 143; Chief Justice of, 37, 39, 50, 51, 140. *And see* Banks, Sir John; Coke, Sir Edward; Finch, Sir John; Heath, Sir Robert; Hobart, Sir Henry; Littleton, Sir Edward; Richardson, Sir Thomas; Justices of, 14, 16, 37, 39, 41, 49, 116, 140. *And see* Coventrye, Sir Thomas; Crawley, Sir Francis; Croke, Sir George; Davenport, Sir Humphrey; Foster, Sir Robert; Harvey, Francis; Hutton, Sir Richard; Jones, William; Manwood, Sir Roger; Reeve, Edmund; Vernon, Sir George; Yelverton, Sir Henry; Prothonotaries of, 110, 112, 116, 118
Constable, the, 146
Conveyancers, 32
Convocation, 52, 81, 138
Cope, Sir Walter, Master of the Wards, 100
Cornwall, Duchy of, 93, 94, 98
Cottington, Francis, Baron Cottington, Master of the Wards, Chancellor of the Exchequer, 27, 100, 101, 102, 103, 119
Cotton, Sir Robert, 88, 94, 114
Council in the Marches of Wales, 16, 17, 18, 106, 107, 108, 144, 145, 146
Council of the North, 16, 17, 18, 106, 107, 108, 132, 137, 144, 145–6
Coventrye, Thomas, Baron Coventrye, Solicitor General, Attorney General, Lord Keeper, 37, 40, 41, 48, 117, 125, 129, 133, 147
Coventrye, Sir Thomas, Justice of Common Pleas, 48
Cowell, Dr John, 30
Cranfield, Lionel, Earl of Middlesex, Master of the Wards, Lord Treasurer, 16, 36, 56, 64, 67, 86, 89, 100, 108, 112, 114
Crawley, Sir Francis, Justice of Common Pleas, 139, 143

Cresey, Hugh Paulinus, 45
Crew, John, 80
Crewe, Sir Ranulph, Chief Justice of King's Bench, 39, 41, 70, 114
Croke, family of, 48
Croke, Sir George, Justice of Common Pleas, Justice of King's Bench, 14, 20, 37, 38, 39, 41, 123 n. 1a, 125, 127, 139, 147
Croke, Sir John, Justice of King's Bench, 42
Cromwell's Case, 59, 60
Cromwell, Oliver, 24, 26, 48
Cromwell, Richard, 48
Culpeper, Sir John, 57
Customs farmers, 76, 77, 89
Cutler's Company, 115–16

Danvers, Henry, Earl of Danby, 87
Danvers, Samuel, 139
Davenport, Sir Humphrey, Justice of Common Pleas, Chief Baron of Exchequer, 37, 39, 126, 127, 139
Davies, Sir John, 35, 36, 55, 74, 94
Dawson, Prof. J. P., 51, 91
Defective titles, 88, 96
Denham, Sir John, Baron of the Exchequer, 127, 137
Devereux, Robert, Earl of Essex, 58
D'Ewes, Sir Symonds, 94, 135
Digby, John, Earl of Bristol, 61, 65, 67
Digges, Sir Dudley, Master of the Rolls, 73, 78, 94, 114, 117, 139
Doctors' Commons, 128
Doddridge, Sir John, Justice of King's Bench, 37, 72, 94
Dudley, John, Duke of Northumberland, 24
Dudley, Robert, Earl of Leicester, 88
Dudley, Sir Robert, 88

Earl Marshal, 16, 19, 146. *And see* Chivalry, court of
Ecclesiastical courts, 118, 144
Edmondes, Sir Thomas, 103
Edward VI, 24, 28
Egerton, John, Earl of Bridgewater, 65
Egerton, Thomas, Baron Ellesmere, Viscount Brackley, Solicitor General, Attorney General, Master of the

Rolls, Lord Keeper, Lord Chancellor, 29, 41, 45, 57, 59, 62, 63, 64, 109, 118
Eliot, Sir John, 13, 19, 45, 51, 53, 56, 71, 74, 76, 78, 80, 84, 94, 99, 120, 122
Elizabeth I, 23, 25, 26, 28, 29, 40, 54, 57, 66, 70, 78, 86, 106
Elton, Prof. G. R., 90
Englefield, Sir Francis, Master of the Wards, 100
Erle, Sir Walter, 93
Escheators, 102, 103, 115
Exchequer Chamber (for debate), 19, 32, 49–50, 100, 127, 128, 129, 141
Exchequer Chamber, courts of, 49 n. 29, 62 n. 17
Exchequer, court of, 16, 18, 29, 54, 56, 59, 75, 76, 77, 85, 86, 88, 93, 100, 107, 114, 117 n. 65, 125; Barons of, 14, 16, 19, 20, 37–8, 39, 49, 53, 55, 77, 90, 114. *And see* Denham, Sir John; Trevor, Sir Thomas; Vernon, Sir George; Weston, Sir Richard; Chancellor of, 16; Chief Baron of, 16, 34, 39, 58, 81, 107. *And see* Davenport, Sir Humphrey; Fleming, Sir Thomas; Manwood, Sir Roger; Tanfield, Sir Lawrence; Walter, Sir John; Clerk of the pipe of, 118
Exeter, mayor of, 146

Fairfax, family of, 107
Fees, commissions of enquiry into, 23, 90, 93, 108–20, 132, 147
Fell, Sir Anthony, 85
Feodaries, 102, 103, 117
Fiennes, William, Viscount Say and Sele, Master of the Wards, 72, 102, 103, 128
Finch, Heneage, Earl of Nottingham, Lord Chancellor, 58
Finch, Sir John, Chief Justice of Common Pleas, Lord Keeper, 20, 21, 32, 37, 41, 48, 77, 78, 93, 95, 97, 109, 125, 129, 139, 140, 141, 143
Five Knights' Case, 41, 70, 144
Fleming, Sir Thomas, Solicitor General, Chief Baron of Exchequer, Chief Justice of King's Bench, 41, 99

Floyd, Edward, 68
Forced Loans, 70, 73, 84, 85, 93, 122, 132
Forests, 52, 86, 88, 95–8, 107, 140, 144, 145
Foster, Robert, Justice of Common Pleas, 143
Foulis, Sir David, 107
Freeman, Francis, 141
Fuller, Nicholas, 28

Gardiner, S. R., 14, 19, 20, 92
Gardiner, Sir Thomas, 46
Godden v. Hales, 50
Goodman, Godfrey, 40
Grand Remonstrance, 21, 102, 104, 105–6, 117, 135, 146
Great Contract, 30, 55, 61, 87, 103, 129
Great Seal, 39, 57; Lord Keeper of, *see* Chancellor, Lord
Greville, Robert, Baron Brooke, 60

Hakewill, William, 93
Hall, G. D. G., 30
Hammersley, G., 95
Hampden, John, 14, 19, 48, 126, 127, 128, 129, 130, 143, 145
Hampden's Case, 15, 22, 32, 50, 51, 123, 126–8, 129, 139, 143, 144, 147, 148
Harrington, James, 34
Harrison, Thomas, 127
Harvey, Francis, Justice of Common Pleas, 36, 48
Harwich, 130
Hausby, Sir Ralph, 98
Heath, Sir Robert, Solicitor General, Attorney General, Chief Justice of Common Pleas, Justice of King's Bench, 39, 41, 46, 71, 79, 116, 140, 143
Henrietta Maria, Queen, 133
Henry, Prince of Wales, 94
Herbert, Sir Edward, Solicitor General, Attorney General, 45, 92
Herbert, Sir Edward, Chief Justice of King's Bench, 50
Herbert, Philip, Earl of Montgomery, Earl of Pembroke, 99

High Commission, 20, 134 n. 18, 136, 144
Hinton, R. W. K., 82
Hobart, Sir Henry, Attorney General, Chief Justice of Common Pleas, 29, 41, 45, 81
Hobart, Sir Miles, 79
Hobbes, Thomas, 20, 52, 148
Holborne, Robert, 126
Holdsworth, Sir William, 14, 17, 18, 113
Holles, Denzil, 14, 80, 145
Holles, John, Earl of Clare, 88
Horsey, Sir Jerome, 81
Hotham, family of, 107
Hotham, Sir John, 80
Houghton, Sir Robert, Justice of King's Bench, 42, 147
Howard faction, 27, 64
Howard, Henry, Earl of Northampton, 27
Howard, Thomas, Earl of Arundel, 61, 65
Hull, 124
Hulme, Prof. H., 79
Hurstfield, Prof. Joel, 16
Hutton, Sir Richard, Justice of Common Pleas, 20, 125, 127, 131
Hyde, Edward, Earl of Clarendon, Lord Chancellor, 24, 25 n. 29, 37, 46, 52, 84, 90, 92, 100, 103, 137, 140, 141, 145, 146, 147
Hyde, family of, 48
Hyde, Sir Nicholas, Chief Justice of King's Bench, 37, 41, 72, 79

Ignoramus, 33–4
Impositions, 19, 20, 30, 31, 54–6, 73, 75, 76, 85, 89, 144
Imprisonment, 19, 21, 59, 70
Inns of Chancery, 128
Inns of Court, 36, 42, 43–8; Benchers of, 32, 43, 47; Readers of, 32, 40, 44, 48, 136; Gray's Inn, 44; Inner Temple, 43, 44, 47, 48, 102; Lincoln's Inn, 44, 48, 134; Middle Temple, 44, 45, 47, 48
Ireland, 26, 42, 44, 52, 133–4, 135
Ireton, Henry, 26
Isle of Man, 90

James I and VI, 14, 19, 22, 23, 24, 25-7, 28, 29, 30, 32, 33, 34, 37, 38, 42, 43, 44, 49, 50, 51, 55, 56, 59, 60, 64, 68, 69, 70, 86, 90, 91, 92, 94, 100, 102, 103, 114, 115, 116, 124, 129, 132, 133, 134, 146

Jeffreys, George, Baron Jeffreys, Chief Justice of King's Bench, Lord Chancellor, 147

Jenings, Alexander, 139

Jones, William, Justice of Common Pleas, Justice of King's Bench, 19, 37, 72, 139

Jonson, Ben, 33

Judson, Prof. Margaret, 14, 15

Justices, 13, 20, 36, 39, 41, 50, 51, 58, 66, 78, 91, 101, 102; attack on, 13-14, 20-1, 22, 23, 52, 53, 137, 140-3. *And see* Common Pleas, Exchequer, King's Bench

Justices of assize, 19, 34, 36, 129

Justices of the peace, 16, 19, 44, 47, 82, 91-2, 96, 134, 135, 136, 137, 138

Juxon, William, Lord Treasurer, 119, 125

Kenyon, Prof. J. P., 31

Kerr, Robert, Earl of Somerset, 27, 88, 109

King, prerogatives of, 15, 18, 19, 23, 27-31, 40, 48, 53, 54, 59, 68, 74, 87, 93

King's Bench, court of, 18, 19, 27, 28, 29, 40, 42, 67, 69, 71, 79, 80, 96, 99, 118, 123, 127, 128, 138 n. 27; Chief Justice of, 37, 38, 39, 41, 42, 51, 58, 78, 106, 113, 114, 116. *And see* Bramston, Sir John; Coke, Sir Edward; Crewe, Sir Ranulph; Fleming, Sir Thomas; Hyde, Sir Nicholas; Jeffreys, George; Ley, James; Montagu, Henry; Popham, Sir John; Richardson, Sir Thomas; Scroggs, Sir William; clerks of, 67, 109, 118; Justices of, 14, 37, 39, 41, 49, 71, 73, 79, 80, 116, 121, 140, 142. *And see* Berkeley, Sir Robert; Croke, Sir George; Croke, Sir John; Doddridge, Sir John; Heath, Sir Robert; Houghton, Sir Robert; Jones, William; Malet,

Sir Thomas; Whitelocke, Sir James

King's counsel, 33, 41

Knighthood, distraint of, 88, 95, 144

Knollys, William, Viscount Wallingford, Master of the Wards, 36, 64, 100

Lambarde, William, 28

Lancaster, county palatine of, 108

Lancaster, Duchy of, 18, 88, 93, 94, 95, 97, 98, 99, 108

Laud, William, Archbishop of Canterbury, 13, 20, 21, 27, 88, 119, 125, 131, 134-6, 137, 140

Lawyers, 14, 19, 32-4, 40, 42-8, 98; canon, 33; civil, 43, 146

Leighton, Alexander, 106

Lenthall, William, 46

Leslie, Alexander, 128, 133

Levant Company, 54

Ley, James, Earl of Marlborough, Attorney of the Wards, Chief Justice of Ireland, Chief Justice of King's Bench, Lord Treasurer, Lord President of Wales, 37, 38, 41, 42, 67, 81

Litigants, 19, 33, 34, 35, 36, 40, 62 n. 17, 65, 66

Littleton, Sir Edward, Recorder of London, Solicitor General, Chief Justice of Common Pleas, Lord Keeper, 41, 94, 126, 143

London, 84, 93, 102, 104, 113, 124, 125, 128; courts of, 18; Customs House of, 76; Guildhall of, 55; Lord Mayor of, 123, 128; recorder of, 46, 143; sheriff of, 77

Long, Walter, 79

Lort, Henry, 105

Lyme Regis, mayor of, 34

McIlwain, C. H., 15

Magna Carta, 71, 73

Malet, Sir Thomas, Justice of King's Bench, 143

Malever, James, 107

Mallet, John, 53

Manwaring, Robert, 74

Manwood, Sir Roger, Justice of

Manwood, Sir Roger—*Continued*
  Common Pleas, Chief Baron of Exchequer, 36, 96
Marshalvea court, 28
Marston, Robert, 121
Marten, Sir Henry, 124, 146
Mary I, 28
Mason, Robert, 79
Merchants, 33, 55, 56, 74, 85, 86, 87, 115, 124
Militia, 88, 130–1, 139
Militia Ordinance, 61, 92 n. 18, 143, 144
Mitchell, Sir Francis, 63, 64
Mompesson, Sir Giles, 63, 64, 68
Monmouth, Chancery at, 18
Montagu, family of, 48
Montagu, Henry, Earl of Manchester, Chief Justice of King's Bench, Lord Treasurer, Lord Privy Seal, 38, 41, 42
Mun, Thomas, 33
Musters, 19, 131
Muster master, 131
Mutton, Peter, 36
Mynne, George, 116

Naunton, Sir Robert, Secretary of State, Master of the Wards, 100, 101
Navy, Treasurer of, 85
Neale, Sir John, 23
Newcastle, 56, 89
Nicholas, Sir Edward, Secretary of State, 125
Norbury, George, 110
Noy, William, Attorney General, 27, 55, 71, 73, 76, 84, 88, 92–5, 97, 99, 114, 119, 124, 132, 139

Offices, 23, 53, 57, 84, 93, 108–20
Opinions, 22, 32, 49, 50–2, 59, 60, 62, 75, 80, 82, 122, 125, 139
Osborne, Sir Edward, 107
Overman, John, 139
Oxford, 44, 70, 74, 143

Palatinate courts, 18, 108 n. 49
Pargiter, William, 139
Parliament, 13, 14, 16, 18, 20, 22, 23, 25, 30–1, 33, 44, 47, 48, 50, 51, 52, 53, 55, 56, 57–83, 84, 85, 86–8, 94, 96, 100, 104, 110, 111, 112, 123, 126, 127, 128, 129, 130, 135, 138, 148; definition of, 52, 80–3; House of Commons, 13, 19, 21, 23, 24, 30, 33, 39, 42, 45–6, 47, 48, 49, 51, 53, 55, 57, 58, 59, 61, 62, 63, 64, 65, 68, 69, 71, 73, 74, 75, 76, 77, 79, 80, 81, 87, 88, 93, 102, 103, 104, 106, 111, 114, 128, 132, 135, 137, 138, 139, 141, 142, 145, 146; clerk of, 87 n. 4; Speaker of, 45, 46, 70, 77, 78, 79, 142; House of Lords, 13, 21, 24, 44, 45, 48, 53, 57–69, 70, 71–2, 73, 74, 86, 93, 101, 128, 135, 136, 137, 138, 140, 141, 142, 143, 144, 145; Members of, 20, 21, 23, 44, 48, 49, 54, 56, 62, 63, 68, 70, 76, 77–80, 82, 134, 137, 138, 145; lawyers as, 14, 21, 45–7, 142
Parliamentary statutes, 15, 17, 18, 21, 22, 24, 36, 52, 57, 61, 63, 66, 73, 80–2, 93, 120, 136, 144, 146
Parliaments (Eliz.), 45, 46, 57, 59, 60, 61, 80; (1604–11) 30, 45, 55, 56, 59, 61, 62, 63, 74, 92, 97, 103, 105; (1614) 20, 27, 45, 46, 54, 56, 59, 60, 61, 62, 64, 78, 81, 82, 83, 103, 114; (1621–2) 27, 48, 49, 53, 54, 57, 59, 61, 63, 64, 65, 66, 67, 78, 80, 81, 86, 93, 103, 108, 114, 115, 119, 135, 137; (1624) 23, 54, 56, 57, 64, 65, 66, 70, 81, 82, 86, 93, 96; (1625) 56, 61, 74, 78, 82, 84, 102; (1626) 61, 65, 66, 67, 74, 78, 84, 115; (1628–9) 52, 53, 55, 59, 60, 67, 71, 75, 76, 78, 87, 88, 93; (Short) 48, 57, 60, 80, 82, 89, 128, 129, 131, 133, 138, 140, 146; (Long) 13, 20–1, 22, 31, 32, 45, 46, 48, 52, 60, 61, 89, 92 n. 18, 96, 98, 99, 100, 101, 103, 104, 105, 106, 108, 128, 136, 137, 138–47
Parry, Sir Thomas, Master of the Wards, 64, 100
Patents and monopolies, 23, 28, 29, 54, 56–7, 89, 95, 104, 108, 138, 144
Peacham's Case, 147
Peers, Great Council of, 89
Peers, privileges of, 57–60
Petition of Right, 51, 56, 73–7, 85, 89, 119, 122, 137, 141
Petre, William, 135

Petty sessions, 35
Peveril, Honor of, 95
Phelips, Sir Edward, Master of the Rolls, 37
Phelips, Sir Robert, 73, 74
Pierrepont, William, 13, 22, 23, 134
Pleaders, 32
Plucknett, T. F. T., 28
Popham, Sir John, Attorney General, Chief Justice of King's Bench, 37, 39, 58
Prisoners, 52, 71, 77, 79, 121
Prisons, 52, 80, 115, 118, 120–2; (Fleet) 60, 115, 118, 120, 121; (Gatehouse) 121, 122; (Marshalsea) 76, 118, 121, 122; (Tower) 77, 78, 79, 80, 141, 143
Privy Council, 18, 28, 36, 39–40, 41, 52, 60, 71, 76, 77, 85, 88, 89, 90, 94, 96, 99, 104, 114, 115, 120, 121, 122, 129, 131, 134, 137, 138, 144, 145
Privy Councillors, 21, 40, 90, 91, 114, 132
Privy Seal, Lord, 42
Privy Seal, writs under, 116, 119
Proclamations, 16, 19, 70, 81, 83 n. 52, 84, 92, 104, 105, 106, 128
Proctor, Sir Stephen, 63, 106
Prynne, William, 44, 92, 106, 136
Puckering, Sir John, Lord Keeper, 41
Purveyance, 54
Pym, John, 14, 31, 48, 73, 74, 78, 104, 123, 131, 134, 138, 139, 142, 146
Pyne, Hugh, 71

Quarter sessions, 35, 71, 81, 129

Reading, 45
Reeve, Edmund, Justice of Common Pleas, 143
Requests, court of, 18, 27–8, 34, 42, 65
Rich, Henry, Earl of Holland, 97
Rich, Robert, Earl of Warwick, 60
Richardson, Sir Thomas, Chief Justice of Common Pleas, Chief Justice of King's Bench, 37, 38, 41, 137
Rigby, Alexander, 32, 140
Rolle, John, 75, 76, 137, 143

Rolls, Master of the, 38, 66, 109, 117, 139. And see Digges, Sir Dudley; Egerton, Thomas; Phelips, Sir Edward
Rudyerd, Sir Benjamin, surveyor of the Wards, 101
Rushworth, John, 25, 131
Russell, Francis, Earl of Bedford, 88

Sackville, Edward, Earl of Dorset, 72, 114
Sackville, Thomas, Earl of Dorset, Lord Treasurer, 130
St John, Oliver, Solicitor General, 126
Sandys, Sir Edwin, 78, 114
Saville, Sir George, 121
Scotland, 24, 25–6, 131, 135, 144
Scroggs, Sir William, Chief Justice of King's Bench, 147
Secretaries of State, 39, 87 n. 4. And see Carleton, Dudley; Cecil, Robert; Cecil, William; Coke, Sir John; Naunton, Sir Robert; Nicholas, Sir Edward; Vane, Sir Henry; Windebank, Sir Francis
Sergeants, 32–3, 34, 37, 38, 40–1, 42–3, 102; Inns of, 42, 49 n. 29, 128
Sewers, commissioner of, 53
Seymour, Edward, Duke of Somerset, 24
Sheffield, Edmund, Baron Sheffield, 36
Sheldon, Sir Richard, Solicitor General, 45–6
Shelley's Case, 49 n. 29
Sherfield, Henry, 92
Sheriffs, 19, 61, 76, 84, 91, 95, 105, 115, 129
Ship money, 13, 20, 21, 52, 53, 84, 87, 89, 94, 104, 107, 122, 123–31, 134 n. 18, 135, 138, 139, 140, 141, 143, 144
Shirley, James, 44
Shirley's Case, 77
Slade's Case, 50
Soames, Thomas, 138 n. 27
Solicitors, 32, 35, 36, 47
Solicitor General, 29, 33, 38, 40, 41, 43, 45, 46, 47. And see Coventrye, Thomas; Egerton, Thomas; Fleming, Sir Thomas; Heath, Sir Robert; Herbert, Sir Edward; Littleton, Sir

Solicitor General—*Continued*
  Edward; St John, Oliver; Sheldon, Sir Richard
Southampton, courts at, 47
Southcote, Sir Popham, 146
Spelman, Sir Henry, 94, 101, 113, 114, 116, 117, 118, 132
Stannaries, the, 52, 84, 98–9, 144
Star Chamber, court of, 16, 18, 28, 40, 43, 52, 59, 60, 67, 76, 77, 78, 79, 84, 98, 103–7, 116, 117, 118, 135, 138, 144, 145
Steward, Lord High, 58
Strode, Sir Richard, 128
Strode, William, 79, 80
Swanherd's courts, 96
Swift, Jonathan, 33

Tanfield, Sir Lawrence, Chief Baron of the Exchequer, 96
Taunton, courts at, 18
Touchet, Mervyn, Earl of Castlehaven, 58
Treasurer, Lord, 16, 39, 42, 67, 100, 121. *And see* Cecil, Robert; Cecil, William; Cranfield, Lionel; Juxon, William; Ley, James; Montagu, Henry; Sackville, Thomas; Weston, Richard
Treasury commission, 125, 134
Trevor, Sir Thomas, Baron of the Exchequer, 41–2, 143
Trevor-Roper, Prof. H. R., 27
Tunnage and poundage, 19, 30, 56, 74, 75, 76, 77, 87, 89, 93, 137, 144

Valentine, Benjamin, 80
Vane, family of, 107
Vane, Sir Henry, Secretary of State, 60
Vassall, Samuel, 56
Vermuyden, Sir Cornelius, 143
Vernon, Sir George, Baron of the Exchequer, Justice of Common Pleas, 38, 39, 143
Villiers, George, Duke of Buckingham, 24, 25, 27, 36, 38–41, 57, 61, 64, 65, 66, 69, 70, 72, 74, 78, 86, 90, 93, 94, 97, 109, 130, 132

Wadham College, Warden of, 34

Wales, Lord President of, 42
Waller, Edmund, 13, 20
Walter, Sir John, Chief Baron of the Exchequer, 19, 39, 51, 79, 93
Wards, court of, 18, 60 n. 13, 65, 69, 84, 99–103; Attorney of, 36, 41, 42, 101; Master of, 16, 39, 100, 101. *And see* Carew, Sir George; Cecil, Robert; Cecil, William; Cope, Sir Walter; Cottington, Francis; Cranfield, Lionel; Englefield, Sir Francis; Fiennes, William; Knollys, William; Naunton, Sir Robert; Parry, Sir Thomas; Surveyor of, 101, 112
Wentworth, Paul, 59
Wentworth, Peter, 59
Wentworth, Thomas, Earl of Strafford, 13, 14, 20, 21, 26, 31, 48, 73, 74, 87, 91, 92, 92 n. 18, 107, 114, 117, 119, 121, 131–4, 135, 137, 139, 140, 142, 144
Westminster courts, 18, 51, 63, 99, 112, 115, 118, 119, 138, 145
Westminster Hall, 42, 58, 63, 103, 141
Weston, Richard, Earl of Portland, Lord Treasurer, 16, 27, 75, 95, 119
Weston, Sir Richard, Baron of Exchequer, 143
Weymouth, 71, 124
Whitelocke, Sir James, Justice of King's Bench, 37, 38, 39, 71, 72, 80, 129
Williams, John, Lord Keeper, Bishop of Lincoln, 16, 34, 41, 60, 64, 66, 72, 106
Williams, Dr P. H., 107
Wilson, Sir Thomas, 37, 90
Windebank, Sir Francis, Secretary of State, 21, 38, 60, 125, 135, 138
Wiseman, Sir Thomas, 106
Wray, Sir John, 141
Wriothesley, Henry, Earl of Southampton, 78

Yelverton, Sir Henry, Attorney General, Justice of Common Pleas, 38, 45, 68, 116
Yelverton, family of, 48
Yonge, Walter, 80
York, 107, 123, 124